THE CAMBRIDGE COMPANION TO
FRANCES BURNEY

Frances Burney (1752–1840) was the most successful female novelist of the eighteenth century. Her first novel *Evelina* was a publishing sensation; her follow-up novels *Cecilia* and *Camilla* were regarded as among the best fiction of the time and were much admired by Jane Austen. Burney's life was equally remarkable: a protégée of Samuel Johnson, lady-in-waiting at the Court of George III, later wife of an emigré aristocrat and stranded in France during the Napoleonic Wars, she lived on into the reign of Queen Victoria. Her journals and letters are now widely read as a rich source of information about the Court, social conditions and cultural changes over her long lifetime. This Companion is the first volume to cover all her works, including her novels, plays, journals and letters, in a comprehensive and accessible way. It also includes critical discussion of her reputation, and a guide to further reading.

PETER SABOR is Director of the Burney Centre and Canada Research Chair in Eighteenth-Century Studies at McGill University. He is one of the General Editors of the Cambridge edition of the works of Samuel Richardson and the editor of Jane Austen's *Juvenilia* in the Cambridge edition of Austen. With Thomas Keymer, he is the co-author of *'Pamela' in the Marketplace: Literary Controversy and Print Culture in Eighteenth-Century Britain and Ireland* (Cambridge, 2005).

D0148758

THE CAMBRIDGE
COMPANION TO
FRANCES BURNEY

EDITED BY
PETER SABOR
McGill University

![Cambridge University Press logo] **CAMBRIDGE**
UNIVERSITY PRESS

COMMONWEALTH CAMPUS LIBRARIES
DELAWARE COUNTY

CAMBRIDGE UNIVERSITY PRESS
Cambridge, New York, Melbourne, Madrid, Cape Town, Singapore, São Paulo

Cambridge University Press
The Edinburgh Building, Cambridge CB2 2RU, UK

Published in the United States of America by Cambridge University Press, New York

www.cambridge.org
Information on this title: www.cambridge.org/9780521615488

© Cambridge University Press 2007

This publication is in copyright. Subject to statutory exception
and to the provisions of relevant collective licensing agreements,
no reproduction of any part may take place without
the written permission of Cambridge University Press.

First published 2007

Printed in the United Kingdom at the University Press, Cambridge

A catalogue record for this publication is available from the British Library

ISBN 978-0-521-85034-6 hardback
ISBN 978-0-521-61548-8 paperback

Cambridge University Press has no responsibility for
the persistence or accuracy of URLs for external or
third-party internet websites referred to in this publication,
and does not guarantee that any content on such
websites is, or will remain, accurate or appropriate.

CONTENTS

CONTENTS

ACKNOWLEDGEMENTS

I wish to thank the contributors to *The Cambridge Companion to Frances Burney* for making this volume possible. For their valuable help with the editing, I am grateful to three assistants at McGill University's Burney Centre: Laura Kopp, Alexis McQuigge and (visiting from Harvard) Hilary Havens. Linda Bree at Cambridge University Press has made many astute suggestions. I am indebted in various ways to Kate Chisholm, Stewart Cooke, Hester Davenport, Thomas Keymer and Paul Yachnin. For financial support, I thank the Social Sciences and Humanities Research Council of Canada and the Canada Research Chairs programme. My largest debt, as ever, is to Marie, my own companion.

CONTRIBUTORS

KATE CHISHOLM read history at Edinburgh University before training as a copy-editor at Cambridge University Press. She is the author of *Fanny Burney; Her Life* (1998) and *Hungry Hell* (2002). She is currently working on a book about the women in Dr Johnson's circle, 'Dr Johnson's Female Army', and has contributed an essay, 'Best Bakery in Town', to *The Last Bungalow: Writings on Allahabad* (2006).

LORNA CLARK is Research Adjunct Professor at Carleton University in Ottawa, Canada. Editor of *The Letters of Sarah Harriet Burney* (1997), she has contributed to the *New Dictionary of National Biography* and the *Encyclopedia of British Women Writers*. Editor of the *Burney Letter* since 1999, she is currently working on two volumes of *The Court Journals of Frances Burney*.

MARGARET ANNE DOODY is currently Director of the PhD Program in Literature at the University of Notre Dame, where she is the John and Barbara Glynn Family Professor of Literature. She is the author of a biography *Frances Burney: The Life in the Works*. She has published several works of fiction, including her latest novel *Mysteries of Eleusis* (2005). Her forthcoming non-fiction book is *Tropic of Venice*.

VIVIEN JONES is Professor of Eighteenth-Century Gender and Culture in the School of English, University of Leeds. She has published widely on gender and writing in the period, including, as editor, *Women in the Eighteenth Century: Constructions of Femininity* (1990), *Women and Literature in Britain, 1700–1800* (2000), *Jane Austen's Selected Letters* (2004), and the Oxford World's Classics *Evelina* (2002).

GEORGE JUSTICE is Associate Professor of English at the University of Missouri-Columbia. He is the author of *The Manufacturers of Literature: Writing and the Literary Marketplace in Eighteenth-Century England* and the co-editor of *Women's Writing and the Circulation of Ideas: Manuscript Publication in England 1550–1800*. Justice co-edits *The Eighteenth-Century Novel: A Scholarly Annual*.

BETTY RIZZO is Emerita Professor of The City College of New York and the CUNY Graduate Center. She is the editor of Volume IV of Burney's *Early Journals and*

Letters and author of *Companions without Vows: Relationships among Eighteenth-Century British Women* and many other books and essays.

PETER SABOR is Director of the Burney Centre and Canada Research Chair in Eighteenth-Century Studies at McGill University, Montreal. He has edited Burney's *Complete Plays* and co-edited *Cecilia* and *The Wanderer*, as well as a selection of her *Journals and Letters*. He is general editor of *The Court Journals of Frances Burney*, in progress.

SARA SALIH is Associate Professor of English at the University of Toronto. She has edited *The History of Mary Prince* and *The Wonderful Adventures of Mrs Seacole*. She is currently working on a book on 'brown' women in Jamaica and England from the Abolition era to the present day.

JANE SPENCER is Professor of English at the University of Exeter. She has published widely on the eighteenth-century novel and on women's literary history from the Restoration to the nineteenth century. Her latest book is *Literary Relations: Kinship and the Canon, 1660–1830* (2005). She is currently working on animals in eighteenth-century writing.

TARA GHOSHAL WALLACE is Associate Professor of English and Director of Graduate Studies at The George Washington University, Washington D.C. Her publications include *Jane Austen and Narrative Authority*, an edition of Burney's *A Busy Day*, and, as co-editor, *Women Critics, 1660–1820*. She has published articles on Smollett, Johnson, Austen and Scott, and is currently writing *Imperial Characters*.

JOHN WILTSHIRE is Professor of English at La Trobe University, Melbourne. He is the author, among other books, of *Samuel Johnson in the Medical World*, *Jane Austen and the Body*, *Recreating Jane Austen* and editor of *Mansfield Park* in the Cambridge edition of Austen's *Works*.

CHRONOLOGY

1752:   *13 June* Frances ('Fanny') Burney, the third of six children of Charles Burney, musicologist, and Esther Sleepe Burney, born in King's Lynn, Norfolk. Siblings are James and Esther.

1755:   *4 January* Sister Susanna ('Susan') born.

1757:   *4 December* Brother Charles born.

1760:   *c. April* Burney family moves to Poland Street, Westminster, where Charles Burney becomes a fashionable music master.

1761:   *4 November* Sister Charlotte Ann born.

1762:   *27 September* Death of mother.

1763:   Samuel Crisp becomes a close friend of the Burney family.

1767:   *13 June* Destroys juvenilia, including poetry, plays, and novel, 'The History of Caroline Evelyn', in bonfire on her birthday.
2 October Father marries Elizabeth Allen. Burney acquires three step-siblings: Stephen, Maria and Elizabeth.

1768:   *27 March* Begins new journal, addressed to 'Nobody'.
20 November Half-brother Richard born.

1769:   *23 June* Father receives degree of Doctor of Music, Oxford; Burney writes commemorative verses 'To Doctor Last'.

1770:   *20 September* Esther marries her cousin Charles Rousseau Burney.
November Burney family moves to Queen Square, Bloomsbury.

1771:   *30 June* Plays Lady Easy and Lady Graveairs in family performance of scenes from Colley Cibber's comedy *The Careless Husband*.

29 September Plays Lady Truman in family performance of Addison's comedy *The Drummer*.

1772: *16 May* Step-sister Maria Allen secretly marries Martin Rishton in Ypres.

29 August Half-sister Sarah Harriet born.

1774: *8 October* Burney family moves to Isaac Newton's former house, St Martin's Street, Leicester Square.

1777: *13 January* Epilogue, probably by Burney, to John Jackson's tragedy *Gerilda: or the Siege of Harlech*, spoken by Jane Barsanti at Crow Street Theatre, Dublin and published in *Walker's Hibernian Magazine*.

7 April Plays Mrs Lovemore in elaborate family performance of Arthur Murphy's *The Way to Keep Him*, including an additional scene probably written by herself; and Huncamunca in Henry Fielding's *Tom Thumb*.

12 October Step-sister Elizabeth Allen secretly marries Samuel Meeke in Ypres.

Late October Brother Charles expelled from Caius College, Cambridge, for stealing library books.

1778: *29 January* Publishes first novel, *Evelina; or, A Young Lady's Entrance into the World*.

Begins writing first comedy, *The Witlings*.

August Begins friendships with Samuel Johnson, members of the Johnson circle and Hester Lynch Thrale.

1779: *4 May* Completes first draft of *The Witlings*, encouraged by dramatists Richard Brinsley Sheridan and Arthur Murphy, as well as by Samuel Johnson, Joshua Reynolds and Hester Thrale.

2 August After reading a revised draft of *The Witlings*, her father and family friend Samuel Crisp urge her to suppress it, for fear of offending the London Bluestockings.

1780: *January* Revises Act IV of *The Witlings*, with a view to showing the whole play to Sheridan. Plans further revisions, but is persuaded by Dr Burney and Crisp to abandon it.

March–June Visits Bath with Hester and Henry Thrale.

10 June When Gordon Riots reach Bath, Burney and the Thrales flee to Brighton.

1782: *10 January* Susanna Burney marries Molesworth Phillips.

12 July Publishes second novel, *Cecilia, or Memoirs of an Heiress*.

1783:   *24 April* Death of Samuel Crisp.

1784:   *23 July* Rupture of friendship with Hester Thrale over her marriage to Gabriel Piozzi.
13 December Death of Johnson.

1786:   *17 July* Begins five years of service at Court, as Keeper of the Robes to Queen Charlotte, with an annual salary of £200.

1788:   *October* Begins writing her first tragedy, *Edwy and Elgiva*, during a period of insanity of King George III.

1790:   *August* Completes first draft of *Edwy and Elgiva*; begins writing two more tragedies, *Hubert De Vere* and *The Siege of Pevensey*.

1791:   *June* Completes first draft of *Hubert De Vere*; begins writing fourth tragedy, *Elberta*, which will remain incomplete.
7 July Ill health impels her to leave service of the Queen; granted annual pension of £100.

1793:   *January* Visits the Lockes of Norbury Park, Surrey, where she meets Alexandre d'Arblay, exiled Adjutant-General of the Marquis de Lafayette; secret courtship follows.
5 July *Hubert De Vere* accepted by John Philip Kemble for production at Drury Lane; later withdrawn in favour of *Edwy and Elgiva*.
28 July Marries d'Arblay in Protestant ceremony, followed by Catholic rite two days later.
19 November Publishes pamphlet, *Brief Reflections Relative to the Emigrant French Clergy*; proceeds given to charity.

1794:   *December* Revised version of *Edwy and Elgiva* accepted by Kemble and Sheridan for production at Drury Lane.
18 December Birth of only child, Alexander.

1795:   *21 March* *Edwy and Elgiva* produced at Drury Lane, with prologue by brother Charles; withdrawn after only one performance.

1796:   *12 July* Publishes by subscription third novel, *Camilla, or, A Picture of Youth*.
20 October Death of stepmother Elizabeth Allen Burney.

1797:   'Camilla Cottage' in Surrey built with the proceeds of *Camilla*.

1798:   Writes second comedy, *Love and Fashion*.

1799:   *30 March Love and Fashion* accepted by Thomas Harris for March 1800 production at Covent Garden Theatre.

1800:   *6 January* Death of sister Susanna, upon her arrival in England from Ireland.
          2 February At father's urging, *Love and Fashion* withdrawn from production. Begins writing two more comedies, *The Woman-Hater*, intended for Drury Lane, and *A Busy Day*, intended for Covent Garden; neither produced.

1802:   *February* Publishes heavily revised second edition of *Camilla*.
          15 April Burney and Alexander follow General d'Arblay to France, arriving in Paris on 20 April.

1803:   *12 May* Outbreak of war between France and England; d'Arblays unable to return to England.

1811:   *30 September* Undergoes mastectomy for breast cancer, without anaesthetic, at home in Paris.

1812:   *14 August* Returns surreptitiously to England with Alexander, on an American ship that is seized by the English; disembarks at Deal.

1814:   *28 March* Publishes fourth novel, *The Wanderer; or, Female Difficulties*.
          12 April Death of father.
          November Returns to France, leaving Alexander at Cambridge.

1815:   *19 March* Flees from France to Belgium, while General d'Arblay fights in army opposing Napoleon.
          17 October Returns to England with wounded husband.
          2 November Takes lodgings with husband in Bath.
          16 December Partial reconciliation with Hester Piozzi at Bath.

1817:   *24 September* Narrowly escapes drowning when trapped by the tide at Ilfracombe.
          28 December Death of brother Charles.

1818:   *6 March* Alexander elected Fellow of Christ's College, Cambridge.

3 May Death of General d'Arblay at home in Bath.

30 September Moves from Bath to London, settling in Bolton Street, Piccadilly.

1819:   *11 April* Alexander ordained priest in Church of England.

1821:   *19 July* Brother James appointed Rear-Admiral.

17 November Death of James.

1824:   *June* Alexander presented as Perpetual Curate to a new chapel in Camden Town.

1832:   *17 February* Death of sister Esther.

6 November Death of closest friend, Frederica Locke.

24 November Publishes final work, *Memoirs of Doctor Burney*.

1836:   *November* Alexander presented as Perpetual Curate to the Chapel of Ely in High Holborn.

1837:   *19 January* Death of Alexander. His fiancée, Mary Ann Smith, comes to live with Burney.

1838:   *12 September* Death of sister Charlotte.

1840:   *6 January*. Death of Burney in London, aged 87. Buried in Walcot Churchyard, Bath, beside husband and son.

1842–46:   Niece and literary executrix Charlotte Barrett edits *Diary and Letters of Madame d'Arblay* (7 vols.).

ABBREVIATIONS

Brief Reflections:	Frances Burney, *Brief Reflections Relative to the Emigrant French Clergy: Earnestly Submitted to the Humane Consideration of the Ladies of Great Britain, By the Author of Evelina and Cecilia* (1793).
Camilla:	Frances Burney, *Camilla*, ed. Edward A. Bloom and Lillian D. Bloom (Oxford: Oxford University Press, 1972).
Cecilia:	Frances Burney, *Cecilia*, ed. Peter Sabor and Margaret Anne Doody (Oxford: Oxford University Press, 1988).
DL:	*Diary and Letters of Madame d'Arblay (1778–1840)*, ed. Austin Dobson, 6 vols. (London: Macmillan, 1904–05).
ED:	*The Early Diary of Frances Burney, 1768–1778*, ed. Annie Raine Ellis, 2 vols. (London: George Bell, 1907).
EJL:	*The Early Journals and Letters of Fanny Burney*, ed. Lars E. Troide et al., 6 vols. (Oxford: Oxford University Press; Montreal: McGill-Queen's University Press, 1988–).
Evelina:	Frances Burney, *Evelina*, ed. Edward A. Bloom and Vivien Jones (Oxford: Oxford University Press, 2002).
JL:	*The Journals and Letters of Fanny Burney (Madame d'Arblay), 1791–1840*, ed. Joyce Hemlow et al., 12 vols. (Oxford: Oxford University Press, 1972–84).
Memoirs:	*Memoirs of Doctor Burney, Arranged from His Own Manuscripts, from Family Papers, and from Personal Recollections*, by his daughter, Madame d'Arblay, 3 vols. (London, 1832).
Plays:	*The Complete Plays of Frances Burney*, ed. Peter Sabor, 2 vols. (London: Pickering and Montreal: McGill-Queen's University Press, 1995).
Wanderer:	Frances Burney, *The Wanderer*, ed. Margaret Anne Doody, Robert Mack and Peter Sabor (Oxford: Oxford University Press, 1991).

PETER SABOR

Introduction

In 1991, the journal *Eighteenth-Century Fiction* devoted a special issue to *Evelina*, Frances Burney's first novel, with an introduction by Julia Epstein, four substantial essays, and an afterword by Margaret Anne Doody. It was a pivotal moment for Burney studies. Both Epstein and Doody had recently published major books on the author, and the special issue, the first that *Eighteenth-Century Fiction* had dedicated to any single novel, suggested that *Evelina* was a truly significant advance in the development of prose fiction, not merely a resting place on the long march from Samuel Richardson to Jane Austen. Doody's afterword, however, entitled 'Beyond *Evelina*', struck a cautionary note. While acknowledging that the collection was a timely recognition of Burney's rapidly rising critical standing, Doody questioned why *Evelina* alone of her four novels was being awarded such attention, both here and in other literary journals. We need, she concluded, to consider Burney's work as a whole, not to make of her 'the one-book little novelist' (371). Austen herself, after all, in her fine tribute to Burney in *Northanger Abbey* (I, ch. 5), singled out for particular mention not *Evelina* but Burney's second and third novels, *Cecilia* and *Camilla*.

In the years since the publication of the special issue, Burney studies – like studies of the eighteenth-century novel in general – have undergone radical change. No longer is one of her four novels privileged at the expense of its three more ambitious and demanding successors, and no longer is Burney regarded only as a novelist. Since 1995, when her eight plays – four comedies and four tragedies – were published in a collected edition for the first time, Burney has become increasingly well known to readers of drama and, most recently, to theatregoers: *A Busy Day*, the last of her comedies, enjoyed a three-month run at the Lyric Theatre in London's West End in summer 2000. And with sixteen out of twenty-four projected volumes of her journals and letters now available in a modern scholarly edition, Burney's importance as a chronicler of her age, from 1768 until the late 1830s, is becoming fully apparent. Another development is a better understanding of the roles, both supportive and counterproductive, that the remarkably talented and productive Burney family played in the composition of her novels and plays, as well as her journals and letters. Recent work on her father Charles Burney, the music historian, on her journal-writing sister Susanna, and on her novelist half-sister, Sarah Harriet, as well as on other family members, has thrown new light on the nature of Frances Burney's achievement.

No agreement, however, has been reached on the best way to name the author. For over half of her life, following her marriage to Alexandre d'Arblay in 1793, she was known as Madame d'Arblay, and although all of her novels were published anonymously, she signed the dedication to *Camilla* as 'F. d'Arblay' and that to *The Wanderer* as 'F.B. d'Arblay'. Nineteenth-century critics referred to her as Madame d'Arblay or, occasionally, as Frances Burney, but, for most of the twentieth century, Fanny Burney was preferred. In the mid-1980s, however, feminist critics, led by Margaret Anne Doody and Janice Farrar Thaddeus, argued strongly in favour of 'Frances', on the grounds that the diminutive 'Fanny' belittled the author. Most contributors to this volume prefer the formal 'Frances' to 'Fanny', but discussions of Burney in her family setting, in which she was known by the diminutive, naturally adopt this usage. To avoid confusion, Burney is called by her maiden name, even after her marriage, unless she is named in conjunction with her husband; here 'the d'Arblays' is preferred to the anachronistic 'Burney and d'Arblay'.

As the conflict over Burney's naming shows, there are few aspects of her life unexplored by critical discourse. Thus, it is fitting that, drawing on the latest research, *The Cambridge Companion to Frances Burney* deals with every aspect of her writing. The four novels are given the prominence they deserve, with substantial chapters devoted to the earlier pair – *Evelina* and *Cecilia* – and to the later, more complex *Camilla* and *The Wanderer*. But the *Companion* also gives full attention to Burney's eight plays, her seventy years of journal and letter-writing, her polemical *Brief Reflections Relative to the Emigrant French Clergy* (1793), and her final publication, the much-criticised *Memoirs of Doctor Burney* (1832). Chapters on the novels, plays and journals are complemented by two that consider her work in relation to political and gender issues. There are also chapters on the Burney family, on her fraught position in late eighteenth- and early nineteenth-century English (and French) society, on the commercial fortunes and misfortunes of her authorial career, and on her critical reception from the 1840s to the present. Due attention is paid to *Evelina*, the novel that made Burney famous, and to some repeatedly anthologised pieces from her journals, such as the address 'to Nobody' with which her earliest surviving journal begins and the much later, appallingly vivid account of her mastectomy, performed without anaesthetic. But the *Companion* goes far beyond these familiar writings, presenting incisive discussions of Burney's lesser-known later novels and her still neglected, unperformed tragedies, *Hubert De Vere*, *The Siege of Pevensey* and *Elberta*.

The great majority of Burney's journals were addressed to members of her family, especially to her father Charles Burney and her sister Susanna Burney Phillips. Kate Chisholm's chapter opens the *Companion* by studying Frances Burney in the context of her family, paying particular attention to her formative years in London. The Burneys, devoted to music, art, book-collecting and travel, as well as to literature, appear as a microcosm of eighteenth-century culture. Jane Spencer's chapter on *Evelina* and *Cecilia* is also concerned with Burney's early life, examining her relationship to her mentor Samuel Johnson and showing how, in her second novel, Burney moved beyond the Richardsonian epistolary model used in *Evelina* to blend the formal gravity of Johnson's style with free indirect discourse. Sara Salih's chapter on *Camilla* and *The Wanderer* considers how these two very long and complex novels can reward the reader today. While recognising their ostensibly conservative contribution to the war of ideas in the 1790s and early 1800s, Salih contends that they also give expression to a radical moral agenda. Tara Ghoshal Wallace examines Burney's involvement with the eighteenth-century stage both through the disastrous production of her tragedy *Edwy and Elgiva*, performed at Drury Lane for a single night in 1795, and through her dealings with Richard Brinsley Sheridan, Arthur Murphy and other contemporary dramatists. Wallace gives as much attention to Burney's tragedies as to her comedies, finding hitherto unrecognised links between her concerns in both forms of drama.

John Wiltshire's chapter on Burney's journals and letters takes in the full extent of her private writings: the early journals, when she was part of the Johnson circle; the Court journals, with their eyewitness insights into the madness of George III and the trial of Warren Hastings; and those written, after her marriage to the exiled French army officer Alexandre d'Arblay, during the French Revolution, the Napoleonic wars and thereafter. Wiltshire also pays attention to Burney's retrospective accounts of her life in *Memoirs of Doctor Burney*, comparing its embellished, amplified versions of events with their more spontaneous, vivacious originals. Margaret Anne Doody, in a chapter on Burney and politics, briefly considers Burney as a journal-writer and dramatist, but her primary concern is with the four novels and especially with *The Wanderer*, Burney's most overtly political work. Doody's analysis is complemented by Vivien Jones's exploration of gender issues in Burney's novels, and the ways in which her reputation was determined, in part, by contemporary critics insistent on depicting her as, in Hazlitt's words, 'a very woman'.

The last three chapters in the *Companion* are concerned with the vicissitudes of Burney's place in society, in the literary marketplace, and (posthumously) in the literary canon. In Burney's novels, as Betty Rizzo remarks, kindred spirits recognise one another through a *cri de l'âme*, or call of the soul: a mutual sympathy that recognises the claims of merit over those of rank. In Burney's life, however, the social structure proved to be more intractable; like her close friend (before their estrangement) Hester Thrale, Burney was unable, finally, to transcend the social limitations placed on her at birth. In his chapter on Burney's authorial career, George Justice examines her dealings with a series of hard-headed publishers, from Thomas Lowndes to Longman and Co., who proved to be as obdurate as the system of rank. Although Burney earned about £5,000 for her last three publications – *Camilla*, *The Wanderer* and *Memoirs of Doctor Burney* – her novels, representing many years of arduous composition under difficult circumstances, were more profitable for her publishers and for the proprietors of circulating libraries than they were for their author.

In her chapter on Burney's afterlife, Lorna Clark examines the reception of her writings from the 1840s, when the posthumous *Diary and Letters of Madame d'Arblay* was first published, to the first years of the present century. The chapter, and the *Companion*, concludes on a positive note. Despite her inability to rise through the ranks of English society and despite the limited success of her arduous negotiations with the book-trade, Burney has achieved greater fame in the twenty-first century than she ever possessed during her lifetime. In June 2002, on the 250th anniversary of her birth, a memorial panel was dedicated to her in the East Window of Poet's Corner, Westminster Abbey. Burney herself wrote the epitaph for a memorial to her father, placed in Westminster Abbey in 1817. It took almost two centuries for the two most famous of the Burneys to be memorialised together. Burney dedicated her first and her last novel to her father, and in her dedication of *The Wanderer* to Dr Burney she expressed the hope that, one day, prose fiction might stand on an equal footing with more exalted genres, such as epic poetry. Epic poets such as Virgil, Homer and Milton already have Cambridge Companions of their own. So too do the eighteenth-century authors whom Burney most admired, such as Swift and Johnson. With the publication of this volume, Burney joins their exalted ranks.

In her journal for March 1778, Burney wrote, with a self-mockery that is not entirely mocking:

> This Year was ushered in by a grand & most important Event, – for ... the Literary World was favoured with the first publication of the ingenious, learned, & most profound Fanny Burney! – I doubt not but this memorable

affair will, in future Times, mark the period whence chronologers will date the
Zenith of the polite arts in this Island! (*EJL* III, 1)

Burney's novels, plays and journals have come to occupy a more central
position in the English canon than their author, outside the confines of
playful fantasies in her private communications, could ever have envisaged.
This *Cambridge Companion*, with chapters by British, American, Canadian
and Australian scholars, reflects the depth and range of interest in Frances
Burney.

I

KATE CHISHOLM

The Burney family

A few weeks before he died in December 1784, the great lexicographer and essayist Samuel Johnson wrote a short note to his friend Charles Burney which he ends by sending his respects 'to dear Doctor Burney, and all the dear Burneys little and great'.[1] Johnson, without a family himself, was intrigued by and enamoured of the Burneys, 'little and great'. By 1784, the family comprised Charles Burney, the musician and scholar, and his second wife Elizabeth, along with their combined household of six children from Charles's first marriage and the two much younger children from his second. The second Mrs Burney also had three children from her first marriage. Such a blended family of siblings, half-siblings and step-siblings was not unusual, but the Burneys appear to have been peculiarly close-knit, drawn together by the powerful personality of their father. Johnson declared of them, 'I love all of that breed whom I can be said to know, and one or two whom I hardly know I love upon credit, and love them because they love each other.'[2]

The Burneys were a talented clan of musicians, writers, scholars, geographers and artists. And their shared habit of 'journalising', recording their encounters in vivid, as-they-happened letters and diaries that were written for each other but with an awareness, too, of their potential historical significance, has ensured that they will never be forgotten. Between them, the Burneys left behind more than 10,000 items of correspondence.[3] Reading through this enormous written record is to be entertained by an everyday saga of family life that is not so very different from our own: Dr Burney is mugged, his house is burgled, and his daughters fall out with their stepmother. His younger son is expelled from Cambridge for petty theft, another is reprimanded by the Admiralty for insubordination. One daughter dies tragically after enduring for years an unhappy marriage, two stepdaughters waste themselves on unsuitable men, while a third is destined for penurious spinsterdom.

We discover that there is nothing new about vegetarian diets, share the excitement of Fanny and her sisters as they prepare for their first masquerade, and marvel at a ballgown trimmed with grebe feathers and gold ribbon. But these quotidian concerns are transformed by the stage on which the Burneys lived out their lives. They shared a knack for being in the right place at the right time so that between them they knew many of the remarkable characters of their age. Dr Burney calls on Voltaire at his home in Ferney in Switzerland; his son James travels to the South Seas with Captain Cook; Susan befriends Pacchierotti, the leading Italian castrato of his time; Charles junior swaps Latin epigrams with William Hazlitt; and Sarah Harriet winters in Rome with the poet Walter Savage Landor and Henry Crabb Robinson, friend of Wordsworth and Coleridge. Richard, too, has his own intriguing tale, setting up a school for orphan children in Calcutta.

But it was Frances (or 'Fanny') Burney who most successfully cultivated her life-chances as one of the daughters of the sociable Dr Burney. Her novels, best-sellers in their time, are read and enjoyed now not for the elegance of her prose style or her ingenious plotting, but for the range and depth of her characters – Captain Mirvan, Elinor Joddrel, Sir Sedley Clarendel, Mr Dubster – inspired by the rich variety of her father's circle of acquaintance. When her diaries were eventually published after her death by her niece and great-niece, she earned a new wave of admirers, among them the novelist William Thackeray, who based his account of the battle of Waterloo in *Vanity Fair* on Fanny's gripping version of the events as she had witnessed them. The historian Macaulay, too, remarked on the extraordinary role which her father had played in London society in the 1770s and 1780s: 'few nobles could assemble in the most stately mansions of Grosvenor Square or Saint James's Square, a society so various and so brilliant as was sometime to be found in Dr Burney's cabin'.[4] Fanny, from an early age, flexed her skills as a writer to capture this 'brilliant' world in word-portraits that are as compelling today as when she first penned them.

She was born on 13 June 1752 in the Norfolk river port of King's Lynn, the third child and second daughter of Charles Burney and his first wife Esther. Charles was the parish organist, supplementing his income by giving private lessons on the harpsichord to the sons and daughters of the local gentry. But life in a provincial town was too limiting for a man of his ambition and talent. 'It Shames me to think How little I knew my self, when I fancy'd I should be Happy in this Place', he told Esther. 'O God! I find it impossible I should ever be so ... Nothing but the Hope of acquiring an independent Fortune in a Short Space of Time will keep me Here.'[5]

He was one of thirteen children to survive (seven, or perhaps as many as nine, of his siblings died in infancy, including his twin sister Susanna), and for most of his childhood he was sent away from home to board at school while his father struggled to make a living as a portrait painter and dancing master of no fixed address. Charles Burney was determined to live a very different kind of life. He taught himself French and Italian, wrote letters to Dr Johnson and other leading scholars, and cultivated friendships with the 'ton', those with inherited wealth and genteel status. Ill health had forced him to leave London, where he had hoped to establish himself as a professional musician, and to retreat to the less polluted air of King's Lynn, but by September 1760 he was back in the capital with his young and growing family. In addition to his first child Esther, born rather shockingly before her parents were married (just one of many Burney family secrets that remained hidden for generations),[6] there were also James, Frances, Susan and Charles (two earlier babies named after their father had died in infancy). Charlotte, the youngest of Charles's six children with his first wife, arrived in November 1761.

They were a boisterous, playful and imaginative family, living first in Poland Street in the heart of the bustling West End, then in quieter Queen Square, in a large and elegant house that from its windows looked across fields to the hilltop villages of Hampstead and Highgate. Esther (also known as 'Hetty') excelled on the harpsichord, and by the age of ten was performing in front of a paying audience. Susan, too, had a fine ear for music and an ability to sing as if she were Italian-born (the Italians were then regarded as the finest musicians in London). Their father inspired in all of them a love of books; even James, who was more of a mathematician than a reader and who was sent away to sea at the age of ten, spent his boyhood pennies at the bookstall in the market on 'a pennyworth of *Roderick Random*' (at least if his proud father is to be believed).[7] Dr Burney had always been careful to nurture his contacts with playwrights, composers and actors (he was named after his godfather Charles Fleetwood, a leading theatre manager); in 1750 he had worked with David Garrick, the most prominent and charismatic actor–manager of his day, on a 'pantomime' version of *A Midsummer Night's Dream*. He encouraged his children in their love of dressing up and play-acting, leading to the infamous occasion of 'Fanny and the Wig'.

Next door to the Burney home in Poland Street lived a wig-maker, or perruquier, also with young children, who often joined the Burneys in their amateur dramatics. On one occasion, talked about for years afterwards, they found some old wigs, which added greatly to their make-believe until one of them fell off and into a tub of rainwater. Only Fanny, aged ten, was prepared to challenge the irate wig-maker by declaring, 'What signifies talking so much about an accident. The wig is wet, to be sure; and the wig was a good wig, to be sure; but it's of no use to speak of it any more; because what's done cannot be undone.'[8] 'The wig is wet' became a standing joke in the family, a kind of secret code between them, while wigs often feature in Fanny's fictions, almost as a personal signature.

Dr Burney was preoccupied during these years with his flourishing career, giving as many as fifty-seven lessons a week, dashing from house to house in his private coach. The increasing wealth and leisure time of the burgeoning middle class from the 1760s onwards meant 'there was hardly a private family ... without its flute, its fiddle, its harpsichord, or guitar',[9] and Dr Burney was a remarkably successful tutor. He had devised his own technique of striking the keys of the harpsichord, which gave his performances, and those of his pupils, a distinctive quality.

His musical ability gave him the opportunity to better himself, becoming as socially mobile as if he had been born rich and well connected. But it was his determined self-education and energetic self-promotion, whether it be writing a history of the comets that had been seen in Britain or publishing an account of his travels in France and Italy or compiling his five-volume *General History of Music*, which ensured that in June 1769 he was awarded a doctorate of music by Oxford University and later was invited to join the most prestigious of all social and intellectual circles – Dr Johnson's Literary Club.

By October 1774 he had moved his family to an even more convenient and fashionable address in St Martin's Street, just around the corner from Leicester Fields, where Sir Joshua Reynolds lived, and conveniently close to the Opera House and the theatres on the Haymarket and Drury Lane. London in these years was at the heart of musical life, not just in England but also in Europe, singers from the Continent finding work in the theatres and assembly rooms of the West End and also at the pleasure gardens of Ranelagh, Marylebone and Vauxhall. The success of his book *The Present State of Music in France and Italy* (published in 1771) meant that Dr Burney was well known throughout this musical community, and his home became a popular rendezvous, especially on Sunday evenings when he organised informal concerts in his 'music room', starring the latest operatic sensations to have arrived in the capital. Dr Burney and his guests were lampooned by the caricaturist Charles Loraine Smith in his *A Sunday Concert, 1782*, depicting an evening in June when the guests included the tall, gangly castrato Pacchierotti and the statuesque Lady Mary Duncan.

At first there was nothing to suggest that Fanny would become the most renowned of all the Burneys. On the contrary, it was Hetty who inherited her father's abilities on the harpsichord, while Susan could astonish her father by repeating a musical air after hearing it just once. Fanny had little or no musical talent, and was teased by her boisterous brothers for not being able to read until she was eight. She was the quiet and retiring middle child who allowed her siblings to shine rather than competing with them for attention and praise. 'I ... was so peculiarly backward', she wrote later to

Hetty, 'that even our Susan [who was three years younger than Fanny] stood before me. She could read when I knew not my Letters' (*JL* XI, 286).

Fanny, however, had two key weapons at her disposal: her 'gnat-like eyes' – as Virginia Woolf so memorably depicted them in her essay on the Burney family[10] – and her acutely tuned memory. Fanny was short-sighted, and without spectacles saw everything through a myopic blur. She taught herself instead to catch the nuances or quirks of behaviour that betray a person's true character. She was by nature highly-strung: 'What a slight piece of machinery is the terrestrial part of thee, our Fannikin!' wrote her father's friend, Samuel Crisp, who became a kind of adopted uncle to the Burney children. 'A mere nothing; a blast, a vapour disorders the spring of thy watch' (*ED* I, lxxxii). But all the time she was quietly absorbing every detail of the conversation as it ebbed and flowed, storing it up before retreating to her room to write down as much as she could remember. In this way she trained her mind to recall an entire evening of dialogue with such accuracy that reading her letters and diaries is to be there with her in the room, listening to Dr Johnson, laughing with David Garrick, marvelling at the exploits of the explorer James Bruce or the scandalous character of Count Aleksei Orlov, who had arrived in England from the court of Catherine the Great, tainted by his involvement in the plot to murder the Tsar.

Fanny discovered in writing down 'my opinion of people when I first see them, & *how* I alter, or *how* confirm myself in it' (*EJL* I, 14) that she had a talent for word-spinning and character assassination, and that this was an effective outlet for her stifled emotions. The Burney household had become a complicated family unit, and Fanny, as a hypersensitive teenager, needed a secret vice. (Letter-writing was approved of, but private journals and fictions were not deemed suitable for young women of imagination but without an inheritance, who might otherwise become distracted from the task in hand: to find a socially acceptable and wealthy husband.) 'Our way of life is prodigiously altered', wrote Fanny in 1773, 'our Family is now very large' (*EJL* I, 315).

Her much-beloved mother had died shortly after the birth of Charlotte, leaving Charles with six children, the eldest of whom was only thirteen and the youngest just ten months. James was already away at sea, but the other five were left at home with a father who was for a time so upset by the loss of his wife that he was unable to carry on teaching. After several months of this inertia, he decided to travel to Paris, taking Hetty and Susan with him so that he could arrange for them to be educated on the Continent. Concerned for their future (without the prospect of a marriage dowry), he wanted to ensure that they acquired a proper French accent, 'to enable them to shift for themselves, as *I* had done'.[11] Fanny stayed behind with just Charles and baby Charlotte for company. We do not know why Susan (rather than her elder sister Fanny) accompanied Hetty, but can only assume that Dr Burney thought she would benefit more from the experience than Fanny. Unlike her sisters, Fanny never received any formal schooling, but instead taught herself French and Italian (just as her father had done) and kept firmly to a timetable of her own devising – her 'Lessons of Conduct and Sentiment' – which included 'Religion', 'Duty', 'Sincerity', 'Charity', 'Self-denial' and 'Delicacy'.

By 1767 Dr Burney had married again, a wealthy widow whom he had known in King's Lynn called Elizabeth Allen. The second Mrs Burney brought with her three children, and then had two more children: Richard (or 'Dick'), born in 1768, and Sarah Harriet, born in 1772. There was a 20-year age difference between Sarah Harriet and Fanny, creating a generation gap between the siblings, let alone between parent and child. As Virginia Woolf suggested in her essay on the Burneys, they became 'a mixed composite, oddly assorted family'.

Fanny was fifteen when her father remarried and she never really accepted the intrusion of the second Mrs Burney, nor did her siblings. In her memoir of her father, written when she was in her seventies, the elderly Madame d'Arblay (as Fanny became after marrying the French chevalier, Alexandre d'Arblay) describes her stepmother as having 'wit at will' and 'spirits the most vivacious and entertaining'. But she adds 'from a passionate fondness for reading, she had collected stores of knowledge which she was always able, and "nothing loath" to display' (*Memoirs*, I, 97). It's that 'nothing loath' (alluding to a line in Milton's *Paradise Lost*) which is so telling. Fanny could still conjure up many years later the antagonism that she had felt as a teenager towards her stepmother. In her novels, the heroines always have to grow up without a maternal influence, and are often thwarted by a repressive or misguided older woman.

Dr Burney, admirably, was aware that mixing up the two families could produce tensions: 'It was my wish & hope that our children would not be in each other's way, & that the children of my former marriage would be loved and regarded by my new partner as her own, being myself perfectly disposed & resolved to treat Mrs Allen's children with the same care and tenderness as my own.'[12] For some years the new Mrs Burney kept on her own home in King's Lynn and divided her time, and her children, between London and Norfolk, in an attempt to defuse the difficulties. But the Burney girls were always suspicious of their stepmother, who, in turn, resented their devotion to their father and did not approve of them spending hours hidden away in their rooms, writing page after page of 'secret thoughts'.

Fanny's diary, significantly, begins on 27 March 1768, six months after the marriage, by which time Mrs Burney was already pregnant with Richard (born in November). 'To Nobody', she says, she will write down, 'my *every* thought, must open my whole Heart!' It reads as though written by a conflicted teenager who is looking for a way to define her character, make her mark, set herself up against her 'nearest Relations'. 'The love, the esteem I entertain for Nobody, No-body's self has not power to destroy', she writes on that first day. 'From Nobody I have nothing to fear ... When the affair is doubtful, Nobody will not look towards the side least favourable' (*EJL* I, 1–2).

There's nothing unusual in this teenage desire for self-expression, or the fact that Fanny satisfied it by painstakingly recording 'my wonderful, surprising & interesting adventures' (*EJL* I, 2) in self-conscious imitation of Defoe's *Robinson Crusoe*.[13] (Her half-sister Sarah Harriet later severely criticised 'the tautology and vanity' of these early diaries.) But Fanny transforms her self-absorption into something much more discerning; she trains herself to write as a reporter, not a self-therapist. Her letters from Streatham Park, the home of Henry and Hester Thrale, which form part of that early journal, were fuelled by her egotistical excitement about the enthusiastic reception of her literary début, *Evelina*. But they also give us new insights into the character of the Thrales' other house guest, Dr Johnson.

Through Fanny's sharply drawn scenes, we see Johnson at play, writing silly verses with Hester Thrale, teasing, bantering, telling off the ladies for not dressing up more fashionably. There was, she writes, 'more *fun*, & comical humour, & Laughable & ... nonsense about him, than almost any body I ever saw' (*EJL* III, 255–6). Many years later when Boswell came to write his biography of Johnson, he begged Fanny to give him some of these insights into the 'Gay Sam', the 'Agreeable Sam', the private man whom she had known at Streatham. She refused, and it was not until her diaries were published after her death in 1840 that this aspect of Johnson's personality was brought fully into public view, amplifying and reinforcing the impression that Hester Thrale had already given in 1786 when her *Anecdotes of the late Samuel Johnson* first appeared.

Fanny became 'a Character-monger', as Dr Johnson teased her. 'I am more pleased with Pacchierotti than ever', she writes on 4 December 1778 of the Italian castrato whose eagerly awaited first performance in London had taken place just six days earlier.

> He seems to be perfectly amiable, gentle & *good*: his Countenance is extremely benevolent; & his manners, infinitely interesting. We are all become very good friends, & talked *English, French & Italian* by *commodious* starts, just as phrases occurred: – an excellent device for *appearing* a good linguist.
>
> (*EJL* III, 184)

But she was not the only Burney to write a diary. Susan had begun her own habit of daily 'journalising' long before Fanny, when she was sent away with Hetty to France after the death of their mother. Charlotte, too, was an amusing letter-writer, with her own inimitable style. The Burney household had become a virtual factory of words, with Dr Burney writing up his travel journals and preparing his history of music while his daughters worked as his team of secretaries, copying out material and preparing his manuscripts for the printer. At night, in the seclusion of their bedrooms, they kept their own diaries, sketched their own plays, or wrote novels. 'The Family of the Burneys are a very surprizing Set of People', declared Hester Thrale. 'Their Esteem & fondness for the Dr seems to inspire them all with a Desire not to disgrace him; & so every individual of it must write and read & be literary'.[14]

Susan's diaries from the late 1770s, still largely unpublished, are a unique record of the musical life of the capital at that time, giving details and insights not observed by Fanny, or by anyone else. Through her father, she knew all the great singers of the day and made obsessively detailed notes on operas that were brought from Italy, performed on just a few occasions and never afterwards published. 'Every line of the Opera [*Rinaldo*]', she told Fanny, 'is beautifully set by Sacchini, and Pacchierotti, not only in his airs, but in every word of the Recitative delighted me. So much sense, so much *sensibility*.'[15] (The score of *Rinaldo* has since disappeared, as have many of Antonio Sacchini's other works, despite his popularity at that time.)

While Fanny caught the essence of the singer's personality, Susan tells us more about his musicality:

> I never heard him so *well* in voice or in better Spirits ... He played all sorts of tricks with his voice running up & down as high or low as he could – I knew his compass to be such that he could sing *Tenor* songs but I did not before *suspect* he could vie with Agujari & Danzi [two well-known sopranos] to their *alt-itudes* – will you believe me when I assure you, & with great truth, that in one of his runs he ran fairly up to the highest F of the Harpsichord.[16]

Charlotte was cheekier than her sisters, and more daring in her opinions. Her account of the Gordon Riots that erupted in late June 1780 after the attempt to push a Bill through Parliament restoring to Catholics their rights to attend Oxford and Cambridge and to hold public office is as vivid and historically important as anything written by her elder sister. Fanny was away in Bath and, for once in her life, was not on the spot to witness a dramatic event. It was up to Charlotte and Susan to file reports to Fanny of the fear generated by the rioters (at one point they thought their house was about to be invaded by the mob) and the extent of the violence. On Monday, 12 June, three days after the rioting was over, Charlotte wrote to Fanny,

I hardly know what to tell you that won't be stale News ... however thank
heaven every body says now, that Mr Thrales House & Brewery [in Southwark
and in danger because Mr Thrale as an MP had voted in favour of the Bill] are
as safe as we can wish them – There was a Brewer in Turnstile that had his home
Gutted & Burnt, because the mob said 'he was a Catholic *papish*, & sold
popish Beer!' Did you ever hear of such Diabolical ruffians?

She continues in typical Burney vein,

It sounds almost incredible, but they say on Wednesday night, last, when the
mob were more powerful, more numerous, & more diabolical & outrageous
than ever, there was never the less a number of exceeding genteel people at
Ranelaugh, tho' they knew not, but their houses might be o'fire at the time! –
God bless you, my dear Fanny! – for heavens sake keep up your spirits – you see
there is no occasion to be *Molloncholy* about *us*! (*EJL* IV, 185–7)

The three sisters wrote with the same vivid observation, but yet express
themselves quite differently. Susan in her account of the riots of 5 and 6 June
not only describes, but also dissects the evidence:

One thing was remarkable, & convinced me that the Mob was secretly
directed by Somebody among themselves – they brought an *Engine* with
them, & while they pull'd [Justice] Hyde's House to pieces & threw everything they found in it into the Flames, they order'd the Engine to play on the
neighbouring Houses, to prevent them catching fire – a precaution which it
seems has been taken in every place that these Lawless Rioters have thought
fit to attack. (*EJL* IV, 548)

The sisters spurred each other on, covering page after page with densely
written, sometimes heavily crossed, accounts of their everyday lives – an
attempt to capture their experiences, but also to keep in touch with each
other, so close were the bonds that had been formed between them.
Pacchierotti once said of Fanny and Susan that it was as if there was 'but
one Soul – but one Mind between you – You are two in one' (*ED* I, lxxiv).

Until she married (in January 1782), Susan was also Fanny's most astute
critic. 'There is no wading through such stuff by oneself', Fanny confessed to
her after allowing her second novel *Cecilia* to be published without a final
read-through (Susan was by this time living in Ipswich with her new husband) (9 July 1782). It is highly possible that the sprightly pace of *Evelina*
was achieved by Fanny only because of Susan's constant presence at home,
reading through Fanny's drafts as she wrote them and suggesting revisions,
curbing her sister's tendency to over-write and lose the plot. Fanny, however, had the greater talent and ambition as a writer, with the ability to
flesh out the essence of a person in just a few words. She describes to Susan,

for example, an afternoon tea party in Bath. 'Mrs Montagu and my Mrs Thrale both flashed away admirably' (*EJL* IV, 38) – a beautifully concise exposition of the tension that she had sensed between the rival Bluestockings. (Mrs Montagu was married to one of the richest men in England and was the hostess of a glittering salon, which Hester Thrale struggled to equal.)

The Burney children prospered by their wits and by their mutual support and rivalry, all of them seeking to impress and please their father. That they achieved so much, rising to the topmost ranks of London society, was remarkable, but would somehow be less interesting if they had not also had their imperfections and personal tragedies. James, for instance, the eldest son, from being a captain's servant on an insignificant man-o'-war rose through the ranks to become a lieutenant on board the *Adventure*, one of two ships that sailed to the South Seas under Captain Cook. He later published an account of his travels, and also a complete history of the voyages of exploration in five volumes, complete with charts drawn by him from his own mathematical calculations.[17] He taught himself to speak Otaheitian fluently so that he could communicate with the islanders and, in particular, with the soon-to-be celebrated Omai, who travelled back to Britain with them on the *Adventure* and stayed for two years. Omai was given breeches and a wig to wear as if he were an English lord and taken up by 'society'; the Burneys drew him into their family circle, entertaining him at home. But James's naval career was punctuated by incidents of insubordination, when he refused to carry out orders or became involved in conflicts with his superiors. As a result, he was for many years 'rested' without a ship to command and was forced to remain reluctantly land-bound on half pay.

His younger brother Charles was the clever, bookish son, and won a scholarship to the prominent public school, Charterhouse (his father would never have been able to afford the fees), and then to Cambridge. But Charles threw away the opportunity in an act of criminal stupidity, stealing books from the university library. And not just a few books: ninety-one volumes are known to have gone missing in just a few weeks after Charles's arrival at the university. Nor did he just steal the books; he also removed the title pages, and cut out the catalogue marks with a pair of scissors. When his room was searched after the losses had been discovered – Charles, as the only under-graduate allowed to use the library, was the chief suspect – only thirty-five volumes were recovered; the rest had been sent by Charles to London where it is presumed he had intended to sell them. The volumes were all rare editions of the classics, Tacitus, Ovid, Seneca and Virgil, some from the early sixteenth century. Their loss was deemed so serious that it was still being discussed in Cambridge many years later (a pamphlet published in 1808 listed all the books that had gone missing).[18]

Dr Burney was incensed, refusing even to see Charles, who was sent to stay with friends in Reading. He then began bombarding people of influence with letters to ensure that Charles was eventually readmitted to university, but as far away as possible – Aberdeen. Charles applied himself to his studies and took his MA degree in the spring of 1781, after which he became a classics teacher at a reputable school in Highgate. The affair, however, plagued his life, as the Bishop of London repeatedly refused to ordain him (only Anglican clergymen could teach at Oxford or Cambridge). Undeterred, Charles established his own boarding school for boys in Greenwich that was soon very successful, expanding to accommodate large numbers of pupils. (G. H. Lewes, George Eliot's partner, was educated there in the early 1830s.)

Proof of his scholarly seriousness is shown by the fact that anyone intending to read his letters in the British Library will need to know Latin and Greek. It is intriguing, however, that when he died in 1817 his library was bought for the nation at a cost of £13,500 (or about a million pounds in today's money), an astonishing legacy for a schoolmaster. He also left a priceless collection of newspapers, now lodged in the British Library, which together chart the history of the print revolution of the early eighteenth century, including initial copies of the first newspaper published in London, the *Daily Courant*, as well as of Addison and Steele's *Tatler* and *Spectator* magazines. The core of this collection probably came from the coffee house in Covent Garden owned by Charles's aunts, Rebecca and Ann Burney, from the 1760s (*EJL* III, 457–9).

Less fortunate was their half-brother Dick who was sent off to India, aged sixteen, after some mysterious scandal (now thought to be an inappropriate friendship with a young woman, perhaps Hester Thrale's eldest daughter). He, too, successfully restored his reputation by setting up a school for orphan children in Kidderpore, near Calcutta. When he died in 1808 a monument was erected 'by his pupils' in the Mission Burial Ground, Park Street, Calcutta, which is dedicated to the memory of 'an enlightened tutor and a spiritual guide. By his persevering exertions, his holy example, and impressive counsel, great advantages have arisen to the Church of Christ, and not a few of his pupils have been brought to a saving knowledge of Divine Truth.' But he never returned to England, and never saw his family again.

In the letters and diaries of his sisters left at home with their stepmother, we can trace a history of family tensions, and near disasters. Blended families of step-parents, step-siblings and half-siblings have become very common again (usually caused now by marriage break-ups rather than premature deaths), so that the Burney story has renewed poignancy. 'Mrs Allen is gone to Lynn', wrote Fanny in April 1774, with an almost audible sigh of relief. 'She made her visit here last near 6 months, however the old lady was never at all in our way, for notwithstanding her Caprice, she ever behaved to Susy & me with the utmost civility, & even kindness' (*EJL* II, 24). The sisters obviously neither expected, nor wanted, anything more from the 'old lady' than 'civility' – and the freedom to carry on as if she were not there. They ignored their stepmother as much as possible, while desperately seeking attention from their father, who, according to repeated complaints in Fanny's journals, was hardly ever in the house. (In Fanny's comedy *The Witlings*, which she wrote in 1779–80, there is a character called Jack who is perhaps based on her father: he is always in a rush, dashing about town and never finishing a conversation.)

While the Burney sisters muttered among themselves about their step-mother, the Allen daughters openly rebelled, by eloping with what appears to be casual self-abandonment – something the Burney girls would never, could never, have done, so concerned were they for their father's approval and well-being. Maria Allen was a spirited, lively, self-willed girl, who swapped teasing letters with her stepsister Fanny. 'I like your Plan immensely', she once wrote to Fanny, 'of Extirpating that vile race of beings called man.' Adding a surprising refinement: 'suppose we were to Cut of [*sic*] their *prominent members* and by that means render them Harmless innofencive Little Creatures' (*EJL* I, 331–2).

Maria made the mistake of not distinguishing between her rebellious thoughts and her actual behaviour. Aged nineteen, she eloped to Ypres. At least she chose a man with some prospects; her sister Bessy, in contrast, ran away with 'an adventurer' before she was sixteen. Bessy's tale has the surface glamour of a Georgian romance, but came to a gothic conclusion: the marriage did not last, and she spent the rest of her life on the Continent, choosing poverty abroad rather than ignominy at home.

She created such a scandal that Dr Johnson heard about it (from Hester Thrale): 'Mrs Burney was coming over from Dieppe to Brighthelmstone *all alone*, in great Distress, her fine Daughter having eloped from her at Paris ... She resolved not to go home, however, but to a friend's House where She would stay She said till her Husband came to fetch her, for She could not bear to go tell *her Story* among his Girls.' Johnson's response to the gossip was sympathetic. 'Poor Mrs [Burney]! ... it is impossible for her husband's daughters not to triumph.' But he adds, pertinently if somewhat slyly, 'and her husband will feel ... *something that does not displease him*'.[19]

The novels that Fanny was later to write are sometimes accused of being too full of dramatic incident to be credible, but within the family there were three elopements (her stepbrother, Stephen Allen, also married in haste, running off to Gretna Green), innumerable affairs, disappearing children, and a possibly incestuous relationship. Her fictions fed off the emotional tensions these dramas created. The fragile state of her own 'respectability' gave her stories an ironic edge, an underlying realism. Since none of the girls could expect a dowry (Dr Burney worked hard to make a decent living, but most of it went on maintaining a lifestyle to match that of his clients), they could never be complacent about their prospects. Fanny herself did not marry until she was forty one, when she met and fell in love with an émigré from the French Revolution, the Comte d'Arblay. Her sister closest in age and affection, Susan, married disastrously a naval friend of their brother James.

Molesworth Phillips at first appeared to be an ideal husband – tall, dark, handsome, clever, even a bit of a hero. He had, like James, travelled with Cook to the South Seas, and was reputed to have shot the islander who killed Cook. He claimed, too, that he had saved the life of a fellow sailor by turning back and helping him to swim to the safety of Cook's ship, the *Resolution*, after the violent fracas between the explorers and the native islanders. But other tales brought home by the crew suggested that Captain Phillips had a fiery temper, and after the first few years of domestic happiness, and the birth of three children, Susan was increasingly abandoned by her wandering husband. She never lived in London again, never went to the opera, was always short of money, and finally was threatened with separation from her elder son unless she left England and travelled to a remote farmhouse in County Louth in Ireland which Phillips had inherited. The marriage fell apart so severely that Susan was even frightened to write openly to her family, devising a system instead of cutting up paper and pasting over the gaps to conceal anything that she feared might anger Phillips.

She died in January 1800 in Parkgate, Cheshire, shortly after arriving by open boat from Dublin. The news took three days to reach Fanny, too late for her to travel north for the funeral. She would forever afterwards mourn the loss of her 'darling confidant', the person to whom she had addressed most of her letters and whose instinctive editing skills had played a part in Fanny's literary success. She abandoned the production of her latest comedy, *Love and Fashion*, which had been scheduled for Covent Garden in the next season. As with her earlier drama, *The Witlings*, which was never staged, the comedy was never performed in public. In private, though, Fanny continued to dream of writing for the stage, admitting to her father that she had 'all my life been urged to, & all my life intended, writing a Comedy' (*JL* IV, 394–5).

'In her life, she bottled it all up, & looked and generally spoke with the most refined modesty', commented her half-sister Sarah Harriet in 1842 after the publication of Fanny's diaries (and with the freedom of knowing that Fanny had died). 'But what was kept back, and scarcely suspected in society, wanting a safety valve, found its way to her private journal.'[20] The intensity of these feelings also stoked the imaginative pot from which emerged the great range of characters who people Frances Burney's novels.

Sarah Harriet was herself a successful novelist (beginning in 1796 with *Clarentine*, and ending in 1839 with *The Romance of Private Life*, via *Geraldine Fauconberg*, *Traits of Nature* and *Tales of Fancy*), but lived in the shadow of her more famous half-sister. She carried the Burney name but had a very different experience of family life. Born in the same year, 1772, that her half-sister Hetty gave birth to the first of her father's grandchildren, she was left behind as a baby in King's Lynn, where she was looked after by her mother's relations. When she did finally turn up at St Martin's Street, she was the only child among a tribe of creative and energetic adults (even the baby, Charlotte, was by then aged fourteen). 'Little Sally is come Home', commented Fanny in October 1775, '& is one of the most innocent, artless, *queer* little things you ever saw', adding almost as an afterthought, 'she is a very sweet, & very engaging Child' (*EJL* II, 163).

Sarah Harriet was only six when Fanny's first novel *Evelina* was published. Her distinction from the other Burney daughters, the way she kept herself apart, is reinforced by the fact that their cousin, Edward Francisco (son of Dr Burney's brother), another gifted Burney who was admired as an artist by Reynolds and James Barry,[21] has left us portraits of Fanny, Susan and Charlotte but never painted Sarah Harriet (or at least nothing by him has survived). Her novels reflect the difficulties she experienced as the much-younger and 'different' child. In *Traits of Nature*, for instance, the heroine, Adela, is abandoned by both her parents when she is only six and is taken in by the Hampden family, where, despite their warm-hearted domesticity, she suffers intensely from feeling herself to be an outsider. Her constant ally is her black maid, Amy, whom she has known from before she can remember and from whom she derives the love and comfort that her parents have so unnaturally denied her. When her mother returns at one point to claim her, Adela is faced with the decision of whether she should go with her or stay with the family who have taken her in and with whom after months of misery she now feels comfortable.

Sarah Harriet lived out one of her own heightened fictions when in 1798 she suddenly disappeared from her rooms in Chelsea College where she was living with her father, by then a widower and crippled with arthritis. A few days later, she was found by her stepsister Maria Rishton (née Allen), who had been dispatched by the other siblings to go in search of her, in a lodging house off Tottenham Court Road where she was living with her half-brother James, who had abandoned his wife and two young children. Maria was shocked not so much by their behaviour but by the 'most Grovling mean

Style' in which they were living, with so little money that their rooms were in a shady part of town, 'where they have found out that the Womans Daughter is a Common Prostitute who brings home a different Visitor every Night – and they dare not both leave their Apartments together lest they shou'd be rob'd' (*Letters of Sarah Harriet Burney*, xl).

It is a painfully sad tale, ended only when Sarah Harriet, after several years of happiness, insisted that James must return to his wife and children, while she took a job as a governess. Like Fanny, Sarah Harriet found solace in her pen. 'I *must* scribble, or I *cannot live*', she once wrote (*Letters of Sarah Harriet Burney*, 197). But within the family she suffered constant comparison with her more famous sibling. 'Don't you find considerable merit in her novel', her father rather condescendingly wrote to Fanny after the publication of *Clarentine* in 1796 (just a few days after Fanny's own novel *Camilla*). 'The opening is embarrassed & incorrect; but she afterwards gets on very well' (*Letters of Sarah Harriet Burney*, lxii).

In his essay 'On the Aristocracy of Letters', published in 1821, the critic William Hazlitt, close friend of James and Charles Burney junior, declared, 'There is no end of it [the Burney family] or its pretensions. It produces wits, scholars, novelists, musicians, artists in "numbers numberless". The name is alone a passport to the Temple of Fame.'[22] The Burneys, with their letter-journals, novels, travelogues, book-collecting, people-collecting, musicality and artistry, were an exceptional clan, the diversity of their talents and the broad range of their adventures serving as a microcosm of eighteenth-century life. Our enduring fascination with them lies in the way that together, little and great, they have preserved a whole world for us to spy on.

NOTES

1. 17 November 1784, *The Letters of Samuel Johnson*, ed. Bruce Redford (Princeton: Princeton University Press, 1992–4), IV, 437.
2. From a letter to Mrs Thrale, 14 November 1781, *The Letters of Samuel Johnson*, III, 373.
3. See Joyce Hemlow, with Jeanne M. Burgess and Althea Douglas, *A Catalogue of the Burney Family Correspondence, 1749–1878* (New York: New York Public Library, 1971).
4. *The Works of Lord Macaulay: Essays and Biographies* (London: Longmans, Green & Co., 1898), IV, 7.
5. *The Letters of Dr Charles Burney*, ed. Alvaro Ribeiro (Oxford: Clarendon Press, 1991), I, 1.
6. First unearthed by Hemlow in *The History of Fanny Burney* (Oxford: Clarendon Press, 1958), 6.
7. From an extant scrap of Dr Burney's own reminiscences, in *Memoirs of Dr Charles Burney, 1726–1769*, ed. Slava Klima, Garry Bowers and Kerry S. Grant (Lincoln and London: University of Nebraska Press, 1988), 141.

8. Dr Burney preserved the story, *Memoirs of Dr Charles Burney, 1726–1769*, 142–3. Fanny also recorded the incident in her *Memoirs of Doctor Burney* (London, 1832), II, 168–71. Her work is the source for this quotation.

9. From Dr Burney's *The Present State of Music in France and Italy* (1771), 6.

10. 'Dr Burney's Evening Party', *The Common Reader* (Second Series, London: The Hogarth Press, 1986), 108–25.

11. *Memoirs of Dr Charles Burney, 1726–1769*, 156.

12. *Memoirs of Dr Charles Burney, 1726–1769*, 175.

13. The full title of Defoe's novel, published in 1719, is *The Life and strange and surprising Adventures of Robinson Crusoe*. Fanny was christened in the Chapel of St Nicholas in King's Lynn where lie buried various members of the 'Cruso' family, two of whom were called 'Robinson'.

14. From an entry dated August 1779 in *Thraliana: The Diary of Mrs Hester Lynch Thrale (Later Mrs Piozzi), 1776–1809*, ed. Katharine C. Balderston, 2 vols., 2nd edn (Oxford: Clarendon Press, 1951), I, 399.

15. Letter dated 9 March 1780: BM Eg MS 3691. See also chapter 4 of *Italian Opera in Late Eighteenth-Century London*, by Curtis Price, Judith Milhous and Robert D. Hume (Oxford: Clarendon Press, 1995), for a detailed study of Susan's letter-journals, her 'technical grasp' of the music, and her 'appetite for backstage gossip'.

16. Quoted by Linda Kelly in *Susanna, the Captain and the Castrato: Scenes from the Burney Salon, 1779–80* (London: Starhaven, 2004), 47.

17. *With Captain James Cook in the Antarctic and Pacific. The Private Journal of James Burney, Second Lieutenant of Adventure on Cook's Second Voyage, 1772–1773*, ed. Beverley Hooper (Canberra: National Library of Australia, 1975); *A Chronological History of the Discoveries in the South Sea, or Pacific Ocean*, by James Burney, Captain in the Royal Navy, 5 vols. (London, 1803–17).

18. Ralph S. Walker gives details of the theft and its impact on Charles's career in 'Charles Burney's Theft of Books at Cambridge', *Transactions of the Cambridge Bibliographical Society*, III, iv (1962), 313–26.

19. *The Letters of Samuel Johnson*, 85–7, 91.

20. *The Letters of Sarah Harriet Burney*, ed. Lorna J. Clark (Athens: University of Georgia Press, 1997), 463.

21. Edward Francisco's drawings can be seen at Tate Britain, the British Museum and the Guildhall Library in London, and also at the Huntington Library in San Marino, California, and the Metropolitan Museum in New York. See also H. A. Hammelmann's article, 'Edward Burney's Drawings', *Country Life*, 143 (6 June 1968), 1504–6; and Patricia Crown's *Drawings by E. F. Burney in the Huntington Collection* (San Marino, California: The Huntington Library, 1982).

22. Quoted by Roger Lonsdale, *Dr Charles Burney* (Oxford: Clarendon Press, 1965), 481.

authorship can be helpful. The world of letters which Burney was entering was itself changing as writing for money began to be, for some, a prestigious as well as possible occupation, with Johnson himself foremost among the new professionals. An expanding and diversifying literary market afforded many opportunities for female writers. Yet the national literary canon, the gradual creation of over a hundred years of developing criticism, biography and literary history, was still a largely male affair, constructed as a patrilineage. As John Dryden had explained in the previous century, 'Milton was the poetical son of Spenser, and Mr Waller of Fairfax; for we [poets] have our lineal descents and clans as well as other families'.[1] In the eighteenth century too, literary fathers and literary sons were understood as the originators and inheritors of traditions of poetry, drama, criticism, and even, as the form rose in status, of the novel. It was not immediately clear how women, understood as marginal to the line of paternal descent, as conduits of rather than participators in inheritance, could truly belong to the literary line. The critical success of Burney's first two novels began to alter that picture. As her heroines negotiated their problematic places within families dominated by the patriarchal principle, the author was making her own way as an inheriting daughter within the patriarchal family of English literature.[2]

Burney's well-known devotion to her own father, her wish to emulate and her fear of disgracing him, surrounded the writing and anonymous publication of *Evelina* with daughterly anxieties, evident in the poem prefixed to the novel, addressing Charles Burney as 'Author of my Being', and in a story she afterwards told of the emotional scene between them when he acknowledged her as the author of *Evelina*. In contrast, her assumption of a connection to her literary fathers was relatively untroubled. In the preface to *Evelina*, she defends the respectability of the novel by referring to 'such names as Rousseau, Johnson, Marivaux, Fielding, Richardson, and Smollet', adding that 'no man need blush at starting from the same post' as these writers (8). This apparent confidence in her literary heritage, though, is predicated on the anonymity that allows her to imply male authorship, to imitate the voice of an inheriting son; and on the suppression of a matrilineal inheritance for her novel – none of her female precursors are mentioned in the preface. By the time she wrote *Cecilia*, her authorship was known. Her second novel would be received not only as a woman's, but as the work of Charles Burney's daughter, and as another attempt from the famous author of *Evelina*. Anxieties multiplied in this situation. After the painful experience of abandoning *The Witlings* because of Charles Burney's and Samuel 'Daddy' Crisp's opposition to the play, she was delighted to be working on a project of which they both approved, but her father's hurry to have *Cecilia* finished created new pressures, and her journal entries during composition give the impression of near-panic: 'I am often taken with such fits of terror about it', she wrote to Hester Thrale, 'that, but for my Father, I am sure I should [th]row it behind the Fire!' (*EJL* IV, 256) Nevertheless she continued to work on this much more ambitious second novel, delaying publication to give it the length it needed, and, despite her wish to please her 'Daddies', insisting on qualifying the happiness of the ending in a way that disappointed them.[3] In writing *Cecilia*, in fact, Burney was coming into her own, asserting an independence from the two 'daddies' whose views had been so influential. Following Richardson and Fielding, whose work had raised the status of the novel in a previous generation, she was aiming to give a new moral and philosophical weight to the feminine novel of a young girl's experience of society. In doing this she took on a different daughterly role, staking her claim to be the literary heiress of Samuel Johnson, 'the acknowledged Head of Literature in this kingdom' (*EJL* III, 73).

Johnson's high praise of *Evelina* had been the jewel in the crown of the novel's success, and her friendship with him, growing rapidly during her time at the Thrales' house in Streatham in 1778–9, transformed her understanding of authorship. For all that he sometimes enjoyed treating her as a petted child, Johnson also spoke of her, and to her, as a serious author in the line of Richardson and Fielding, to be compared to them and in some respects surpassing them. For him, the world of letters was an arena in which a woman should compete on the same terms as a man. Moreover, as they stayed together at Streatham, both writing, rumours grew that they were working together. Burney was proud of the association between them, symbolised in one of her cousin's illustrations of *Evelina*. Describing this picture in a letter to Johnson, she triumphantly quoted Pope's *Epistle to Mr Jervas*:

So mix our Studies, & so join our Names.

  Do you not, Sir, recollect how often in sport you have repeated this Line to me? but what will You say when I tell You that *something of that there sort*, in Mr. Norman's phrase, is actually coming to pass? – & that in a stained Drawing designed from a Scene in Evelina, a Print of Dr Johnson is hung up in the Study of Mr. Villars? – I half fear that not all the kindness with which you honour me, nor all the partiality with which you exalt my Book will enable You to bear this with complacency. Nothing, however, is farther from my thoughts than any intention of offering to prevail with the Young Artist, Mr. Edward Burney, to suppress the Drawing, – no, – I am much too proud of our appearing together thus in Public, – for it is meant to be Exhibited at the opening of the Royal Academy in Somerset House – to daintify away my own satisfaction. And indeed should I neglect an opportunity so inviting of joining our Names, none other may offer till we write an Account of our Travels to the Hebrides, to Lapland, or to the peak of Teneriffe. (*EJL* IV, 70–1)

Burney and Johnson never travelled to Lapland or published together, but the literary relationship between them, begun with her preface to *Evelina*, was deepened in her second novel, which consciously echoes Johnson's style and pursues and adapts Johnsonian ideas.

Evelina

By hanging Dr Johnson's portrait in Mr Villars's study, Edward Burney continued an association between the famous moralist and Evelina's moralising foster-father, begun by Charles Burney when he praised the '*sound sense,* & *manly reasoning*' of Mr Villars's letters, and commented 'that Johnson could not have expressed himself better' (*EJL* III, 53). In reading Mr Villars either as a Johnsonian presence or as a pure exponent of sense and goodness, however, Burney's father radically simplified her text. Mr Villars is in fact a most un-Johnsonian moralist. Johnson's influential moral fable, *Rasselas*, had expressed disillusionment with the world, but still insisted on the necessity of human engagement with it; while in his friendship with Burney, Johnson, far from recommending the sort of sequestered existence that is Villars's ideal for Evelina, wanted her to take her place even aggressively in the world of letters by attacking his own rival, Elizabeth Montagu: '[F]ly at the *Eagle!*' he urged her (*EJL* III, 153). By contrast, Mr Villars is a study in obsessive fear of the social world. He can hardly let Evelina out of his sight; at the outset of the novel, even the suggestion that her annual visits to Lady Howard's safe and respectable country house should be resumed is too much (18). He eventually agrees to Evelina's visit to Howard Grove, and later to London, with great uneasiness, invoking the dangers of the world and the brittleness of female reputation, and longing for her to be restored to him with innocence and purity intact. Well aware of his own 'weakness' (18), he admits to Evelina that '[t]o follow the dictates of my own heart, I should instantly recall you to myself, and never more consent to your being separated from me' (130). His greatest desire, mentioned three times in his letters, is to die in her arms (17, 27, 405).

Villars's exaggerated fears and morbid wishes stem from his unhappy experiences with the Evelyn family. First he lost his friend Mr Evelyn, and then Mr Evelyn's daughter, Carolyn Evelyn. Persuaded into a secret marriage by Sir John Belmont, and then disgraced and abandoned in her pregnancy, she died giving birth to Evelina, who like her mother before her was left to Villars's guardianship. To complete his dependence on this third-generation Evelyn, Villars has lost his own wife and has no child. His fears of losing his second ward are roused by Lady Howard's opening letter explaining that Evelina's grandmother, now Madame Duval, has written to her enquiring after her grandchild; and this news would seem to bring on the months of illness that he suffers between the second and third letter of the novel.

Mme Duval's letter triggers the events of the narrative, but is not itself reproduced. Burney is an economical epistolary writer: where Richardson, in *Clarissa* and *Sir Charles Grandison*, multiplied points of view and detailed incidents from several angles, she includes only letters that forward the plot, and in Evelina's correspondence with her friend Maria Mirvan, for example, none of Maria's letters appear. However, more than economy is involved in the suppression of Madame Duval's writing. Her point of view is consistently belittled; her words are given only to be mocked. The contents of her letter are relayed with Lady Howard's hostile commentary, and her words are quoted indirectly, with Lady Howard's sarcastic emphasis. She tells Mr Villars:

> [Madame Duval] has ... lately used her utmost endeavours to obtain a faithful account of whatever related to her *ill-advised* daughter; the result of which giving her *some reason* to apprehend that, upon her death-bed, she bequeathed an infant orphan to the world, she most graciously says that if *you*, with whom *she understands* the child is placed, will procure authentic proofs of its relationship to her, you may send it to Paris, where she will properly provide for it.
>
> (13–14)

Thus we are invited to be sceptical of Mme Duval's claim that Villars has concealed Evelina's existence from her – though the charge, in fact, is never clearly refuted. Mme Duval is given a moment of pathos when she first meets Evelina, crying 'Let me not lose my poor daughter a second time!' (54), and Evelina's later account of her grandmother's dunking in a muddy ditch betrays some uneasiness at her own complicity in the older woman's humiliation; but on the whole the novel shows remarkably little sympathy for a grandmother deprived of her grandchild. With its strong emotional investment in the heroine's relationship to her father and to father figures, *Evelina* honours the patriline and is ambivalent about the matriline, dividing it between a good dead mother and a bad living grandmother.

Villars does have a reason for his initial reluctance to tell Mme Duval of baby Evelina's existence. Mme Duval, through her tyrannical attempt to force Carolyn into an unwanted marriage, was to blame for her elopement, and he could not be expected to be keen to hand the child over to the woman who had persecuted her dead mother. Still, there is a pattern here. Mr Villars has something of a habit of keeping babies from their natural relations. Carolyn herself, as a baby, was kept away from her own mother under the terms of her father's will: having belatedly realised that his wife was 'low-bred and illiberal', Mr Evelyn needed no other reason to leave their daughter to Villars's guardianship instead (16). Here the father's word is law; but when Evelina is born, her own father, having repudiated his marriage, loses his legal rights over her, and he, like Mme Duval, is kept ignorant of her birth. Again Villars has an excuse in Sir John's behaviour to Carolyn and in Carolyn's own stipulation that her child should only go to its father if acknowledged as legitimate. Yet there is a hostile passivity in Villars's apparent failure to contact father or grandmother (his view seems to be that it was up to them to enquire, not up to him to volunteer information). Eventually the reader learns that ever since Evelina's babyhood, Sir John has been bringing up her nurse Dame Green's daughter, believing this child to be his own daughter by Carolyn. If Belmont has contributed to the confusion by keeping his putative daughter out of the way in a convent, Villars unwittingly made the deception possible in the first place. It was because she saw him so keen to hide Evelina from the world that Dame Green considered it safe to offer her own child to Sir John instead.

The theme of Evelina's tragic family history and its threat to her future dominates the early exchanges in the novel, in which the heroine herself plays no part. Once her own voice appears, in the eighth letter, the tone and the narrative concerns change. If Villars is living in the past, hoping to keep Evelina in a static purity, his young ward is making the most of the present moment. Pleading to be allowed to go to London with the Mirvans and Lady Howard, she shows her own desire to view the world Villars finds so danger-ous. Once there, she is brisk and busy: 'This moment arrived. Just going to Drury-Lane theatre' (27). The novel moves into its stride. Accounts of David Garrick's acting, of walks in St James's Park, of shopping expeditions, hair dressing and balls build up the vivid picture of contemporary social life that made it such a fashionable success in Burney's time and make the author, for us, one of the best delineators of the new consumer society. As naive obser-ver, Evelina is a satirical device, her innocent enthusiasm for the acting exposing the foppishness of those who attend the theatre to be seen rather than to watch and her ignorance of the rules of a young lady's behaviour at the ball acting as a covert critique of them. Shy and easily abashed in company, tart and witty in her letters, Evelina manages to combine an innocent appreciation of the world's pleasures with a satire on its follies. Her letters create the other characters; and young men's conceited foppish-ness, Mme Duval's rudeness and ignorance, the Branghtons' inept social airs, and Mrs Selwyn's satiric bite are all conveyed through her dramatisations. She also hints at the nastiness underlying the ordered social world, evident in the barely suppressed violence of Captain Mirvan's practical jokes, and while praising her hostess, Mrs Mirvan, she manages to convey her dismay at the Mirvans' dreadful marriage, in which the wife's 'principal study seems to be healing those wounds which her husband inflicts' (55).

Evelina's discovery of the fashionable and not-so-fashionable world is woven into a courtship plot in which the impossibly decorous Lord Orville proves his superiority to the heroine's other admirers by his ability to see through apparently compromising social appearances and appreciate her true inner worth. When her vulgar cousins commandeer his carriage in her name, his respect for her is not lessened, and when he comes across her walking in Vauxhall Gardens with two prostitutes, his only concern is how to alert her to the truth without upsetting her delicacy. As the relationship with Orville comes more and more to dominate Evelina's consciousness, displacing concern for her tangled family situation, Burney accentuates the effect through a skilful juxtaposition of letters. She generally presents letters in the order of composition and sending, which means, allowing for the time taken in the post, that characters frequently write before having read the letter that, for the reader, immediately precedes theirs. As we approach the climax of protracted negotiations with Sir John Belmont, Villars having finally been convinced that Evelina should confront her father, the heroine herself is too wrapped up in her feelings for Orville to pay much attention. The last letter from Evelina's dying mother to Sir John is enclosed in one of Villars's letters to Evelina; but in the following letter Evelina, not yet having read this, is concerned only with the problem of how she should behave towards Lord Orville, whose intentions are not yet clear to her. By the time she writes again she has read Villars's letter, but swiftly dismisses it, reporting: 'important as is this subject, I am, just now, wholly engrossed with another, which I must hasten to communicate' – the proposal of marriage she has just received from Orville (350).

Yet Evelina cannot escape her family history. It haunts her throughout, from Mme Duval's unwelcome appearance and the social embarrassments caused by her new relatives, the Branghton family, to the complications following her meeting with the young poet Macartney, her illegitimate half-brother. Her uncertain social status, with no father's name to define her identity, leaves her constantly vulnerable to sexual insults, such as Sir Clement Willoughby's half-formed seduction plan or Mr Brown's intimation that he might just persuade himself to marry her. Important though it is that Lord Orville, above such nonsense, offers love and marriage before learning her true identity, Evelina herself needs to have that identity acknowledged before she can be comfortable accepting him. The meeting with her father, when he acknowledges his daughter by seeing her as the image of her mother, forms the emotional climax of the novel.

Burney's first novel is finally ambivalent about its heroine's entrance into the world. The female *Bildungsroman* is bound to be problematic in a society where a woman's maturity is marked by entering a marital relationship in which she is considered a perpetual minor. On the one hand, Evelina does grow and learn to act with a measure of independence. Early in the second volume, Villars, though reluctantly, sends her on a second visit to London under her grandmother's protection with the advice: 'you must learn not only to *judge*, but to *act* for yourself' (166). She does so most decidedly in her relations with Mr Macartney, standing up for him when the Branghtons mock him, rushing in to save him from an apparent act of suicide, giving him money and advice. During a visit to Bristol in the third volume, she pursues her friendship with Macartney even though it causes misunderstandings with Orville. However, much of the heroine's new social confidence is developed under Orville's wing, and as a husband he is clearly going to offer a protection that, if less anxious and obsessive than Villars's, will be all the more effective. Moreover, marriage seems to have added to the number of her protectors rather than replacing one with another. Her final letter reaffirms her bond with her guardian as she rushes to Berry Hill to the arms of 'the best of men' (406) – still, for her, Villars, despite her wedding to Orville and despite the novel's critical analysis of the foster-father's wish to keep the young lady well away from the world.

Cecilia

The 'choice of life', a common classical and neoclassical theme, was central to Johnson's fiction: it is a concern of the stories in the *Rambler* as well as the explicit core of *Rasselas*. It also underlies the *Lives of the Poets*, on which Johnson was working when Burney first got to know him. By structuring her second novel around the heroine's attempts to make her choice of life, Burney was raising the well-known plot of a young lady's entrance into the world from mere romantic story to the status of serious morality. Rasselas, imprisoned in the Happy Valley, wishes to escape in order to 'judge with my own eyes of the various conditions of men, and then to make deliberately my *choice of life*';[4] Cecilia, at the outset of her story, seems to be a Rasselas released, all set to judge and choose. As an orphan heiress, she has unusual power for a young woman. Though she has three guardians until her coming of age, which of them she lives with is left to 'her own choice' (6). Soon tired of fashionable life with the Harrels, she plans a new 'scheme of happiness at once rational and refined': she will give up the usual round of visiting and being visited, see only a select few friends, and spend her time studying music, reading and making the right use of her fortune:

> Many and various, then, soothing to her spirit and grateful to her sensibi-
> lity, were the scenes which her fancy delineated; now she supported an orphan,

now softened the sorrows of a widow, now snatched from iniquity the feeble trembler at poverty, and now rescued from shame the proud struggler with disgrace. (55)

An innovative heroine, keen on her independence and power to do good, Cecilia is like those altruistic eighteenth-century women discussed by Betty Rizzo, who 'had begun to discover in charitable societies and purposes a challenging as well as acceptable use for their talents'.[5] Burney's Johnsonian narrative honours her intentions – and her practical efforts to carry them out – while gently mocking her inflated hopes and revealing the inevitable letdown: 'when the fervour of self-approbation lost its novelty, the pleasure with which her new plan was begun first subsided into tranquility, and then sunk into langour. To a heart formed for friendship and affection, the charms of solitude are very short-lived' (130). Cecilia, 'finding the error into which her ardour of reformation had hurried her', adopts a more moderate programme, aiming for 'that golden mean' which 'always eludes our grasp, yet always invites our wishes' (131).

In her grand dreams and subsequent disappointments Cecilia is very like Rasselas; but where Johnson's hero roams at large observing mankind and considering his choice of life at the most general level, Burney revitalises the theme by embedding it in the concrete particularities of realistic narrative. Her novel, with its contemporary English setting, constrains its characters' choices by class, gender, economics, social convention, individual psychology. Cecilia is a lot less free than at first appears. Her choice of residence turns out to be a choice among the ruinous extravagance practised by the Harrels, the sordid meanness of Mr Briggs, and the cold pride of Mr Delvile. Mr Harrel works so successfully upon her inexperience and benevolence that he cheats her out of her father's fortune, leaving her only the income from her uncle that is tied by the name clause. As the classical theme meets the romantic plot, the heroine's choice of life turns into a choice of husband. When she falls in love with Mortimer Delvile, her conscious will is overtaken by the involuntary 'choice of her heart' (252).

The other character in the novel who is seriously concerned with making a choice of life is Belfield, who acts throughout as Cecilia's foil. As a young man able to enter a profession, he is freer than she is, but he suffers the constraints of his class position. A tradesman's son given a university education, he is too proud to trade, too poor to sustain a gentleman's life and humiliated by his dependence on aristocratic patronage. He often appears in the narrative at points when his choice illuminates Cecilia's. At the outset, when she is on her way to London with the world before her, he praises her for meaning 'to be guided by the light of your own understanding' (14), and starts a debate between the claims of worldly rules and individual judgment that resonates throughout her stay with the Harrels, during which she discovers that to act rightly she has to defy convention. Belfield reappears later, when Cecilia is caught between the conflicting demands of Delvile and his mother. Mrs Delvile has persuaded her that, to save the Delvile family name, she must not only refuse to marry Delvile but decide never to see him again; but Delvile himself is demanding a meeting. At this point Cecilia, wretched with indecision, runs into Belfield and learns of his recent choices. He has left his patron and become a day labourer. Disgusted with the way he was treated by his social superiors, Belfield had wanted to give up human society altogether, but, as he explains:

> No stranger to life, I knew human nature could not exist on such terms; still less a stranger to books, I respected the voice of wisdom and experience in the first of moralists, and most enlightened of men, and reading the letter of Cowley, I saw the vanity and absurdity of *panting after solitude.*
>
> I sought not, therefore, a cell; but, since I purposed to live for myself, I determined for myself also to think ... I found out this cottage, and took up my abode in it. I am here out of the way of all society, yet avoid the great evil of retreat, *having nothing to do.* I am constantly, not capriciously employed, and the exercise which benefits my health imperceptibly raises my spirits in despight of adversity. I am removed from all temptation. I have scarce even the power to do wrong; I have no object for ambition, for repining I have no time: – I have found out, I repeat, the true secret of happiness, Labour with Independence. (663–4)

The ironies of the passage are manifold. Burney's footnotes identify the great moralist, 'Dr JOHNSON', and the reference to his 'Life of Cowley' (663), which prints a miserable letter by the poet as proof that he failed to find happiness in retirement. Cowley's complaints stand as a warning to 'all that may hereafter pant for solitude'.[6] Belfield has seized on Johnson's message and misapplied it, running from one vain hope, solitude, to another, independent labour. Like the characters in *Rasselas*, he speaks a language of Johnsonian balance and gravity while remaining lost in the 'vanity and absurdity' he moralises on; like them, he keeps on expecting to find the true secret of happiness. It is no surprise when, shortly after this, Cecilia learns that Belfield has abandoned his cottage for yet another new hope. Burney is at her most Johnsonian as she reveals the inevitable failure of Johnson's morality to reform even a well-meaning man who believes he understands it.

Yet if Belfield is wrong to think day labour the answer to all problems, his concern for independence is one shared by Burney, who had explicitly held it up as an ideal in *The Witlings*. Cecilia, whose wealth is an 'independence' in the parlance of the times, ostensibly has what Belfield seeks, but her freedom of action is constantly under threat. The abortive marriage with Delvile was an attempt to have him while retaining her uncle's fortune. Once that ceremony is abandoned, Cecilia also abandons her will to Mrs Delvile, writing to her, 'Inform me of your desire, and I will endeavour to fulfil it. As my own Agent I regard myself no longer' (646–7). This abdication leads eventually to the second, successful wedding, on Mrs Delvile's terms, with Cecilia giving up both name and fortune, and the Delviles retaining their family pride. Independence, it would seem, cannot be a woman's lot, and the woman's inheritance must be given up.

Before this, however, Cecilia spends the first months after coming of age believing that she will have to remain single. She becomes a demonstration of the eighteenth-century ideal of the right use of riches: taking possession of her inheritance, she lives moderately, ignores fashion, and helps the poor. 'The system of her œconomy, like that of her liberality, was formed by rules of reason, and her own ideas of right, and not by compliance with example, nor by emulation with the gentry in her neighbourhood' (792). Her independent income matched by independent thought, Cecilia fulfils the ideal to which Belfield erratically aspires. Meanwhile he has left his cottage and tried a new route to independence, writing for money. She meets him in London, extolling the virtues of his new calling, proclaiming his freedom of thought and speech, and intending to do good as well as make a living. He has rejected aristocratic patronage; now he turns down the role of 'hireling scribbler for the purposes of defamation or of flattery', promising that 'My subjects shall be my own' (736). His is the professional model of authorship which Burney found in Johnson's circle; his failure to follow this model for long suggests not so much that it is not viable as that he has no staying power. A few months later they meet again in London. By now Cecilia has forfeited her own independence and secretly married Delvile on his mother's terms, losing her estate without even, so far, gaining his protection. Belfield, meanwhile, has given up his profession and become a book-keeper. He talks of the frustrations of writing for money in terms that could equally apply to Cecilia's conflicts over her marriage: 'what a life of struggle between the head and the heart! How cruel, how unnatural a war between the intellects and the feelings!' (883). Cecilia's version of this war will shortly lead her to temporary insanity.

The novel's downbeat ending, which emphasises the cost to the heroine of the conventional marital resolution, is Burney's illustration of the vanity of human wishes. She brushed aside her father's desire for a happier conclusion, choosing instead to follow her literary father. But she follows him with a difference. *Rasselas* ends with a fine poise between the characters' new schemes for happiness and their own consciousness of inevitable failure. Male and female characters alike continue to form new projects, while 'Of these wishes that they had formed they well knew that none could be obtained' (*Rasselas*, 176). *Cecilia* distributes expectation and wisdom differently. Belfield moves from one project to another, never satisfied, always beginning again, till Delvile helps him to a post in the army – ironically returning him full circle to the first employment he abandoned. The last we hear of him, 'his hopes were revived by ambition, and his prospects were brightened by a view of future honour' (940). Cecilia, however, for all her happiness with Delvile, is conscious of life's imperfections, never forgets the loss of her fortune, and ends the narrative bearing 'partial evil with chearfullest resignation' (941). Hope and resignation, the two poles between which Johnson's characters move, are distributed among Burney's by gender. The young man making his choice of life has greater freedom, greater scope, and keeps on hoping; the young woman's marriage choice limits her forever. Within Burney's moral scheme the young man is clearly deluded, while the young woman has gained the greater wisdom; but her lack of bright hope remains striking.

Burney's second novel was immediately identified as Johnsonian. 'It is related in a style peculiarly nervous and perspicuous, and appears to have been formed on the best model of Dr. Johnson's', explained the *Monthly Review*. A 'nervous' – forceful and succinct – style was understood as manly, and meant that Burney could be taken seriously, as a writer above the usual limitations of lady novelists. 'The Author of Cecilia asks no undue lenity: she doth not plead any privilege of her sex: she stands on firmer ground'.[7] However, the Johnsonian style that earned Burney praise in the 1780s has harmed her reputation since. Thomas Babington Macaulay, in an influential nineteenth-century retrospective of Burney's career, dismissed her as 'one of [Johnson's] most submissive worshippers', foolishly attempting to copy a style that was both flawed in itself and beyond her reach.[8] Recent critics, more appreciative of Burney, still often read her imitation of Johnson negatively. Joanne Cutting-Gray considers that the Johnsonian narrative style of *Cecilia* suppresses feminine discourse (located, for example, in the heroine's deranged speech at the crisis of the novel, when she is alone, unprotected and driven temporarily mad) in favour of masculinist reason. The Johnsonian style, 'built on latinate nominalizations ... [which] stop movement ... create the passive voice ... fix passage', makes for static writing, and Burney's adoption of the 'omniscient authorial voice' is a sign of her capitulation to the 'regulative order of reason'.[9] This is putting it far too bleakly. Burney *was* concerned to find an acceptable, authoritative voice, but she was not forced into some sort of deadly Johnsonian reason. Rather, she developed a distinctive version of the omniscient authorial voice, influenced by Johnson but adapted to her own narrative purposes. By using this style for relating the adventures of a marriageable young woman, Burney helped alter readers' perceptions of the gender of rational discourse. The balanced structure and elevated diction of Johnsonian sentences gave an air of authority to the narrative, making it seem perfectly natural that the experiences of a young girl in London society should carry the weight of general moral reflection. Burney's style encouraged readers to attach a new seriousness to the young woman's moral existence, and to the novel of contemporary life that gave that existence expression.

Omniscient narrative was already common in the novel, and many of Burney's female precursors, including Aphra Behn, Eliza Haywood, Sarah Fielding and Charlotte Lennox, had used it, helping to establish the notion of an authoritative female narrative voice that could command general state-ment and ironic reflection. In particular, *Cecilia* appears to be influenced by the ironic yet fundamentally sympathetic narrative presentation of the heroine in Haywood's *The History of Betsy Thoughtless* and Lennox's *The Female Quixote*. The dominant model for an authoritative narrator, though, was Henry Fielding. His narrator in *Tom Jones* – learned, urbane, facetious, teasing the reader and commenting self-reflexively on the progress of his narrative – was a strong and colourful presence in the novel: emphatically a man, and a highly individualised man, speaking to his readers. Burney neither imitated Fielding's narrator nor developed a female counterpart to him. Johnson offered an alternative narrative style, a less egotistical author-ity. Isobel Grundy has noted how much of Johnson's authority derives from his use of maxims, a habit of style which, she acutely notes, expresses a certain humility: the general pronouncement appears as the distilled wisdom of many thinkers, a collective voice.[10] Such an impersonal voice, not strongly marked by gender, became for Burney a way of taking authoritative control of her narrative without sounding like a man.

Burney did not use Johnsonian style exclusively. Much of the novel is in dialogue form, and her highly dramatic practice of defining many of her characters through their ideolects saves her from the fault critics found with Johnson in *Rasselas*, of making everyone speak in the same elevated manner. Where she narrates in the third person, though, Johnsonian periods and diction are often put to use in her development of a technique in which she is a pioneer – free indirect discourse. This style, in which the third-person narrative takes on a colouring from the character's idiom and con-sciousness, can be used in the representation of speech, but in *Cecilia* is more often used to indicate a character's thoughts, generally the heroine's. Cecilia is an introspective heroine, and the reflective passages, which punctuate her story, chart the movement of her mind and the progress of her feelings as she falls in love with Mortimer Delvile and realises how complicated and difficult their relationship is proving to be. At one point her friendship with Henrietta Belfield is tested by her discovery that Miss Belfield also loves Delvile. 'Her own mind was now in a state of the utmost confusion' (351), and the narrative sticks closely to the workings of that mind as she tries to sort out her feelings and to determine the right course of action:

> But though this curiosity [about Henrietta's acquaintance with Delvile] was both natural and powerful, her principal concern was the arrangement of her own conduct: the next day Miss Belfield was to tell her everything by a voluntary promise; but she doubted if she had any right to accept such a confidence. Miss Belfield, she was sure, knew not she was interested in the tale, since she had not even imagined that Delvile was known to her. She might hope, therefore, not only for advice but assistance, and fancy that while she reposed her secret in the bosom of a friend, she secured herself her best offices and best wishes for ever.
>
> Would she obtain them? no; the most romantic generosity would revolt from such a demand, for however precarious was her own chance with young Delvile, Miss Belfield she was sure could not have any.   (351–2)

The balanced phrases and elevated diction of Cecilia's reflections add a new dignity to the experience of a novel heroine. Like Wollstonecraft a few years later, Burney wants a heroine with 'thinking powers',[11] and a Johnsonian style helps create her.

If the heroine's reflections show the influence of Johnson, they also look forward to Austen, who develops free indirect discourse more fully in *Mansfield Park*, *Emma* and *Persuasion*. Jane Austen took a great deal from *Cecilia* (including the situation of a heroine perturbed by her friend's desire for the man she wants herself – Cecilia's dilemma over Henrietta and Delvile anticipates Emma's over Harriet and Mr Knightley). Austen's free indirect style is much more flexible than Burney's, consistently achieving a combination of sympathy and subtle irony which Burney reaches only occasionally, but Austen's debt to the earlier novelist is considerable. *Cecilia* poses the question of how a young woman makes the choice of life in a world that does not expect her to be independent or in control. Cecilia's experiences illustrate Johnson's maxims, and Burney develops a new narrative medium for reflection on these experiences: one that brings the gravity and balance of Johnson's style into a free indirect discourse that blends narrative commentary with a close rendering of the heroine's consciousness. As Burney, writing her history of an heiress, takes on her own inheritance from Johnson, she simultaneously prepares a rich legacy for Jane Austen.

NOTES

1. *Essays of John Dryden*, ed. W. P. Ker (Oxford: Clarendon, 1900), II, 247.

2. On the English literary tradition as patrilineage and Burney's relation to it see my *Literary Relations: Kinship and the Canon 1660–1830* (Oxford: Oxford University Press, 2005).

3. Margaret Anne Doody, *Frances Burney: The Life in the Works* (Cambridge: Cambridge University Press, 1988), 141, 148.

4. Samuel Johnson, *Rasselas and Other Tales*, ed. Gwin J. Kolb (New Haven: Yale University Press, 1990), 56.

5. Betty Rizzo, *Companions Without Vows: Relationships Among Eighteenth-Century British Women* (Athens and London: University of Georgia Press, 1994), 23.

6. Samuel Johnson, *Lives of the English Poets*, ed. Roger Lonsdale (Oxford: Oxford University Press, 2006) I, 198.

7. Review of *Cecilia*, *Monthly Review* 67 (Dec. 1782), 453, 456.

8. *Edinburgh Review* 76 (Jan. 1843), 564.

9. *Woman as 'Nobody' and the Novels of Fanny Burney* (Gainesville: University Press of Florida, 1992), 47, 52.

10. Isobel Grundy, 'Samuel Johnson: Man of Maxims?', in *Samuel Johnson: New Critical Essays*, ed. Isobel Grundy (London: Vision Press Ltd, 1984), 13–30.

11. *Mary* and *The Wrongs of Woman*, ed. James Kinsley and Gary Kelly (Oxford: Oxford University Press, 1980), 'Advertisement', n. pag.

3

SARA SALIH

Camilla and *The Wanderer*

Do Burney's fictional representations of ineffectual mentors, impracticable conduct book advice, and the social artifice that is required of women constitute a critique of her society? If so, this aspect of her fiction seems to have eluded her original critics, since they praise Burney for purveying 'instructive' and 'illustrating' sentiments in all four of her novels.[1] Even *The Wanderer*, which was pilloried both by the Tory critic John Wilson Croker and by the liberal William Hazlitt for its Francophilia, its stylistic misdemeanours, and its flagging creative energy, was not branded a radical novel, although as one of Burney's recent biographers observes, it contained 'an astringent exposé of Regency Britain'.[2] On the surface at least, *Camilla* (1796) and *The Wanderer* (1814) promote a conservative moral agenda as regards female conduct, social class and feminine identity. Yet it is also true that both novels feature numerous moments of gender construction and disintegration, as well as reflecting contemporary anxieties about the impossibility of interpersonal knowledge in a society where social and moral protocols govern every aspect of conduct and desire. In *Camilla*, the gender distinctions and ideals that eighteenth- and nineteenth-century moralists take for granted are overtly endorsed even as they prove to be unsustainable for the heroine and for the novel's gender-ambiguous characters. Similarly, although *The Wanderer*'s conspicuous didactic components include an all-but-perfect conduct-book heroine, and a chapter of Evangelical Christian doctrine in volume V (ch. 85), the novel's engagements with nationality, culture, race and religion convey a sense of radical ambiguity and confusion. *Camilla* and *The Wanderer* represent social identity and conduct as impersonation or drama, but they also attempt to maintain the distinction between the theatrical surface (called 'semblance' in both novels), and the spiritual essence or soul whose existence is insisted upon by the hero of Burney's last novel (*Wanderer*, 781–94).

Camilla and *The Wanderer* reveal an apparent lack of fit between conventional conservative morality and Burney's witting or unwitting representation of the contradictions inherent in those very morals, leaving the reader to make sense of the apparent conflict between the novels' manifest conservatism and their potentially radical representations of identity. In a perceptive chapter on *Camilla* in her book *Equivocal Beings*, Claudia Johnson points out that Burney never directly challenges the moral system within which her heroines operate. 'The recent renaissance in Burney studies has tended sometimes to overstate Burney's confidence as a social critic, as if she were Wollstonecraft's ideological sister, whereas it seems to me that Burney is distinctive precisely for her retreat from the explicitly oppositional', writes Johnson.[3] The insight is useful, for although it is certainly possible retrospectively to attribute radicalism and rage to Burney as critics such as Margaret Anne Doody and Julia Epstein have done in their influential analyses, it is also important to note that *Camilla* and *The Wanderer* represent social, gender and identity disruptions only to shut them down, to dispel ambiguity and doubt in their conventional, conservative conclusions. Why is it that Burney's late novels so insistently connect identity with theatre and impersonation, while ultimately reaffirming that identity is essentially, ontologically stable? And what are the effects of the novels' displays of gender ambiguity, of failed or factitious gender? How, in other words, does Burney outwardly uphold a conservative moral agenda while simultaneously revealing such formulations of identity to be simply unworkable?

In this chapter I will address these questions by paying close attention to those moments in the novels where conventional gender identities are revealed to be impracticable, theatrical and non-unitary. It will not be useful to condemn Burney as an arch-conservative, nor do I intend to claim her as a crypto-proto-feminist. Rather, I want to scrutinise the ways in which the novels *inevitably* reflect contemporary anxieties about gender roles, social class, national and racial identity, even as they strive to attain the requisite didactic closure in their highly conventional, even perfunctory conclusions. In these two novels, I discern an intriguing non-equivalence between contemporary readers' moral expectations on the one hand, and the complexities of essentialist assumptions on the other. How *Camilla* and *The Wanderer* reflect and seek to resolve this tension will be the subject of this chapter.

Camilla

'We are almost all ... of a nature so pitifully plastic, that we act from circumstances, and are fashioned by situation', Mrs Arlbery declares in *Camilla* (398), during a conversation in which she extends to men Alexander Pope's aphorism, in 'To a Lady' (the second of his *Moral Essays*): 'most women have no characters at all' (l. 2). Until the nineteenth century, 'plastic' could mean 'formative' or 'creative', but Mrs Arlbery uses the word negatively to imply that people are formless and impressionable, willing to be fashioned and moulded by contingencies. It is an apt gloss on *Camilla*'s characters, the majority of whom – including Mrs Arlbery herself – are in some sense fashioned, self-fashioning, or fashionable. As early as Camilla's tenth birthday party, the children's plays anticipate the gender ambiguities, sartorial interludes and cross-dressing episodes that occur with striking frequency throughout the novel (*Camilla*, 18). When Camilla 'metamorphos[es Sir Hugh] into a female' by dressing him in her cap and the maid's apron and giving him a rattle and Eugenia's doll to 'nurse and amuse', we see the ease with which gender identities may be sartorially altered, while Sir Hugh's carelessness towards Eugenia's doll constitutes a grotesque parody of maternity. 'Heigh ho! ... Camilla, my dear, do take away poor Doll, for fear I should let it slip' he declares (*Camilla*, 18). Significantly, the doll is termed an 'it' not a 'she', and thus resembles Sir Hugh, who in Camilla's cap, brown bob, maid's apron and cork whiskers is neither male nor female, aristocrat nor working class. Similarly, six-year-old Eugenia's smallpox and her fall from the see-saw swiftly transform her from female beauty to gender anomaly, placing her, along with Sir Hugh, Doll, and a host of other characters, outside the binary oppositions of gender.

Edward and Lillian Bloom note in passing that Eugenia 'was the name of a third-century Roman martyr', but Burney may well have been thinking of Saint Eugenia when she conceived of her character (*Camilla*, 930). The Alexandrian saint is reputed to have cross-dressed as a man so that she could join an all-male religious community where she eventually rose to the position of abbot. When Eugenia was accused of rape by a lady, she disproved the charge by undressing to reveal a female body beneath her robes.[4] After Sir Hugh has dropped her from the see-saw, however, Burney's Eugenia no longer possesses a body that is identifiably female, so that unlike her namesake, she cannot simply undress in order to prove her sex. Eugenia's deformation at the hands of Sir Hugh excludes her from the system of heterosexual relationships in which clearly defined gender roles such as 'blooming coquette' or 'beauteous prude' are a prerequisite (*Camilla*, 905). '[S]eamed and even scarred' by the smallpox, 'diminutive and deformed' because of the accident on the see-saw, Eugenia is awarded financial and intellectual independence by a contrite Sir Hugh, but her large fortune only compounds her transformation from female to gender anomaly, compensating for her loss of femininity by distancing her even further from a contemporary feminine ideal (*Camilla*, 29, 33).

That Eugenia is disqualified from the heterosexual order of things is vividly illustrated by her cousin Clermont Lynmere's disgust at the prospect of having a classically educated 'cripple' as a life partner. '[B]y the Lord! she's no wife of mine!' he declares when Indiana informs him of Sir Hugh's matchmaking plans: 'I'd as soon as marry the old Doctor himself! and I'm sure he'd make me as pretty a wife. Greek and Latin! why, I'd as soon tie myself to a rod. Pretty sort of dinners she'll give!' (*Camilla*, 579). Clermont is marked in the novel as highly, unacceptably effeminate. His perfect feminine body is indeed represented as the obverse of Eugenia's and the mirror image of his sister, Indiana's, his beauty and his effeminate person suggesting the contiguity of masculine and feminine identities, along with their free-floating nature in relation to sex (so that it is possible to be a manly woman or a womanly man). Indiana remains something of a lacuna in the novel: her physique is not inventoried as her brother's is, and her feminine beauty is only evoked through the positive or negative responses of others. 'Do you know ... when that beautiful automaton, Miss Lynmere, is to marry young Mandlebert?' a stranger asks in Camilla's hearing early in the novel when a match between Edgar and Indiana is still Sir Hugh's dearest wish (*Camilla*, 191). The stranger's characterisation suggests that conventional feminine beauty is unspontaneous and machine-like, while the word 'automaton' links Indiana both to the beautiful young woman Mr Tyrold takes Eugenia to see in volume II, who 'turn[s] round with a velocity that no machine could have exceeded', and to Camilla at the uniformed ball, no more than 'a fair lifeless machine' in Edgar's absence (*Camilla*, 309, 714).

If such depictions of female 'automata' convey the mechanical and con-structed nature of feminine identity as embodied by women, womanly men in the novel similarly reflect contemporary anxieties concerning artificial femininity, effeminacy and emasculation. Clermont Lynmere is not the only character who fails to embody conventional masculine norms: Sir Hugh's riding accident and wound in the side, while not so generous a hint as Uncle Toby's injured groin in *Tristram Shandy*, nonetheless immobilise and, by implication, feminise him, while his 'unalterably sweet' temper, openness, and 'almost infantine artlessness', as well as 'an insuperable want of quick-ness', make him seem like something of a cross between Camilla and Indiana (*Camilla*, 10). The baronet's 'depression', 'despair' and 'self-punishment', along with his attack of gout after Eugenia's accidents, are also signs of his effeminate sentimentality (*Camilla*, 12, 28, 327). Without wife or children and therefore in search of alternative modes of kinship (although Mrs Tyrold considers him to be 'more childish than her children themselves'), Sir Hugh, on his arrival at Etherington, precipitates the rifts in the nuclear family unit which culminate in Mr Tyrold's imprisonment and the eventual desertion of Cleves (*Camilla*, 26, 853).

Sir Hugh constitutes a powerful illustration of the function of the gender ambiguous 'third term' – not, as George E. Haggerty suggests in his essay on

'Defects and Deformity in *Camilla*', to confirm gender binarisms, but to disrupt, to bring to crisis, and destabilise heterosexual assumptions and institutions (here, the family). Like Sir Hugh, Sir Sedley Clarendel is a 'gender outlaw',[5] and his deliberate assumption of an effeminate role is thrown into sharp relief on those occasions when he is startled out of it. It is intriguing that in *Camilla* spontaneous expressions of emotion frequently occur in the presence of animals; indeed, the novel is a veritable menagerie, as a bull, bullfinch, bulldog, several horses and various wild beasts from Africa (with the emphasis apparently on 'bulls' of one kind or another) provide pretexts for the characters involuntarily to depart from their carefully studied social and gendered roles. On one of these occasions, during a trip to Mount Ephraim in the Tunbridge section of the novel, Mrs Arlbery alights from the phaeton, handing the reins to Camilla. The horses take fright and rear up, 'plunging and flouncing incessantly'. It is Sir Sedley who stays them 'at the visible and imminent hazard of his life', allowing him momentarily to forget his theatrical persona. 'His natural courage, which he had nearly annihilated, as well as forgotten, by the effeminate part he was systematically playing, seemed to rejoice in being again exercised; his good nature was delighted by the essential service he had performed', the narrator remarks (*Camilla*, 403–4). The phaeton incident recalls Edgar's earlier encounter with a horse which, frightened by a bee, accidentally kicks him on the shoulder, and his subsequent injury at the fangs of an incensed bulldog (*Camilla*, 346, 538–9). Both of these occasions bring forth Camilla's sensibility and love for Edgar, while demonstrating Edgar's courage as well as his physical weakness (on the first occasion Edgar has to be bled, while on the second, he fails to prevent the bulldog from attacking a spaniel; *Camilla*, 347, 539).

The display of 'natural' gender roles (men defending women and spaniels against horses and bulldogs) during these animal interludes also draws the reader's attention to the fact that men, no less than women in the novel, are acting, dissembling, engaging in social theatre – except when they cannot help involuntarily stepping out of character. A number of the novel's protagonists complain that, while women may depart from conduct-book standards of modesty and virtue, men are artificial and 'effeminate'. 'What a prospect for [Camilla], then, with our present race of young men!' declares Mrs Tyrold during a discussion with her husband: 'their frivolous fickleness nauseates whatever they can reach; they have a weak shame of asserting, or even listening to what is right, and a shallow pride in professing what is wrong' (*Camilla*, 222). It is no coincidence that Mrs Tyrold's comment is followed by a scene in which the 'Modern Ideas of Duty' in the chapter title are illustrated by the news that Lionel has blackmailed his uncle Relvil. The renegade nephew is thrown into a suicidal frame of mind by the discovery of his actions: '[I]f I were a man I should shoot myself!' he tells Camilla (*Camilla*, 228), but Lionel is evidently not a man, for he refrains from placing a gun to his temple (unlike Macartney in *Evelina* and Harrel in *Cecilia*), and his continuing course of 'frivolous fickleness' includes transvestic escapades. It is Lionel who dresses Miss Dennel in military uniform and Macdersey in a bob wig, while 'accoutr[ing himself] in the maid's cloaths', and later, he appears disguised in a cloak, an occasion on which he expresses to his sister a sense of bewilderment at the role he has assumed: 'What has bewitched me, I know no more than you; but I never meant to play this abominable part' (*Camilla*, 264, 727, 739).

Lionel and Sir Sedley's self-conscious role-playing might appear to suggest that there is a grounded, authentic masculinity to which they may return, but characters such as Sir Hugh, or even Mr Tyrold, that ineffective father and mentor, call the notion of gender groundedness into doubt. The sequence of gender roles through which Camilla moves further undermines the notion that gender identities are stable, fixed, or essential, even though the novel may well imply that there are proper and improper modes of femininity. The financial pressures of gender construction for women are revealed as Camilla struggles to perform the roles of coquette and spendthrift and falls into debt as a consequence. When she departs for Tunbridge, Camilla vows to obey the instructions conveyed in her father's 'little sermon', but once she has left his care, it is Mrs Arlbery who furnishes the heroine with her conduct script. Not only does she advise Camilla regarding the best way to win Edgar, but the heroine borrows money from her new mentor, her clothes are modelled on Mrs Arlbery's, and some of Camilla's utterances even echo Mrs Arlbery's (*Camilla*, 484, 462–3, 538). It is only when Camilla is well into her coquettish performance that she realises she has been acting. 'Accident, want of due consideration, and sudden recollection, in an agitated moment, of the worldly doctrine of Mrs. Arlbery, had led Camilla, once more, into the semblance of a character, which, without thinking of, she was acting', the narrator remarks (*Camilla*, 679). This moral retrospection does not put an end to Camilla's performances, however: she still has Lord Pervil's uniformed ball to attend – perhaps the novel's most striking instance of fashionable, fashioned, conformist identity – after which she relinquishes her attempts at coquettishness and takes on the persona of a sentimental madwoman or (in modern parlance) a 'hysteric', instead.

'[H]ysteria is what? *Failed* masquerade', writes Stephen Heath: '[t]he hysteric will not play the game, misses her identity as a woman'.[6] Camilla's failures at playing the feminine game, and the self-conscious, self-induced nature of her illness, are unmistakeable. Having taken lodgings at Mrs Marl's inn (even here, Camilla cannot escape from clothes: marl is a mottled fabric made from two differently coloured threads), the destitute heroine is swiftly 'persuaded [her] life was on its wane' (*Camilla*, 863). She resists sleep, since

> her ever eager imagination made her apprehensive her friends might find her too well, and suspect her representation [a resonant reference to the letter Camilla has sent to her mother] was but to alarm them into returning kindness. A fourth night, therefore, passed without sleep, or the refreshment of taking off her cloaths.   (*Camilla*, 866)

It is only the sight of Bellamy's corpse that makes Camilla realise the 'cruelty of [her] egotism' in wishing to die, but her self-neglect has already produced the desired result, and the heroine is eventually ushered back into the family unit in a final piece of theatre. The novel's concluding scenes are so stagey as to seem almost parodic, and the final chapter, 'The last Touches of the Picture', draws our attention back to the subtitle, and to Camilla's own characterisation of men as pictures, while also reminding us of the artificial nature of the novel itself (*Camilla*, 903).

We have moved from the spectacle of uniform, uniformed femininity at Lord Pervil's ball, to an interlude of physical collapse that runs counter to the contemporary cultural representation of nervous disorder or 'madness' as a form of heightened individuality. For, in precipitating her own illness, Camilla is still playing a part, and at the end of the novel it is evident that she has merely exchanged the feminine scripts which proved so ineffectual (coquette, spendthrift, mad, or dying woman) for another, more convincing role (that of exemplary daughter and wife-to-be).

> 'I will see – or I will avoid whoever you please – ' [Camilla promises her mother shortly after their bedside reconciliation] 'I shall want no fortitude, I shall fear nothing – no one – not even myself – now again under your protection! I will scarcely even think, my beloved Mother, but by your guidance!'. (*Camilla*, 895)

The heroine's repetitive protestations and the novel's highly conventional conclusion suggest that we have not progressed from spectacle to real life, but from spectacle to picture, from one impersonation (or set of impersonations) to another. In that case, the theatrical closing scenes seem highly fitting, since they leave gender identities unstable, contingent and ambiguous. Indeed, it is tempting to see the 'Unsettled Collateral Expectations' which are condemned in the penultimate paragraph as referring not only to fortune, but also to the 'unsettled' nature of gender identity. *Camilla* ends on a note that is itself unsettled and unsettling: having destabilised masculine and feminine gender identities, it is no easy matter simply to reaffirm them for the sake of novelistic closure.

The Wanderer

The typically Burneyan questions raised in *Camilla* (how is it possible to tell when people are acting and when they are not? Can true female virtue be distinguished from its false counterpart? Is female virtue discernible anyway, if it is an invisible essence?) are politically inflected in *The Wanderer*, where 'the dire reign of the terrific Robespierre' is indirectly represented through its reverberations in mid-1790s England (*Wanderer*, 11). Burney's last novel extends the category crises represented in *Camilla* beyond the domestic sphere, so that national, cultural, racial and religious identities overlap somewhat uneasily with sex and gender. Begun by Burney over a decade before its publication in 1814, and reflecting (as Burney says in the preface) the events of the French Revolution, *The Wanderer* is a 1790s novel manqué in which Jacobin and anti-Jacobin debates are re-rehearsed from a safe temporal distance (*Wanderer*, 6). This doubling is replicated at many levels in a text where the heroine is coupled with a radical anti-heroine, and where the theatre and France both reflect and critique non-theatrical, domestic occurrences. Harleigh's insistence that the material world is complemented – *doubled* – by its immaterial counterpart provides a suggestive gloss on the ambiguity arising from these uncanny encounters between self and other, without ultimately reaffirming the opposing categories that are destabilised in *Camilla*. Instead, identities rigidly defined by gender, race and class are undermined through sartorial shifts and cross-dressing interludes, while the presence of actual stages in the novel suggests the degree to which identity is itself a form of theatre.

The doubling of heroines in late eighteenth- and early nineteenth-century novels, such as Elizabeth Hamilton's *Memoirs of Modern Philosophers* (1800) and Maria Edgeworth's *Belinda* (1801), has been identified as a strategy of subversion whereby apparently conservative writers can air a reformist agenda before (apparently) decisively rejecting it.[7] There is certainly a sense in which the virtuous Juliet is defined by her radical other, the phonic similarity of Ellis/Elinor constituting only the most obvious of the equivalences between them. Numerous critics have noted the radical potential of the pairing, and it would certainly be a mistake to consign Elinor to the status of ideologically irrelevant red herring. If Elinor's Wollstonecraftian protests complement Juliet's 'FEMALE DIFFICULTIES', the anti-heroine's confirmatory role is also of metaphorical significance in a novel where so much is defined by what is supplemental, outside, other. I want to focus on the stage as a resonant example of the doubling that informs *The Wanderer* thematically, formally and ideologically. By this I mean both the literal stage, on which the characters perform John Vanbrugh and Colley Cibber's Restoration comedy, and (as in *Camilla*) the figurative stages of identity.

It is surely no coincidence that two other novels published in 1814 – Jane Austen's *Mansfield Park* and Maria Edgeworth's *Patronage* – also feature amateur theatricals. In *The Wanderer*, as in *Mansfield Park*, the temporary conversion of domestic space into theatre reflects contemporary concerns about the drastic political 'conversions' that were occurring outside the household: Austen's novel mirrors the reassigning of political authority during George III's illness, while *The Wanderer* is clearly inflected by the aftermath of the French Revolution in France and in England. I want to emphasise at the outset the stage's allegorical significance in the novel by citing Edward Said's characterisation of the Orient as an appendage to Europe and the site of Orientalist fantasy. '[T]he Orient is the stage on which the whole East is confined', writes Said: 'On this stage will appear figures whose role it is to represent the larger whole from which they emanate.'[8] Although, like *Mansfield Park*, Burney's novel contains a number of allusions to the Caribbean, it is France that is the Saidean stage on which the English characters imaginatively enact their fantasies of violence and despotism in a displacement that permits them to ignore local injustices. That the English use France as a locus of negative identification is signalled by Juliet's suffering at home (i.e. in England), while the novel's introduction of sympathetic and humane French characters who do not at all resemble English constructions of France and Frenchness constitutes an implicit critique of these nationalistic and belligerent English attitudes.

It may seem as though we have moved a long way from the amateur theatricals, but I am suggesting that France's displaced, doubling function in *The Wanderer* is mirrored in the novel's inclusion of a literal theatrical stage on which, as in *Mansfield Park*, the characters enact their impermissible desires. Both Austen and Burney make frequent use of such containment tactics whereby narratives featuring some kind of sexual impropriety are insulated from the body of the text, but nonetheless included in it. In *Sense and Sensibility*, for example, Colonel Brandon tells a scandalous story of two Elizas: the first, once his beloved, who became a prostitute, and the second, her daughter, who was seduced by Willoughby (II, ch. 9). There are thematic parallels between the play staged in *The Wanderer* and the novel itself, just as there are similarities between England and France or Elinor and Juliet. The selection of Vanbrugh and Cibber's *The Provok'd Husband* (1728) seems pointed, since Burney might, for example, have cast Juliet as the virtuous and long-suffering Lady Brute in Vanbrugh's *The Provok'd Wife* (1697). Instead, the role of Lady Townly allows Juliet to depart from her usual restraint to give a jaunty rendition of the dissipated woman who enjoys thwarting the moral demands of her fretful husband – played of course, by a plaintive Harleigh in a role that hints at the frustrations an independent woman might experience as his wife. '[T]he universe knows I am never better company than when I am doing what I have a mind to', Lady Townly retorts in the play, and she dismisses her husband's demands that she give up late nights and gaming, rebelliously asserting her right to a life of pleasure (Act III). Lord Townly declares that he will turn his wife out of doors if she continues in this course, and the estranged couple part acrimoniously without resolving the issue.

Juliet performs this risqué comic role with 'gay intelligence', 'well bred animation' and 'lively variety' (*Wanderer*, 94). She is equally captivating in the last act. Here

> Lady Townly becomes serious, penitent, and pathetic ... the state of [Juliet's] mind accorded with distress, and her fine speaking eyes, her softly touching voice, her dejected air, and penetrating countenance, made quicker passage to the feelings of her auditors, even than the words of the author. (*Wanderer*, 96)

If the role of recalcitrant wife eventually humbled into obedience seems a far cry from *The Wanderer*'s faultless conduct-book heroine, Juliet's enthusiastic comic performance invites us to consider that her mysterious life story may be shadowed in that of the character she is playing. Not only is her true social status hinted at in Lady Townly's title, but the heroine's disobedience towards her husband re-emerges later in the novel, albeit in mutated form, when she tells Sir Jaspar Herrington how she became the 'married wife' of a ruthlessly mercenary French commissary from whom she immediately escaped (significantly, Juliet compares the civil marriage ceremony to a piece of theatre; *Wanderer*, 745–7). Indeed, Juliet's assertive behaviour throughout the novel suggests, like her comic performance of Lady Townly, that the veneer of conduct-book femininity might conceal its opposite. When Harleigh urges Juliet not to perform at Vinstreigle's benefit for fear it might encourage other women to 'deviat[e], alone and unsupported ... from the long-beaten track of female timidity', Juliet defies him out of economic necessity rather than hedonism, but on many occasions she does not behave with the diffidence Harleigh regards as intrinsic to female modesty (*Wanderer*, 343). The alias within an alias printed on the playbills ('Lady Townly by Miss Ellis'; *Wanderer*, 91) suggests, as in *Camilla*, the sequential nature of identity, and it also confirms the ambiguity that has already been introduced with Juliet's racial cross-dressing, her arbitrarily assigned initials 'L.S.' (later corrupted into a name), and her refusal – along with the narrator's – to divulge any information regarding her past.

Juliet's myriad disguises draw attention to the fact that drama in *The Wanderer* is not confined to the stage, while Elinor's theatrical appearances and her frequent pronouncements on the subject of acting also blur the distinction between stage and 'real life'. Although Elinor celebrates spontaneity and the free flow of desire, disparaging those such as 'Ellis' 'who act always by rule ... tame animals of custom, wearied and wearying plodders on of beaten tracks', she also compares her own life to a badly acted 'tragi-comedy' with 'a long last act' (*Wanderer*, 585–6, 581). Elinor's allusions to the dramatic nature of conduct suggest that she too is one of those 'plodders' who follows a script, even though in her case it is an unconventional one.[9] '[W]ithout [passion], I regard and treat the whole of my race as the mere dramatis personæ of a farce; of which I am myself, when performing with such fellow-actors, a principal buffoon' she tells Juliet (*Wanderer*, 153). The anti-heroine's expressions of love for Harleigh might be described as 'passionate', but her carefully staged suicide attempts certainly have farcical, artificial elements about them. It is fitting then that Elinor's first attempt to take her life occurs at Vinstreigle's musical benefit, just as Juliet is preparing to give a harp recital before a large audience. Spotting a 'deaf and dumb' man in 'foreign clothing [with] a foreign servant', Juliet is filled with 'a thousand vague fears and conjectures'. At this point, the reader does not know what these fears and conjectures might be, but in retrospect, it seems clear that Juliet is afraid the 'foreigner' is somehow connected to her husband. '[W]as he watching her from mere common curiosity? or had he any latent motive, or purpose?' Juliet wonders. Of course, the 'deaf and dumb tormentor' turns out to be Elinor in drag, and when Juliet sees 'a glitter of steel' in his/her hand, she reaches the 'horrible surmise' that the anti-heroine has 'come to perpetrate the bloody deed of suicide' in public (*Wanderer*, 357–8).

The scene is remarkably suggestive: Elinor not only shifts the arena of performance from theatrical to non-theatrical stage, but her cross-dressed appearance and Juliet's response also anticipate the latter's encounter with her husband at an inn *en route* to Salisbury later in the novel. On this occasion, the heroine once again spots an oddly dressed 'foreign gentleman', fears the worst and falls to the floor (she faints at the benefit, but not at the inn; *Wanderer*, 724). A queer theorist such as Eve Sedgwick might say that Harleigh, Elinor and 'Ellis' constitute a homosocial triangle in which the bond linking the two female protagonists (rivals for Harleigh) is at least as powerful as that between male/female lovers.[10] Similarly, a Freudian critic might argue that Elinor, cross-dressed as a foreigner, constitutes the return of Juliet's repressed, the uncanny double of the brutish Frenchman Juliet has been forced to marry, while also shadowing Juliet's *own* cross-dressing experiences and the other 'unfeminine' activities in which she has been compelled to engage as a matter of self-survival.

Camilla has already demonstrated the interrelatedness of hyper-femininity and hyper-masculinity, and the Ellis/Elinor coupling raises similar questions about the conduct-book ideal apparently embodied by Juliet. If Camilla's appearance at the uniformed ball highlights the artificial nature of femininity, Juliet takes the destabilisation of categories to another level through her sequential acts of racial, gendered and social transvestism. Her appearance in racial drag in the first scene of the novel is only the first in a series of transformations (narrated and represented) from white to black, from female to male, from aristocrat to working class – and back again. 'I changed my clothing for some tattered old garments; stained my face, throat, and arms ... [and on the French coast] added patches and bandages to my stained skin, and garb of poverty', Juliet tells Sir Jaspar in her lengthy retrospective account (*Wanderer*, 748–50). Significantly, the clothes out of which Juliet has changed are 'a man's great coat, ... a black wig, and a round hat', so that in narrative time, the heroine's act of gender transvestism precedes Elinor's (*Wanderer*, 747). Later, wandering through the New Forest, Juliet engages in class cross-dressing when she assumes a 'rustic and ordinary garb' that includes Debby Dyson's bonnet. The disguise is so effective that Harleigh thinks the heroine is 'some light nymph of the inn' when he encounters her on the way to Salisbury (*Wanderer*, 692–3, 702, 726).

How stable are class, gender, nationality – even race – when they can be donned and discarded as easily as a bonnet or a collection of patches? As transvestic figures who repeatedly cross from one category to another, Juliet and Elinor possess an extraordinary ability to disrupt the apparent fixity of male/female, white, English, middle- and upper-class identity. After all, once Juliet's black skin has faded and her bandages and patches have fallen off, none of the characters, apart from Harleigh, is willing to take her at face value (literally). Mrs Ireton makes numerous spiteful references to Juliet's change of complexion, suggesting that she has 'metamorphosed' herself from black to white with the help of make up and skin enamelling (*Wanderer*, 43, 485–6). Such vituperative comments reveal the discomfort and confusion caused by the heroine's frequent category shifts, while raising broader questions about the relationship of self to other, and the effects of introducing 'difference' into an early nineteenth-century white, English, middle-class milieu.

Elsewhere I have suggested that in *The Wanderer*, Burney problematically and opportunistically equates slavery with the oppression of white middle-class women, occluding the former to the ideological advantage of the latter as she shifts the reader's attention from the characters' Negrophobia to their Francophobia.[11] Margaret Doody expresses her disappointment that Burney 'did not give us a black heroine',[12] but it is unlikely that Burney's original readers would have responded with quite the same ideological wishful thinking (and I know of no contemporary novel that features a black heroine, although writers such as Amelia Opie, Maria Edgeworth, Sarah Harriet

Burney and even Jane Austen do include characters of colour in their fiction). Indeed, it is likely that a reader in 1814 would have been *relieved* that a gleaming white heroine – albeit culturally French – emerges from the 'stained' skin that the heroine wears in the novel's opening pages. Still, although the racial attitudes displayed in *The Wanderer* are likely to trouble modern readers, critiquing the author for what she fails to do may not yield useful insights. Instead, we must make sense of the fact that the plea for the integration of otherness embedded in the novel extends only as far as the other side of the Channel, with the wider application of Harleigh's Evangelical doctrine applying solely to the French. When the hero exclaims '[w]hat new countries we visit! what strange sights we see!' he is not talking about actual travel to foreign lands, but about dreaming, the metaphysical nightly phenomenon which he takes as evidence of the soul's existence (*Wanderer*, 789). In Harleigh's analogy, sleep, like travel, is adduced as proof of the existence of the other (the soul and also, by implication, the cultural/racial other) while throwing into sharp relief the limits of the 'corporeal machine' that hides our unseen essence (*Wanderer*, 788). The arrival of the French characters on Teignmouth beach at the end of the novel tacitly suggests the failure of Harleigh's anti-materialist doctrine as it applies to social relations. French goodness is not taken on trust, necessitating an act of ideological *habeas corpus* in which their bodies and beings are produced to establish that they do not fit the English construction of them as bloodthirsty demons. Similarly, while Harleigh eschews the need for 'documents', both in his religious discourse and with regard to Juliet, it is only once the Admiral has produced the 'documents, certificates' proving the heroine's birth that she is assigned her proper place in the upper echelons of society.

Paradoxically though, Harleigh's conservative doctrine (we must believe in the existence of what we cannot see) invokes a non-unitary mode of identity whereby a person's semblance is not all there is to know of her. '[H]ow can I expect to be judged but by what is seen, what is known?' Juliet laments earlier in the novel, foreshadowing Elinor's question '[H]ow can we reason but from what we know?' (*Wanderer*, 297, 786). Later, the heroine asks herself: '[W]hat is woman unprotected? She is pronounced upon only from outward semblance: – and, indeed, what other criterion has the world? Can it read the heart?' (*Wanderer*, 344). Of course, *The Wanderer* suggests that people (particularly women) should *not* be judged solely from 'outward semblance', and Juliet throws English materialist epistemological assumptions into sharp relief through her numerous costumes, her shifts in complexion and her social mobility, all of which scramble social signifiers. The heroine's thematic pairing with Elinor further compounds her plurality, and even the codicil to her father's will, produced by the Admiral at the end of the novel, suggests that far from being singular, people are defined by what is supplemental to them (documents and codicils to documents) or perhaps even invisible (other countries, other people, the soul).

The novel's final characterisation of the heroine as 'a female Robinson Crusoe' condenses these ambiguities. As a Robinson Crusoe (the word 'female' suggesting that we need to be *reminded* of Juliet's gender), Juliet is transgendered, transvestic, transnational and insistently doubled with her others – whether it be the anti-heroine, her French adoptive relatives, or the numerous personae she has assumed in the course of her wanderings (*Wanderer*, 873). Like *Camilla*, *The Wanderer* does not leave the reader with the comforting sense that stability is finally and fully restored, even though both novels work hard to seal off the uncertainties they have opened up. *The Wanderer*'s beach scenes display all the perfunctoriness of a Shakespearean comic conclusion, where noble birth is rapidly established and the characters relinquish their disguises before organising themselves into traditional heterosexual configurations. All Burney's novels capitulate to narrative convention in the end, but they also leave the tensions between conservative morality and ontological reality unresolved. *The Wanderer* echoes Elinor in its final lines by reminding the reader of the 'mighty ... DIFFICULTIES with which a FEMALE has to struggle' (*Wanderer*, 873). '[Elinor] will return to the habits of society and common life, as one awakening from a dream in which she has acted some strange and improbable part', Harleigh reassures Juliet, and yet the anti-heroine's capitulation to convention is not represented, nor does the reader witness her assumption of these societal 'habits' (*Wanderer*, 863). Instead, *The Wanderer*'s protracted social critique makes it unclear as to what reality Elinor will embrace, while Harleigh's dream analogy recalls (and apparently contradicts) his earlier advocacy of an oneiric model of spirituality and social relating. Deliberately or unwittingly, then, Burney suggests in *Camilla* and *The Wanderer* that the society in which her characters are inscribed is compromised and profoundly unstable.

NOTES

1. See for example *The English Review* 1 (1783), 16; *The New Annual Register* 3 (1782), 247; *The Critical Review* 54 (1782), 414; *The Gentleman's Magazine* 52 (1782), 485; *The Monthly Review* 21 (1796), 163.
2. See Hazlitt's review in *The Edinburgh Review* 24 (1815), 320–38, and Croker's in *The Quarterly Review* 11 (1814), 123–30; Kate Chisholm, *Fanny Burney: Her Life, 1752–1840* (London: Chatto & Windus, 1998), 229.
3. Claudia Johnson, *Equivocal Beings: Politics, Gender and Sentimentality in the 1790s; Wollstonecraft, Radcliffe, Burney, Austen* (Chicago: University of Chicago Press, 1995), 144.

4. Marjorie Garber, *Vested Interests: Cross-Dressing and Cultural Anxiety* (New York: Routledge, 1992), 213–14.

5. George E. Haggerty, *Unnatural Affections: Women and Fiction in the Later Eighteenth Century* (Bloomington: Indiana University Press, 1998), 146.

6. Stephen Heath, 'Joan Riviere and the Masquerade', in *Formations of Fantasy*, ed. Victor Burgin, James Donald and Cora Kaplan (London: Methuen, 1986), 51.

7. Claudia Johnson, *Jane Austen: Women, Politics, and the Novel* (Chicago: University of Chicago Press, 1988), 20–1.

8. Edward Said, *Orientalism: Western Conceptions of the Orient* (London: Routledge & Kegan Paul, 1978), 63. *Zara*, a play with a Turkish setting, is staged in *Patronage*.

9. Cf. for example *Wanderer*, 585, where Elinor compares herself to a Tragedy Queen with a bowl and dagger.

10. Eve Kosofsky Sedgwick, *Between Men: English Literature and Male Homosocial Desire* (New York: Columbia University Press, 1985), 1, 21.

11. Sara Salih, ' "Her Blacks, her whites and her double face!" Altering Alterity in *The Wanderer*', *Eighteenth-Century Fiction* 11.3 (1999), 301–15.

12. Margaret Anne Doody, *Frances Burney: The Life in the Works* (Cambridge: Cambridge University Press, 1988), 324.

4

TARA GHOSHAL WALLACE

Burney as dramatist

When a significant body of work by a major author emerges from obscurity, scholarship and dissemination follow a fairly predictable trajectory. The first wave, necessarily biographical and bibliographical, places the material within the author's life and career and makes it accessible through careful editorial work. Burney's plays have been fortunate in this regard: the plays first came to our attention through the work of Joyce Hemlow, whose deep knowledge of Burney contextualised them within her biography and literary corpus. Hemlow's 'Fanny Burney: Playwright' and her subsequent *The History of Fanny Burney* described the manuscripts, summarised the plots, connected them to Burney's personal literary life, and initiated a scholarly focus on Burney's dramatic output.[1] When Margaret Anne Doody took up the plays in her literary biography of Burney, she gave them the kind of serious consideration that ensured that they would never again be relegated to the margins of Burney's work.[2] Uncovering in them innovative techniques, acerbic social commentary and a rich source of information on Burney's growth as an artist, Doody makes the plays full partners with the better-known novels and journals.

Recent scholarship has continued the ground-breaking work of Hemlow and Doody. Barbara Darby, in the only book dealing wholly with Burney's plays, reads them from a feminist perspective, arguing that all the plays represent the oppression of women by male-dominated institutions and practices, whether in the political conflicts depicted in the tragedies or in the domestic discords enacted in the comedies.[3] Sandra Sherman and Deidre Shauna Lynch discover in *The Witlings* material for other kinds of cultural criticism: Sherman makes a compelling case for reading the play as an articulation of new class divisions produced by the 'time-as-discipline' protocols of the industrial age, and Lynch locates the play at the intersection of consumer culture and the emerging public sphere.[4] Scholarly attention to Burney's plays has been accompanied by increasing public circulation, most notably in the highly successful productions of *A Busy Day*, first mounted by

Alan Coveney in Bristol in 1993, and subsequently produced in London in 1994 and 2000. The elaborate programme for the 2000 Lyric Theatre production, including maps and descriptions of eighteenth-century London, a brief social history and contemporary cartoons, attests to the play's significance as cultural artefact.

Of course, we will always lament that Burney's plays were so ill-fated in her own lifetime, for she was manifestly equipped to write drama, both by experience and inclination. The Burney family's intimacy with David Garrick meant that not only did they have access to his private box at Drury Lane, but that they also witnessed his playful theatrics in private life. Burney describes, for example, Garrick's antic performance while Dr Burney was having his hair dressed. Donning 'a most odious scratch Wig', Garrick oversees the procedure with 'a look ... of *envy* & sadness', before shifting to 'a *raree* show man's Voice' to hawk his host's *History of Music* (*EJL* II, 95–6). Young Fanny learned early in life the pleasures of ludic performance, both on stage and off. Her wide knowledge of plays (she mentions some 150 she has seen or read[5]) was supplemented by the Burney family's private theatricals, though Fanny's shyness made public performance an ordeal. Despite her stage fright, however, Fanny clearly entered into these family projects with gusto, as she makes clear in a fifteen-page account of their double bill of Arthur Murphy's *The Way to Keep Him* and Henry Fielding's *Tom Thumb*. She herself played Huncamunca with 'Tragic pomp & greatness', and 'The whole concluded with great spirit, – all the performers dying, & all the Audience Laughing' (*EJL* II, 249–50). Burney's journals consistently present 'scenes', as when she recounts the Reverend Michael Lort's disparaging view of the anonymous new novel *Evelina*. His declaration, during a Streatham supper, that he has 'no great desire to see it, because it has such a foolish Name', evokes a series of bodily responses from the assembled company: Burney herself 'munched my Biscuit as if I had not Eaten for a fortnight', while

> Dr. Johnson began *see-sawing*; Mr. Thrale awoke; Mr. Embry, who I fear has picked up some Notion of the affair from being so much in the House, *Grinned* amazingly; & Mr. Seward, biting his Nails, & flinging himself back in his Chair, I am sure had wickedness enough to enjoy the whole scene.

Having given her actors stage directions, Burney follows with a dialogue in which the clueless Rev. Lort, firmly put in his place by Dr Johnson and Mrs Thrale, decides to begin reading the novel that very night (*EJL* III, 113–5).

These same admirers of *Evelina* urged Burney to turn to writing for the stage. In 1778, simultaneously enjoying and intimidated by her own authorial fame, Burney found herself among a circle of wits and *literati*, who would provide both encouragement and material for her new project. She was further prodded by two eminent theatrical professionals: Arthur Murphy promised he would 'most readily, & with great pleasure, give any advice or assistance', and Richard Brinsley Sheridan offered to produce anything she cared to write – '*Unsight unseen*', as Sir Joshua Reynolds put it – '& make her a Bow & my best Thanks into the Bargain!' (*EJL* III, 246, 235). As Burney rightly concluded, such a commitment from a '*manager*, who must, of course, be *loaded* with Pieces & recommendations' could not be resisted: 'this Evening seems to have been *decisive*, my many & encreasing scruples *all* give way to encouragement so warm from so experienced a Judge, who is himself *interested* in not making such a request *par pure complaisance*' (*EJL* III, 236).

Burney's scruples were, in part, imposed from without, specifically in the form of the somewhat hysterical fears of Samuel Crisp, who, after congratulating himself on having foreseen that she would be pressed by her new friends to write a comedy, proceeds to enumerate the difficulties lying in her way. He cautions her that the 'frequently lively Freedoms' necessary to successful comedy would be inappropriate coming from 'Ladies of the strictest Character', while simultaneously counselling against writing one of the 'all-delicate, Sentimental Comedies ... so Void Of blood & Spirits' which have recently entered the repertoire. In a fairly impressive display of verbal gymnastics, he assures her that the task of writing with both verve and propriety is '*difficult* not *impracticable* – at least to your dexterity'; warns her that novelists as gifted as Fielding and Marivaux have a history of failing as playwrights; and ends with an ambiguous expression of confidence – 'if You have not the united Talents I demand, I don't know who has' (*EJL* III, 187–90). Burney responds to this confusing set of exhortations with an equivocation of her own: affirming that she 'would a thousand Times rather forfeit my character as a *Writer*, than risk ridicule or censure as a *Female*', she yet concludes, 'If I *should* try, I must e'en take my chance' (*EJL* III, 212). One can only smile appreciatively when Burney's next communication to Crisp on the subject, some four months later, is a terse 'I have finished a Play' (*EJL* III, 262). In the end, Crisp and Dr Burney are the ones who finish *The Witlings*, 'in *every* sense of the Word ... when my two Daddys put their Heads together to concert for me that Hissing, groaning, catcalling Epistle' (*EJL* III, 347, 350). Despite continuing importunities from Sheridan and Murphy, Burney obeyed the injunctions of her two male guardians, '& down among the Dead Men [sank] the poor Witlings, – for-ever & for-ever & for-ever!' (*EJL* III, 345).

That mournful farewell to Burney's first play is echoed in the germination of her next dramatic ventures, the four tragedies she embarked upon while unhappily employed as Queen Charlotte's Keeper of the Robes. Burney's journals during George III's illness indicate how deeply she participated in the general gloom afflicting the Court. In October 1788, immured at Kew with the royal family, she found herself 'in mere desperation for employment', composing tragedy (*DL* IV, 118). Both Hemlow and Doody suggest that these tragedies represent a reflection of and a release from the almost unbearable social and psychological burdens of her life at Court: the texts describe 'the dreariness of her own mind, the pomp and circumstance of court, and perhaps the cabals and political intrigues of the proposed regency', and they show Burney 'lost in the dark wood and savaged by her own terrors . . . It was not so much imagination as a kind of obsession which pushed these writings into the light.'[6] By the end of 1788, overwhelmed by the real tragedy unfolding in the royal household, Burney put *Edwy and Elgiva* away, but she took it up again at a moment of high personal tension and resulting illness. In 1790, while anxiously awaiting release from an employment which was destroying her health and mental stability, she finished *Edwy and Elgiva*, and went on to write *Hubert De Vere*, *The Siege of Pevensey* and notes toward *Elberta*. All these plays are set in medieval England, and all contain an unusual mixture of gothic trappings and actual historical events. Whatever their subsequent public fate would be, Burney clearly found in them a way to manage grief and stress; at the same time, however, Burney never ceased to consider her tragedies as part of her artistic *oeuvre* and continued to revise them, albeit fitfully, well into the nineteenth century.[7]

Unfortunately, Burney's one foray into public presentation of her tragic drama was an unmitigated disaster. The auguries for the Drury Lane production of *Edwy* in 1795 were both encouraging and alarming. Though the celebrated actor–manager John Philip Kemble 'instantly & warmly pronounced for its acceptance', and though he and his sister, the equally celebrated tragic actress Sarah Siddons, took the leading roles, the play was neither ready for performance nor given adequate attention by the company. Burney herself had not had time to provide the 'intended divers corrections & alterations' (she had recently given birth to her son Alexander and remained ill for some weeks); Sheridan and Kemble had not addressed the 'many *undramatic* [ef]fects, from my inexperience of Theatrical requisites & demands'; and many of the actors neglected to learn their parts, most egregiously John Palmer, who 'had *but 2 lines* of his part by Heart! he made all the rest at random – & such nonsense as put all the other actors out as much as himself' (*JL* III, 98–100). Mrs Siddons's compassionate but damning appraisal – 'Oh there never was so wretched a thing as Mrs. D'arblaye's Tragedy . . . The Audience were quite angelic and only laughed where it was *impossible* to avoid it' – was echoed by reviewers and given a mean-spirited twist by Hester Piozzi: 'Poor Fanny Burney's Tragedy called Edwy and Elgiva is hooted off the Stage I find . . . how it must gall her Pride!!'[8] Astonishingly, even after such a humiliating failure, Burney not only retained thoughts of revising *Edwy and Elgiva*, but also harboured hopes of publishing her tragedies as closet dramas. Such tenacious allegiance to works which she had begun as therapy argues either a deplorable lack of self-criticism or a conviction that these tragedies had something important to say. I will argue that the tragedies, with all their flaws, vindicate Burney's faith in them.

Burney made one more attempt at the London stage in 1798, when once again propitious beginnings ended in disappointment. Thomas Harris, manager of Covent Garden, was eager to produce a Burney comedy, but this project too was doomed to oblivion. In two letters dated 11 February 1800, Burney gives somewhat contradictory reasons for withdrawing the script. A letter to her sister Esther implies that the postponement resulted from her grief and her sense of impropriety in 'bringing out a Comedy at this period' (*JL* IV, 397) – i.e. so soon after the death of her beloved sister Susanna. But one to her father deploys the double-voiced discourse she had used twenty years before in replying to Crisp's strictures, and does so much more aggressively. She submits to Dr Burney's desire that she abort the attempt, but at every stage of the letter she argues against his directive and asserts her right to produce comedies. His displeasure, she says, is 'unaccountable', and prevents her from 'doing what I have all my life been urged to, & all my life intended, writing a Comedy'; his concern about her reputation is misplaced, for she knows the failure of this wholly moral work 'can only cause *disappointment*', not disgrace; his determination to limit her writing projects to a single genre is, on its face, unreasonable (*JL* IV, 394–5). It is a daring assertion of her own desire, but *Love and Fashion* never did find its way to the stage, perhaps because Harris changed his mind about reviving the project – in March 1801 Burney writes 'I know not what is purposed as to *time*, or even whether at ANY it will be heard of! – My Agent [her brother Charles] is *dead silent*' (*JL* IV, 477). Nevertheless, Burney was already embarked on her last two comedies, *A Busy Day* and *The Woman-Hater*. Once again, external forces prevented public trial of her comic talents. In 1802, she travelled to France to join General d'Arblay, only to be trapped there for ten years by the military conflicts between France and England. As Doody has remarked, 'Events, even international affairs, seemed to conspire against her getting a comedy on the London stage.'[9]

Burney's tragedies have fared little better in our time than they did in hers, and it is only very recently that they have elicited critical attention. Even sympathetic readers have either neglected them – and here I cite (and retract) my own casual dismissal of their 'contrived action and stilted language' – or depreciated them, as Hemlow does, as 'experiments in blank verse, scarcely to be considered as poetry'.[10] It is probably still the case that they would not prosper on stage today (and how many eighteenth-century tragedies do?), but they certainly reward the kind of scrupulous readings they have begun to accrue. Darby explicitly sets out to recuperate the tragedies, in particular by considering their deployment of conventional generic elements in service of a powerful critique of patriarchal power. Indeed, Burney's tragic drama, like that of her contemporaries Hanna More, Hannah Cowley and Joanna Baillie, dwells on institutional (male) cruelty to women, often seeming to revel in the details of physical and mental agony.

In *Edwy and Elgiva*, Elgiva is punished for her secret marriage to her cousin/King by being kidnapped and murdered by Dunstan's ruffians. Her crime, in the eyes of Dunstan and his supporters, lies not only in contracting a marriage against canon law, but in tempting Edwy away from the legitimate (male) companionship of nobles and clergy. When Dunstan discovers that Edwy has stolen away from his own coronation feast to seek Elgiva's company, he thunders, 'See England's King in base seduction's arms!' and accuses her of being the king's concubine (II.iii.4, 44). As both cause and symbol of Edwy's resistance to papal authority, Elgiva must be excommunicated and eliminated, thereby replacing sexuality/domesticity with religion/politics. Elgiva, caught between Edwy's passion and Dunstan's rigidity, is destroyed by forces outside the romantic, domestic space she inhabits. In her last moments, she expresses the hope that her death concludes the struggle between King and Bishop:

> Ah! bear the coming blow! –
> Brings it not peace? (V.xi.17–18)

It does not. Elgiva's death provides a momentary lull in hostilities which can end only with the death of the King himself, as we see when Dunstan insists that Edwy must be replaced by his malleable brother:

> Edwy will bear no yoke,
> Not ev'n Ecclesiastic ... Edgar is better fram'd to serve our cause.
> Contented with his own pursuits, the burthen
> Of State affairs on us would soon devolve. (III.i.18–25)

Edgar displaces Elgiva in the consciousness of both combatants; Dunstan, after being informed of her death, vows, 'These Eyes shall close no more till Edgar reign!' (V.ii.20), while Edwy, grieving over her body, becomes reanimated by news of Edgar's betrayal:

> Thou calls't me back to life! – I'm wondrous glad! ... Glorious scenes of bloodshed
> Fire with new energy my torpid mind. (V.xiv.7–10)

Even Elgiva's posthumous affect is minimised; although Dunstan recoils in pain when he sees her corpse, it is regicide which evokes his horrified remorse: 'I feel petrified! – My King!' (V.xviii.4). Elgiva's role as the cause of civil war becomes secondary; and we note that unlike Dryden's Mark Antony and a more recent monarch, Edwy never contemplates abdication, never considers the 'World Well Lost' for 'the woman I love'.

The vision of women suffering or dying, though dramatic in representation, is similarly marginalised or avoided in Burney's other tragedies. In *Hubert De Vere*, both central female characters serve as pawns in the plots of the villain de Mowbray, whose niece Geralda is coerced into marrying Lord Glanville in order to save her uncle from the charge of treason against King John. Not content with exploiting one kinswoman, de Mowbray also plots a match between his unacknowledged daughter Cerulia and his enemy De Vere, in order to prevent De Vere and the widowed Geralda from rekindling their romance and to position Cerulia as his new shield against De Vere's wrath. Geralda's painful marriage remains entirely off stage, but in Cerulia's madness and death, we do witness the kind of iconic female suffering enacted in Otway's *Venice Preserv'd* or Rowe's *Jane Shore*. Cerulia's unaffected passion for Hubert and her despair when she discovers his abiding love for Geralda unseat her reason and lead to her death, which she welcomes as release from a blighted life:

> No Father's smile foster'd my opening days;
> No Mother's votive Flowers will sooth my Manes:
> Him who I lov'd – I have lost ... Oh balmy sleep
> of Death, come, come – in pity! (V.391–7)

Cerulia's death temporarily moves de Mowbray to repentance and self-loathing, but he quickly reverts to violence in the cause of self-preservation; as for Hubert and Geralda, they gain in Cerulia's death yet another tie that binds: Hubert's pangs for 'hapless' Cerulia find solace in 'Matchless Geralda', whose 'noble pity' he interprets as 'Celestial omen! Sympathy divine!' (V.438–42). The death of Cerulia, far from ravaging the soul of the hero, frees him to marry the woman of his choice.

Adela and Elberta do not even die, so their stories cannot be considered she-tragedies in the literal sense,[11] but they do suffer on stage. Adela, in *The Siege of Pevensey*, anguishes over the choice between a forced marriage such as Geralda incurs and a secret, unsanctioned marriage such as Elgiva embraces. Adela's father Chester, however, unlike de Mowbray, values her emotional autonomy and resists the temptation to ransom her from the besieged castle only 'To chain her to an harder, longer bondage' to William

Rufus's favourite William de Warenne (I.i.62). Even when King William demands the marriage as the price of his life, Chester rejects the exchange:

> Horrour is in her Face! – I will not live! –
> What has my remnant life to pay this sacrifice? (V.xii.50–1)

Unlike Geralda (or Juliet in *The Wanderer*), Adela escapes the sacrificial marriage, and does so through her own ingenuity: perceiving William's greed, she offers her dowry to the King's treasury in exchange for safe harbour in 'some convent's lone retreat' (V.xii.62). In the end, Robert of Normandy's sudden capitulation rescues her from the cloister as it saves England from continued civil war, allowing her to marry Robert de Belesme, who has been fighting against William's forces.

Adela's love for de Belesme, in conflict with her filial devotion, gives rise to the other episode of feminine suffering in this play. Reluctantly acceding to a secret marriage with de Belesme, she is devastated by guilt when Chester suddenly appears. The scene which follows is indeed overwrought and does end in Adela's absolute submission to 'my single duties! / My undivided ties!' (IV.v.129–30) to her father. But however we choose to decode Burney's depiction of the father–daughter bond in *The Siege of Pevensey*, we need to keep in mind that Burney chooses to allow her heroine not only life, not only an affective marriage, but also the ingenuity to save her father without capitulating to de Warenne's demands. As Janice Farrar Thaddeus has said, *Pevensey* 'is a dream of control, where a woman seizes her own fate'.[12]

Despite Stewart Cooke's meticulous reconstruction of *Elberta* from a mass of surviving draft scraps, our readings of it must remain more speculative than those of the other tragedies. We know that Burney contemplated, for the first time, a heroine who is also a mother and that, to some extent, Elberta's difficulties combine those of Elgiva and Adela. She is both secretly married (to Arnulph, who serves the Norman King) and the victim of a threatened coerced marriage (to Arnulph's uncle Offa, who covets her Saxon estates). Elberta echoes Geralda's and Adela's revulsion from a loveless marriage, articulating the blindness of a despised but exigent suitor:

> How can he view her cold, averted Eye
> And even wish to claim her? –
>
> . . .
>
> Short-sighted such presumption! ill they scan
> The delicate female Heart, and ill conceive
> It's secret agony, its latent horrour,
> It's bitter pangs, from exquisite disgust –   (I.x.30–48)

Elberta's agonies, however, are more materially (and maternally) grounded; whereas Chester only imagines the slow starvation of his daughter in besieged Pevensey (I.iii.13–15), Elberta must witness her babies waste away from want of food (IV.iii.5–7). Unlike other Burney heroines, Elberta suffers from no inner conflict, for the danger to her children – as her legitimate heirs, they threaten Offa's designs on her property – makes her single-minded and ferocious. As her servant Wilfred notes, the mother cancels the natural timidity of the woman,

> Turning aside
> The gentle stream that timid flowed
> Through every vein – for the rough, tumbling torrent
> Of more than manly force –   (IV.xiv.13–16)

Paradoxically, motherhood re-genders her, so that she appropriates the physical courage and mental endurance of the typical tragic hero. Her final ringing assertion after the death of Arnulph attests to her dominant will:

> Yes! I will live! – to Heaven's high will resign'd –
> I'm wondrous glad he's dead – for now I'm calm –
> 'Tis marvellous how I'm changed! I grieve at nothing.
>   (V.xiii.16–18)

She echoes Edwy's wondrous gladness that Edgar's treachery has invigorated him. Just as Cerulia's death liberates Hubert and Geralda, Arnulph's death frees Elberta to fulfil her destiny as a mother – and powerful female.

As the foregoing discussion shows, I cannot entirely subscribe to a reading of the tragedies that focuses exclusively, or even primarily, on the victimisation of women. While Burney surely means to represent ways in which society oppresses women, these plays also give them agency, sometimes to behave heroically (as when Adela returns to Pevensey to save de Belesme or when Elberta fiercely guards her children) and sometimes to choose less worthy paths (clandestine marriages are never entirely admirable). In any case, Burney's feminist agenda should be read alongside other issues equally central to her tragedies – monarchy and national character as understood through English political history.

It is now a truism that many fictional texts of the late eighteenth century encode responses to the French Revolution and its effect on Britain. Burney's engagement with the French Revolution, explicitly taken up in *The Wanderer*, is more obliquely present in the plays. To some extent, she writes into them the conservative, Royalist viewpoint which eschews popular uprisings. Indeed, *Edwy and Elgiva* includes multiple criticisms of insurrection, from Edwy's reproach to his barons 'That Me, your Sovereign, you thus dare pursue / Ev'n on the Day when every legal tie / Invests Me with acknowldg'd power superior' (II.v.6–8) to Dunstan's contemptuous characterisation of the very populace which confirms his power. To Dunstan, 'the people' are like Dryden's 'headstrong, moody, murmuring race':[13]

> The crowd require illusion, not conviction.
> Entic'd by Terror, caught by Ambiguity,
> Weakly beguil'd, and eagerly amaz'd,
> To them 'twere useless to discuss opinions;
> They must be led more vigourously to action
> By calling forth their passions, and their interests,
> By raising fears unnam'd, and Hopes mysterious. (III.i.28–34)

The restless and gullible mob joins with the unruly barons, whose 'Noisy festivity, repasts luxurious, / Spirits inflam'd by Reason's conflagration, / Loud, frantic, vehement, discordant sallies' drive Edwy away from his own coronation feast (II.ii.47–49). Together, these different classes, 'Confus'dly mixing' (IV.xx.11), ignite the civil war which kills the King, but we should also note some counter-currents in the text. The monarch in question has not only impulsively and secretly contracted an interdicted marriage, but he also imperiously demands that Aldhelm bring him the 'full, unanimous consent ... of my united people' (I.ix.91–2). Flinging away Aldhelm's prudent counsel against convening the synod, Edwy rages at his one loyal follower: 'Nay, reason not; – obey Me! – or be silent! – ' (III.vi.20). As choleric as Lear, without the excuse of age and long habits of power, Edwy demands absolute submission, ignoring both pragmatic politics and his own culpability. Like the British government's repressive, legislated patriotism in the 1790s, Edwy's definition of loyalty is silent acquiescence. This is not to claim that Burney is a closet Jacobin who wishes the end of monarchy; we know that she was in fact a loyal and affectionate subject. It is, rather, to suggest that not only was she aware of the political divisions of her time, but she was also fully aware of the dangers of unbridled royal power, whether French or English.

Indeed, in *Hubert De Vere* and *The Siege of Pevensey*, monarchs serve as examples for their corrupt followers. John makes no personal appearance in *Hubert*, but for Burney's readers as well as for us, he is the epitome of malicious and ineffective rule. John's turbulent reign provides not just a background, but the occasion for the plot of *Hubert*, since the multiple personal betrayals in the play originate in conspiracies against the king:

> Glanville, returning from the Court of Philip
> With articles of peace 'twixt France and England,
> Betray'd a Writing, signed by sundry Barons

> Yet unenroll'd in treason's open records,
> Offering to France this interdicted Kingdom,
> By secret treaty, from the unpopular John.   (III.285–90)

Philip's intrigues with English peers serve as the impetus for de Mowbray and Glanville's plot against Hubert, and John's own arbitrary judgment allows them to succeed. At the very beginning of the play, Beauchamp laments finding 'Hubert De Vere, the first on Valour's list, / Exiled, unheard, by John, to this small Isle' (I.19–20). Hubert himself, while he dwells on Geralda's perfidy, also berates 'Ungrateful John! – so lightly to discard me!' (I.113). John's own faithlessness incites treachery in his subjects, who follow his lead in advancing their own interests at the cost of national security. And at the end of the play, John's soldiers arrive to escort both hero and villain to Court, not because John has repented his harsh treatment of Hubert, but because, in a kind of parody of Louis XIV's omniscience in Molière's *Tartuffe*, 'The King has been much mov'd by varying rumours … Doubts arise / Of Fraud – of Perjury' (V.425–8).

The Siege of Pevensey places the monarch squarely at the centre of civil war and its multiple betrayals. While the officer Fitz Hammon assigns equal claims (and equal blame) to Robert and William – one is the 'elder born' while the other is the choice of the 'Conqueror's will' (I.i.13–15) – it is William Rufus who exercises arbitrary power, plotting against his own barons, coveting the estates of his followers, and inverting all chivalric codes: 'When War's abroad … Treachery is honour, then, and plunder, patriotism' (II.ii.15–16). To Chester's pleas that Robert's supporters are 'your subjects! … your children … still your fellow-Creatures!' (II.ii.55–9), he opposes an unrelenting will to vengeance, swearing to 'make the Nation feel the Norman Yoke, / Till every rebel spirit is crush'd for-ever' (II.ii.82–3). William's confidantes, like John's, engage in multiple manipulations and betrayals and William too abandons his few principled and truly patriotic followers. In the end, England is saved from the ravages of war only because 'The noble Duke, griev'd at the ills of War, / Wishes to spare th'effusion of more blood / Ev'n at the proper cost of his own interest' (V.xiv.11–13). Amid the general celebration of peace, even during de Belesme's submission to 'England's lawful Sovereign', and William's declaration that Robert is 'my Brother – and we war no more!' (V.xv.5, V.xiv.23), we remember William's premeditated treachery:

> Would the spendthrift Robert
> Cede England as my due, Peace should be sign'd:
> And his lax discipline, when least aware,
> With scarce a blow, would give me Normandy.   (II.iv.8–11)

With the possible exception of Offa in *Elberta*, William is the most despicable character in all of Burney's tragedies. Burney bases her contemptible William Rufus on David Hume's characterisation of him as 'violent, haughty, tyrannical',[14] but the range and intensity of his malice are her own invention. It is possible that Burney embodies in William the oppressive *ancien regime* in France, but she might also be reacting to the beginnings of repressive practices in England, practices which would lead to the attacks on free speech and the Treason Trials of the 1790s. In either case, Burney's portraits of John and William can hardly be said to reflect straightforward Royalist sympathies.

Burney undertakes in the tragedies an ambitious and historically grounded project. She chooses to write about pressure points in English political history: the violent deposition of a legitimate monarch, and the survival of problematic and unpopular monarchies. These are dark moments in English history, and, despite the 'happy' personal endings for the lovers in *Hubert* and *Pevensey*, all the plays leave the kingdom in the hands of tyrannical, treacherous leaders. The noble sentiments of Hubert, who declares, 'for my country's peace, repress my murmurs' (V.435), and Chester, who exclaims, 'O sire! Faith and loyalty / Be all thy own!' (V.xiv.27–8), seem singularly naive within the plays' context of double-dealing and violent conflict. Peace itself, as Burney demonstrates in the fragments which constitute *Elberta*, can occasion rapaciousness; winners are no more likely to be magnanimous than losers to be resigned. The cycles of violence continue under Edwy, or William, or John.

Burney opts for these problematic moments in English history because they provide material for serious meditation on the nature of virtuous rule and responsible citizenship. They allow for a broad range of cultural analysis, from the treatment of women who become pawns in political intrigue, to the monarch's complicity in creating a nation in which violence and betrayal have become the rule. These plays issue from a deeply serious, historicised understanding of a nation's past. Burney's tragedies may have originated in her painful private life at George III's Court, but they engage, confidently and subtly, with significant public moments in England's tumultuous past.

Burney's tragedies depict a dark world in which the sins of the monarch lead to civil war, dishonourable practices and excruciating deaths. No wonder then that her biographers detect in them an expression of her misery at Court, and that one of them concludes that 'Her tragedies contain various and variegated characters, but no humor.'[15] When critics have noticed humour, it has been mortifyingly inadvertent: Sabor points out that a line in the Drury Lane performance of *Edwy and Elgiva* unfortunately echoed the call for a popular tavern liquor, while equal hilarity was elicited by transporting the wounded Elgiva on 'an elegant couch' (I.vii.1n.; V.xi.sdn). But even in these bleak plays, written during a period of personal gloom, Burney does retain some lightness. For example, Mowbray sounds remarkably like Deborah in *A Busy Day* when Adela and de Belesme dispense with his attendance: 'Methinks / Thou art wond'rous eager to dismiss me hence: / But as I once was young myself' (III.xi.12–14), he genially accommodates their desire to be alone. Even *Edwy and Elgiva*, perhaps the most unrelieved of the tragedies, contains at least one flash of wit, when Aldhelm responds to Dunstan's misogynist tirade with a piece of theological logic: 'If Woman is our scorn, Wedlock, our horrour, / Where dwells the virtue of our self denial?' (III.iv.63–4). *Hubert De Vere* gives us more sustained comic episodes: Agatha and Geoffry, like the shepherds in *As You Like It*, comically mirror the heroes' star-crossed love, while Geoffry and his friends enact a parodic knightly combat when they rescue Geralda from de Mowbray's ruffians: 'Like ravenous Wolves for rage we sprang at them / With our stout weapons of good husbandry' (I.218–19). Cerulia's peasant friends exasperate Hubert when they flock around him, just as the Watts family dismays the upper-class Tilneys in *A Busy Day*, and he, like Lady Wilhelmina, exclaims, 'What strange, uncouth annoyance!' (IV.109).

The moments of humour in *Hubert De Vere* derive from the clash of social classes so central in Burney's comic plays and novels, but we need to note that Burney's signature confrontation of classes takes more than one form; she doesn't always repeat the winning formula of brash Branghtons disconcerting snobbish upper classes. In *The Witlings*, class distinctions are thematised through a consideration of leisure. Just as there is little difference between the bad manners of Mr Briggs and of Mr Delvile in *Cecilia*, there is little to choose between the milliner's casual disdain for middle-class clients – a spoiled cap 'will do well enough for the City' (I.15) – and the careless damage inflicted by 'fine Ladies [who] ... keep ordering and ordering, and think no more of paying than if one could Live upon a needle and Thread' (V.4–6). *The Witlings* exposes predatory practices on both sides of the counter.

An even more significant commonality, I believe, exists in the dependence of all classes on a volatile economy which can destroy fortunes of all sizes. The plot hinges on Cecilia's loss of fortune when her banker Stipend fails, but she is by no means the only person at risk in a system relying on mysterious financial transactions. Mrs Sapient worries that 'I may be myself concerned in this transaction', and adds that Stipend 'has concerns with half my acquaintance! ... I think one hears some bad news or other every Day' (II.471–2, 478–80). Mrs Voluble consoles Cecilia by assuring her that her plight is universal: 'Times are very bad! ... all the Gentlefolk breaking ... poor Mr. Mite, the rich cheesemonger at the Corner is quite knocked up ... as to Breaking, and so forth, why I think it happens to every body ... there's Mr. Grease, the Tallow Chandler ... is quite upon the very point of ruination' (V.7–9, 124–8). At every level of society, it seems, bankruptcy and ruin are widespread. No wonder, then, that Mrs Wheedle's first reaction to Cecilia's trouble is to present her own bill before other creditors can make claims. In this economy of mutual dependence of labour and capital, of provider and consumer, there is both absolute reciprocity and absolute self-interest; Beaufort's closing paean to 'the most useful of all practical precepts That Self-dependance is the first of Earthly Blessings' (V.951–2) is thus doubly ironic. Not only do Beaufort and Cecilia return to the dependence secured by blackmailing Lady Smatter, but also there is in fact no 'Self-dependance' available to citizens of an imperial nation engaged in global trade.

In *Love and Fashion*, the new economy has defeated the old land-based system, and the victory has not gone to the deserving. The servants Dawson and Innis articulate this contest (conquest) in the first scene of the play, when they compare the amiable Lord Exbury with his self-important brother Lord Ardville, who 'was not half so proud before he got his title, upon going that last time to the Indies, where he made his great fortune':

> Lauk! to see his elder Brother, Mr. Exbury, that's only got his natural Estate as one may say, being no more than what comes from Father to son, so genteel-behaved, and agreeable! – while this, that only got his topping income by fortune-hunting, in comparison, to be so *highty* and *imperial*! (I.31–8)

Ardville represents the bad colonial, whose misbegotten wealth serves only to augment his pride and ill temper, and who is despised by the very people he employs. In contrast, Lord Exbury's devoted valet, discovering that his master has been ruined by his son Mordaunt's extravagance, vows to 'serve him without the lucre of gain ... I would not but serve him, now he can hardly pay me, to be made forty Emperors' (I.ii.187, 191–2). Lord Ardville's imperial fortune does tempt Hilaria, who loves Exbury's son Valentine but cannot resist 'jewels and nabob muslins' (III.ii.34–5) and 'the finest Gems of the East' (IV.iii.158–9). The spoils of colonial conquest, in *Love and Fashion*, are deployed to seduce the heroine away from her true love and her own integrity. The happy ending comes about only because Hilaria openly offers to barter her hand in exchange for Valentine's release from debt and because Lord Ardville, like Lady Smatter in *The Witlings*, fears public ridicule. Both are cornered into a generosity neither natural nor graceful.

Love and Fashion, like *The Witlings*, ends with a singularly inapposite speech about independence, when Lord Exbury predicts Valentine's inevitable success: 'Is This a Land where spirit and Virtue shall want Protection?

What is there of Fortune or distinction unattainable in Britain by Talents, probity, and Courage?' (V.iv.291–3). Since Valentine has just been rescued from poverty, disgrace and imminent imprisonment by the pity of a woman and the shame of her rejected suitor, the speech seems somewhat misapplied. Similarly, since Beaufort has shown no sign of knowing how to earn a living and Cecilia has passionately declined to 'expose myself, like a common Servant, to be Hired' (V.239–40), the hymn to self-dependence in *The Witlings* sounds like mere rhetoric. Moreover, the self-made Ardville accrues scorn and mockery, making the exaltation of individual advancement inappropriate and even hypocritical. Burney's first two comedies, though separated by two decades and life-changing experiences, both articulate Burney's suspicion of the new economic system. *The Witlings* may represent the real labour of working women, and *Love and Fashion* may idealise the pastoral romance of woodcutters and haymakers, but, in the end, both plays point to the dangers of a new world order based on an unstable system of global commerce.

In her last two comedies, Burney shifts to a very different view of class and the imperial economy. While she continues her characteristic comic deployment of class antagonisms, she no longer inscribes in her work a fear of the new economy. The Wattses in *A Busy Day* are undoubtedly vulgar, ostentatious and self-centred, but there is much pathos in their failed attempts to encroach and much validation of their complaints against the boorish ruling class. The Watts family originates far down the social scale; as Cousin Tibbs so mortifyingly recalls, they had been 'styed in such a little dirty hole!' and Mrs Watts 'used to scrub the floor upon her knees' before she married (III.223, 235–6). Their rise to affluence illustrates Lord Exbury's speech about Britain as the land of opportunity, and their appalling vulgarity does not prevent the upper-class wastrel Frank from wanting to marry their money. That their wealth has bought them at least limited access to 'polite' company is attested to by the very complaints Mr Watts makes about the contemptuous rudeness of the upper classes:

> They'll eat up all the best things, one after another, without caring for not leaving you a scrap: and they'll take all the best places, without minding if you have not a bit as big as my hand to sit upon . . . and they'll let one speak half an hour, before they'll give an answer; and they'll clean their teeth full in one's face, as if one was nothing but a looking glass. (III.546–52)

Our sympathy for Mr Watts – insulted by his social superiors, bullied by his wife and daughter, made lonely and useless by leisure – is undercut by his own coarse indifference to the less fortunate, but the fact remains that he has earned his way up and participates, however marginally and unhappily, in the fashionable world. At the end of the play, when the match between Eliza

Watts and Cleveland is confirmed, the two families (and the two classes) become linked by blood; Lady Wilhelmina may sputter and Miss Percival may shriek, but the cross-pollinating marriage will occur nevertheless.

To some extent Burney cheats in *A Busy Day*, making the class miscegenation palatable by creating a heroine whose personal qualities transcend both the class she is born into and the one into which she is about to marry. As Cleveland rhapsodises, 'Sweet lovely Eliza! from weeds so coarse can a flower so fragrant bloom?' (III.599–600). Eliza's social and mental elegance overcomes Cleveland's own revulsion from 'the whole vulgar crew' (III.594) and mitigates the radicalism of such an unequal match. Significantly, Eliza's personal and financial assets come from her connection with the Empire: she has been raised in India by her adoptive father Mr Alderson, and has brought back to England the gentle manners and the £80,000 acquired there. Unlike Lord Ardville, Mr Alderson possesses 'virtues … benevolence … unceasing kindness' (I.418–19) and has bequeathed them to Eliza. He has also given her an appreciation for the people she lived among: her tenderness toward the Indian servant Mungo contrasts with the contempt of the English waiter, and her sentimentalised characterisation of Indians rebukes the racism of her sister:

MISS WATTS.	Pray, Sister, do the Indins do much mischief?
ELIZA.	Mischief?
MISS WATTS.	What kind of look have they? Do they let 'em run about wild? Wa'n't you monstrous frightened at first?
ELIZA.	Frightened? the native Gentoos are the mildest and gentlest of human beings.
MISS WATTS.	La, nasty black things! I can't abide the Indins. I'm sure I should do nothing but squeal if I was among 'em.

(I.455–62)

In *A Busy Day*, only the ignorant and the vulgar configure India merely as a source of wealth and muslins; the imperial experience, in this text, inculcates cosmopolitanism while it produces fortunes.

Burney's representation of the imperial adventure takes yet another turn in *The Woman-Hater*. The melodramatic tale of jealousy and false accusation is enabled by a colonial narrative much deployed by eighteenth-century writers – captivity by Amerindians. In this case, the object of Wilmot's jealousy, Captain Ludlow, 'had been surprised, with his whole party, by a large body of Indians, carried up the Country a Prisoner, and detained, a Slave, not a Captive' for sixteen years (III.viii.58–60). His disappearance, unluckily coinciding with Eleanor's flight to England, has kept Wilmot in a state of rage against his wife, who in turn has assumed that he has utterly discarded her and their daughter Sophia. The action of *The Woman-Hater* is precipitated by the convergence in the same vicinity of a repentant Wilmot and a destitute Eleanora, each seeking help from their respective siblings: Lady Smatter (a witling resurrected from the earlier play) and Sir Roderick.

The arrival from the West Indies, however, contains none of the happy baggage seen in *A Busy Day*. Wilmot, obviously an official sufficiently important that his voyage has been announced in the newspapers (III.ii.72), has merely endured his 'gloomy career in the West Indies' (III.viii.6–7) and remains culturally removed from the place he has inhabited and governed for so many years. His supposed daughter Joyce also appears indifferent to the culture in which she grew up, offering no corrective to Lady Smatter's prejudices: 'The part of the World you have left is, I fancy, rather … uncivilized? You have been forced to live pretty much, I imagine, among savages?' (III.x.4–5). Joyce and Wilmot seem equally untouched by their corner of the empire, cocooned in their narrow emotional and social lives. Only Nurse is eager to return, urging Joyce to 'coax your Papa to go back to the West Indies' (III.x.111–12), but of course her attachment to the colony is motivated by self-preservation. 'O that I was safe back in the Indies!' (III.x.120) she exclaims, fearing that her exchange of babies will be detected if they stay in England. And it is Nurse who refers to the newest outpost of the British Empire, when she begs Joyce not to reveal the truth, for 'you'll get me sent to Botany Bay!' (V.xvi.4). The somewhat sentimentalised and certainly laudatory representation of imperial service in *A Busy Day* is replaced in *The Woman-Hater* with a highly problematised elision of representation.

In these two comedies, written at about the same time, Burney constructs a hierarchy of British possessions, in which India holds a privileged place. Such differentiation indicates that Burney has thought carefully about the multiple manifestations of the imperial enterprise, and that she encodes in her work her judgment of them. The positive view of India in *A Busy Day* reflects, in part, her support for Warren Hastings and his participation in Sir William Jones's project to preserve Indian cultures; the relative indifference or perhaps even distaste for the West Indian colonies may reflect a general sense that the slave-owning plantation elite as well as the 'backward' population they ruled were less valuable than those who travelled to India to administer and preserve an ancient civilisation. And Botany Bay, the convict colony which replaced North America as a repository for criminals the home country wanted to exile, merits no more than an invocation as dreaded punishment. While these far reaches of the British Empire may not occupy a central place in *A Busy Day* and *The Woman-Hater*, they indicate how seriously Burney has reflected on their role in contemporary British life.

Burney's assessment of these different colonial civilisations informs the sort of heroine connected with them. Eliza's sojourn in Calcutta has in fact raised her socially and intellectually above her ill-bred English family. Joyce, on the other hand, remains essentially 'uncivilised,' retaining a kind of genetic propensity for hoydenish behaviour, inherited from her low-class parents. Rejecting the scholarly tendencies of Wilmot (parodied in his sister's display of bookishness), Joyce rejoices in the carnivalesque – ballads, jigs, and food. It is also possible to see her disruptive presence as a figure for the untamed colonial; unlike Eliza, educated out of her lower-class origins by her colonial experience, Joyce finds no path out of her social class. At the same time, Joyce's deflationary rhetoric provides a welcome corrective to melodramatic narratives, whether they originate in the West Indies or in England:

> Well! I have lost two Papas; but I have learned one thing as perfect as if I had read all the Books and authors in the Universe! – and that is – what is meant by a Woman-Hater! It is, – to hate a woman – if she won't let you love her: to run away from her – if you can't run to her: to swear she is made up of faults – unless she allows you to be made up of perfections: and to vow she shall never cross your Threshhold, – unless she'll come to be mistress of your whole house!
>
> (V.xxiii.103–9)

Perhaps the uncivilised West Indies has value after all.

In *A Busy Day* and *The Woman-Hater*, Burney demonstrates the range of her dramatic powers, deftly combining sentiment with farce, gothic melodrama with social satire, and contextualising it all within a consideration of how Britain's imperial reach affects its domestic spaces, thereby changing class hierarchies and the economic system. After all, Cleveland and Wilmot embody a radical shift in being upper-class men who actually work for a living; they are imperial servants who have not in fact amassed ill-gotten fortunes. At the same time, Eliza and Joyce, two women who have grown up in the peripheries, represent women who make themselves independent of their families, each claiming for herself the power to choose a husband and a way of life. When Eliza decides to use her fortune to enable the match with Cleveland, when Joyce opts for 'my liberty' (V.xii.25) by marrying the illiterate servant Bob Sapling, they energetically reject the traditional, passive role of the dependent woman. The self-dependence so inappropriately lauded by Beaufort and Lord Exbury can, in these last plays by Burney, apply to female as well as male characters. Moreover, just as she had reached back to early English history to trace the links between monarchical and national character, Burney now stretches far beyond the borders of Britain to show how imperial power has changed the world at home.

NOTES

1. Joyce Hemlow, 'Fanny Burney: Playwright', *University of Toronto Quarterly* 19 (1950), 170–89; Hemlow, *The History of Fanny Burney* (Oxford: Clarendon Press, 1958).

2. Margaret Anne Doody, *Frances Burney: The Life in the Works* (Cambridge: Cambridge University Press, 1988).

3. Barbara Darby, *Frances Burney, Dramatist: Gender, Performance, and the Late-Eighteenth-Century Stage* (Lexington: University Press of Kentucky, 1997).

4. Sandra Sherman, '"Does Your Ladyship Mean an Extempore?" Wit, Leisure, and the Mode of Production in Frances Burney's *The Witlings*', *Centennial Review* 40.2 (1996), 401–28; Deidre Shauna Lynch, 'Counter Publics: Shopping and Women's Sociability', in *Romantic Sociability: Social Networks and Literary Culture in Britain, 1770–1840*, ed. Gillian Russell and Clara Tuite (Cambridge: Cambridge University Press, 2002), 211–36.

5. See *A Busy Day*, ed. Tara Ghoshal Wallace (New Brunswick: Rutgers University Press, 1984), 195–9.

6. Hemlow, *History*, 206; Doody, *Life in the Works*, 178–9.

7. See Sabor's notes to the tragedies; he finds, for example, that Burney was tinkering with *Hubert De Vere* as late as 1836 (*Plays* II, 95).

8. Hester Lynch Piozzi, *Thraliana: The Diary of Mrs Hester Lynch Thrale (Later Mrs Piozzi), 1776–1809*, ed. Katharine C. Balderston, 2 vols., 2nd edn (Oxford: Clarendon Press, 1951), II, 916 and n. 1.

9. Doody, *Life in the Works*, 289.

10. Wallace (ed.), *Busy Day*, 157; Hemlow, *History*, 220.

11. Hemlow applies the term to Burney's tragic drama, while Sabor urges that the term, 'which has had so constricting an effect on the study of Burney', be dropped (Hemlow, 'Fanny Burney: Playwright', 176; Sabor, 'General Introduction' to *Plays* I, xxxi).

12. Janice Farrar Thaddeus, *Frances Burney: A Literary Life* (Basingstoke: Macmillan, 2000), 106.

13. John Dryden, 'Absalom and Achitophel', l. 44.

14. David Hume, *The History of England from the Invasion of Julius Caesar to the Abdication of James the Second, 1688*, 6 vols. (London, 1754–62), I, 221.

15. Thaddeus, *Frances Burney*, 108.

incidents into miniature dramas. Burney wrote, at a much later phase of her life, and in a very different mood, 'I returned to my pen, with which alone I was able in pouring forth my fears to attract back my hopes, & in recording my miseries, to imbibe instinctively the sympathy which had the power, magnetic, to sooth them' (*JL* VIII, 438). In other words, she was inspired to write for someone such as Susan, her 'Daddy' Samuel Crisp, later her sister Esther or, later still, her son Alexander: for the family, in short.

Yet Burney's life-writings exist simultaneously in two different genres – as letters (their recipients addressed as 'you') and as historical records, compiled with a half-conscious eye to the future. Originating as brief notes on her erasable writing 'tablets', they are amplified, ordered and many of them retrospectively revised. The historical dimension becomes formalised in her later invention of the short 'Narrative', a title she gives to autobiographical writings focusing on specific events or episodes, which are yet still enclosed within the convention of the letter. These documents thus epitomise a paradox: they are private communications which at the same time parade Burney's experiences and write their author into history. Sheltered within the family, they are annunciations by a person who felt her own experiences to be intensely important and, increasingly, matters of public interest. In this account, the broad term 'journal' is used for all her life-writings, diaries, letters, 'journal-letters', narratives (as her editors have variously called them).

Burney refuses to hand over the documents to Boswell on the grounds of the sacredness of privacy. 'I cannot consent to print private letters, even of a man so justly celebrated', she declares (*DL* IV, 433). So, although she recorded many incidents like this one, they were, in the first instance, private accounts kept, during Burney's lifetime, within the family. In 1843, after her death, some of the voluminous material she had accumulated and prepared, or in some cases doctored, was edited by her niece Charlotte Barrett and published as *The Diary and Letters of Madame d'Arblay*. The tradition, inaugurated by these volumes, in which an autobiographical narrative, loosely in the manner of an epistolary novel, is constructed out of diverse materials, including letters from correspondents, is continued to some extent in the scholarly edition of *The Journals and Letters of Fanny Burney* (12 vols., 1972–84), which takes 1791 as its starting point, and in the ongoing editions of *The Early Journals and Letters of Fanny Burney* (1988–) and *The Court Journals and Letters of Frances Burney* (in progress) which begin in 1768. The entire account of Burney's miserable time at court between 1786 and 1791, as well as the years before, from 1782, when she was the confidante of Dr Johnson, is currently obtainable only in the incomplete earlier editions. Barrett's was edited, and to a small extent supplemented, by Austin Dobson in 1904–5, and these are the volumes used here for those years.

One day in 1789, Burney confides to one of her fellow courtiers that Dr Johnson, in that earlier phase of her life, had offered to teach her Latin: 'and I proceeded to the speedy conclusion – my great apprehension, *conviction* rather, that what I learnt of so great a man could never be *private* . . . which to me was sufficient motive for relinquishing the scheme' (*DL* IV, 223). Privacy was an essential attribute of female gentility, augmented in her case by great personal shyness. Nevertheless it was Burney's fate that her privacy should be constantly tested or infringed. The contest between the desire for privacy and the lionising of a successful author is the substance of many of the incidents, both excruciating and comic, that she recorded after the publication of *Evelina* in 1778. During those years at Court, guarding her privacy is supremely important to her, but she is dragged into the full glare of history when the King, recovering from his 'madness', catches sight of her in Kew gardens, runs after her and gives her a hearty embrace (*DL* IV, 242–50: February 1789). Not the least of the trials of her Court life was that, with its livelong 'toil(ette)', it is a parody of those genteel female occupations – dressing, hair-dressing, gossip, the tea table and cards – that were soon to be derided by Mary Wollstonecraft in her *Vindication of the Rights of Woman* (1792). And yet, with the King's illness, the feminised circle of the Queen's attendants is no longer insulated from the masculine world of politics, as the crisis of the Regency – with the King temporarily replaced by his son, the Prince of Wales – unfolds. As a woman and a lady, Burney is an apolitical person: yet her life is caught up in and invaded by politics in each of its episodes. As I shall suggest, Burney – though writing within a mode which privileges personal relationships – becomes an embodiment of that condition of modernity in which history is enacted through the experience of the private subject.

Burney began her earliest surviving journal at the age of fifteen. From the first, it was filled with conversations, sometimes dramatised in stage-play form. She gives graphic accounts, for example, of Garrick's talk (*EJL* II, 94–7) and of the conversation about him at the family party where she first saw Dr Johnson, making also a vivid sketch of Johnson's appearance, as she usually did of any new acquaintance (*EJL* II, 225–9). In May 1775, there is a long and very interesting episode in which she is courted by a young Mr Barlow, a gentleman who will not take no for answer (*EJL* II, 115–29). With its accumulation of family pressures, this is a miniature Richardsonian drama: but, like Jane Austen's Elizabeth Bennet, Burney is not much disturbed, and presents her admirer's preposterous letters for her family readers' amusement. Later, on the anonymous publication of *Evelina* (1778), the journal repeatedly makes comedy out of the speculations about its authorship, writing 'Nothing can be more ridiculous than the scenes in which I am almost perpetually engaged' (*EJL* III, 58). Burney gets a lot of mileage, for months, out of these 'scenes'. Soon, the secret being told her, Hester Lynch Thrale, hostess and friend of Dr Johnson, takes up the successful young author, and an important phase of her autobiographical writing begins.

The records of life at Streatham, the Thrales' residence in south London, are known as the 'Streatham Journals'. It was there that Burney became a close friend of Johnson and recorded his domestic behaviour and conversation more vividly and intimately than even Mrs Thrale herself was to do in the *Anecdotes* published after his death.[1] Burney has the advantage over Mrs Thrale in her sense of theatre and situation, and she also has a key advantage over Boswell. '[H]e will be seen in this work more completely than any man who has ever yet lived', Boswell was to claim in the first pages of his biography,[2] but in fact he showed Johnson almost exclusively in the company of men. Burney records a Johnson who is sportive and benign, delighting in the company of the two clever women, full of teasing and repartee, but she also witnessed Johnson in his most ferociously disputatious mood – as when he went for a Mr Pepys who had the temerity to criticise his 'Life' of Lord Lyttelton (*EJL* IV, 366–71: June 1781). Burney's shock at this 'frightful scene' as she called it, even when recalling it two years later, is the greater because, it seems, she was an innocent onlooker, largely unaware of the quarrel's political undercurrents. It was an innocence – or an appearance of it – that she was long careful to retain.

Johnson is old and in much pain throughout their friendship. When he arrives late for dinner at the Burney home in St Martin's Street, Burney records a confidence that typifies their closeness.

> When I went up to him, to tell how sorry I was to find him so unwell, – 'Ah!' he cried, taking my hand and kissing it, 'who shall ail anything when "Cecilia" is so near? Yet you do not think how poorly I am!' This was quite melancholy, and all dinner time he hardly opened his mouth but to repeat to me, – 'Ah! you little know how ill I am.'   (*DL* II, 171: 4 January 1783)

This is not a side of Johnson given much attention in Boswell's biography. Burney's record of her last meeting with Johnson – sent to her sister – is an intimate account of a public figure. Johnson is 'very ill' and is thinking of trying what 'sleeping out of town might do for him'.

> 'I remember,' said he, 'that my wife, when she was near her end, poor woman, was also advised to sleep out of town; and when she was carried to the lodgings that had been prepared for her, she complained that the staircase was in very bad condition – for the plaster was beaten off the walls in many places. "Oh," said the man of the house, "that's nothing but by the knocks against it of the coffins of the poor souls that have died in the lodgings!"'
>
> (*DL* II, 270: 28 November 1784)

Burney's comment is: 'He laughed, though not without apparent secret anguish, in telling me this. I felt extremely shocked, but, willing to confine my words at least to the literal story, I only exclaimed against the unfeeling absurdity of such a confession.' She understands that this 'absurdity', which must have been told to Johnson by his wife Hetty herself, a witty woman, is a macabre joke that covers – for Johnson as it must have for Hetty – a recognition of the imminence of death. 'Such a confession' is perhaps a slip: this is Johnson's confession, made to a woman with whom in this dialogue he speaks his most private thoughts.

Burney had been close to Johnson's once dear friend (she was taken to Brighton by Mrs Thrale in 1779, and gives a lively account of their journey and three-month stay (*EJL* IV, 23–174)), but the friendship was ruptured when the widow fell in love with the musician Gabriel Piozzi. Burney sided with her daughters, who vehemently opposed their marriage. The break left Burney with painful feelings, only partially assuaged many years later in 1817 when the two women met again in Bath. With Johnson's death and the loss of Mrs Thrale, the scene of the journals changes. Burney is apparently depressed, and it is in this state of depression that she succumbs to the accumulated pressures of her friends, especially Mary Delany, which drive her into accepting the position of Queen Charlotte's Keeper of the Robes at Court:

> I now took the most vigorous resolutions to observe the promise I had made my dear father. Now all was finally settled, to borrow my own words, I needed no monitor to tell me it would be foolish, useless, even wicked, not to reconcile myself to my destiny.
>
> The many now wishing for just the same – Oh! could they look within me. I am *married*, my dearest Susan – I look upon it in that light – I was averse to forming the union, and I endeavoured to escape it; but my friends interfered – they prevailed – and the knot is tied. What then now remains but to make the best wife in my power? I am bound to it in duty, and I will strain every nerve to succeed. (*DL* II, 382: 17 July 1786)

These resolutions were to need repeated renewal in the coming months. The conception of her appointment as an arranged marriage is also reiterated, the metaphor becoming more bitter as she begins to realise how much her new life cuts her off from her friends, her position, as the Queen declares, 'permanent', her betrothal tantamount to entombment. Her life is made the more intolerable by Mrs Schwellenberg, her fellow Keeper of the Robes, the Queen's old servant, a German spinster whose jealousy and envy of her colleague is to blight the whole time of her 'servitude' (*DL* II, 400). Burney had assumed that the Court day, though long, tedious and tiring, would allow her some hours to herself; instead she finds her company demanded when the two are off duty, whilst she is treated with contempt in the presence of others. Mrs Schwellenberg is 'noxious and persecuting' (*DL* III, 10) but Burney's plight is the more extreme because honour forbids her speaking of her persecutor to the Queen.

Much of the journal from July 1786 is occupied with Burney's attempts to negotiate the elaborate repertoire of conventions and unspoken rules which govern Court life, both in the presence of the royals and in the behaviour of the courtiers amongst themselves. She reports 'these little details of interior royalty' (*DL* II, 436) to Susan. As with Mrs Schwellenberg's announcement that 'you are to have a gown' – 'a favour [made] through the vehicle of insolent ostentation' (*DL* II, 436–7) – and the Court's visit to the great house, Stanton Harcourt, where no provision at all is made for her reception, she finds that her position, the source of so much pride to her father, occasions many mortifying experiences. The journals turn often, in fact, on embarrassing social situations, such as when Burney's French visitors Madame la Fîte and Madame la Roche broadly hint that they would like to stay to tea (especially as it begins to rain outside) but Burney dreads to invite them, knowing that Court protocol forbids her having anyone to dine with her without the prior permission of the Queen (*DL* III, 27–34).

When Fanny finds herself lost in St James's Palace (*DL* III, 163–70), her relation of her bewilderment is similarly aware of its comic elements, despite the 'agony of fright' it also contains. The artist in Burney builds up such scenes' tension and awkwardness, enjoying the dilemmas of the same self whose distress she is relating to her correspondent. The Court she reports on is an extreme version of eighteenth-century polite society in general, its protocols and hierarchies merely more complex, arbitrary and absurd. Burney's imagination here, as in the novels, is especially attuned to occasions in which conventions of polite behaviour are tested or accidentally transgressed. It is not merely the etiquette of a ball, or of courtship, but a far more complex network of prohibitions and regulations that produces situations which the writer can exploit for her characteristic enfolding of embarrassment and amusement. And, as the poet James Beattie was to remark to her, that 'species of distress' in which 'people of high cultivation and elegance [are] forced to associate with those of gross and inferior capacities and manners', which she had introduced into the novel, had now become true of her life (*DL* III, 286: 13 July 1787).

Despite her constant underlying misery, Burney succeeds in finding episodes which will amuse her correspondents. (Though she certainly shared the Evangelical tendencies of her time, religion is surprisingly absent from these accounts.) The journals still characteristically take the form of dramatic action, with extensive dialogue and the representation of 'characters' through their speech, as when she hits off the equerry Colonel Goldsworthy's 'style of rattle':

> 'I vow, ma'am,' cried the Colonel, 'I would not have taken such a liberty on any account; though all the comfort of my life, in this house, is one half-hour a day spent in this room. After all one's labours, riding, and walking, and standing, and bowing – what a life it is? Well! it's honour! that's one comfort; it's all honour! royal honour! – one has the honour to stand till one has not a foot left; and to ride till one's stiff, and to walk till one's ready to drop, – and then one makes one's lowest bow, d'ye see, and blesses one's self with joy for the honour!'
> (DL III, 64–5: c. 6 October 1786)

The 'entertainment' Burney declares such figures (often disguised under pseudonyms reminiscent of eighteenth-century theatre comedy such as 'Colonel Welbred') provide in the relative privacy of the tea room has a poignant undertow, since these are all unhappy people, imprisoned by protocol. Already, before she took up her position, Burney had provided Susan with a satirical 'Directions for coughing, sneezing, or moving, before the King and Queen' (DL II, 352–4) in which the cost of preserving the decorums of the Court was depicted with uncommonly macabre humour: 'If, by chance, a black pin runs into your head, you must not take it out ... If the blood should gush from your head by means of the black pin, you must let it gush ... If, however, the agony is very great, you may, privately, bite the inside of your cheek' (DL II, 353). These are disciplined bodies, genteel subjects subjected to constraints and surveillance of a kind undreamt of by Foucault. But the term discipline is inadequate: as Fanny soon learned, the Court and courtiers might exact physical demands that amounted to no less than torture.

The attractions of teatime to the male courtiers must have been partly due to Miss Burney's capacity to provide them with the stimuli of repartee that drew out such speeches as Colonel Goldsworthy's. Demure as she represents herself, she stands up to them, and to no one more sturdily than to the Queen's Reader, the Rev. Charles de Guiffardière, who goes under the name of 'Mr Turbulent'. This 'character', which Fanny introduces with some relish to her correspondents (DL III, 93), is the more intriguing because he seems to seek out Burney's company unremittingly, to engage her in arguments about morality and religion, and to delight in catching her out, with an apparent defiance of decorum and protocol that simultaneously alarms, embarrasses and amuses her – a complexity of responses, oscillating and intermittent, that she is never able to compose into a settled opinion. This 'importunate casuist' thus, in the course of the many pages given to their 'war', remains puzzling – but very vivid – and hence becomes something more than a 'character' constructed on repetitious and formulaic grounds – well beyond the stable, predictable and caricature-like quality of similar figures in the novels. He exits the journal as oddly as he entered it; the disturbance, possibly sexual, that he aroused is unassuaged.

Mr Turbulent is another gentleman who won't take no for an answer. At one moment, when Fanny is trying to persuade him that she doesn't need his escort in the coach, he throws himself on his knees, and declares himself her slave: a display at once ridiculous and terrifying in its defiance of conventional behaviour (*DL* III, 212). Other scenes of the 'interior' of the Court are bleak, not comic, as when Mrs Schwellenberg on a November journey insists that the 'glass' be kept down in the carriage, so that the icy wind blows unceasingly into Fanny's eyes. Here, as on other occasions, Burney is the victim of unremitting domestic tyranny. Its witnesses consider Mrs Schwellenberg's treatment of her outrageous, but Burney bows her head, 'considering [herself] as *married to her*, ... all rebellion could but end in disturbance, ... Oh what reluctant nuptials! – how often did I say to myself – Were these chains voluntary, how could I bear them! – how forgive myself that I put them on!' (*DL* III, 347: December 1787). All that can be salvaged is an identification with the tragic heroine, Antigone, married to and 'buried' within the Court.

In February 1788 began the state trial of Warren Hastings, accused of corruption and atrocities as Governor-General of Bengal, which was to last for seven years. Burney procured a ticket for the great spectacle in Westminster Hall. The innate tendency of her training and sensibility compels her not to describe the 'show', as her sailor brother James calls it, but the dialogues that take place in her private box. Burney, having met and liked Hastings, is convinced of his innocence, but she is approached by the statesman William Windham, who like herself had been a young friend of Johnson. He is a passionate advocate of the prosecution. The reports of their ensuing conversations take up many pages of the journal (*DL* III 421–34; III 437–46; IV 367–71). Though Burney's easily derided assumption that Hastings's gentlemanly address guarantees his integrity appears remarkable, Burney's courageous declaration of allegiance to the accused, to Windham's disturbance and disbelief, is nothing short of extraordinary. Later in the day he returns to her, perhaps drawn by the skill of her advocacy: though he is certainly not a suitor, there is an undercurrent of mutual attraction. Their encounter, as she records it, has a plausible rhythm: other subjects sometimes divert them, but underlying the dialogue is a tension that finally builds up to a crisis. Burney, at a moment when Windham expresses empathy for Hastings's ignominious position, seizes her opportunity, and her speech goes home:

'I must shake all this off; I must have done with it – dismiss it – forget that he is there.'

'Oh, no,' cried I, earnestly, 'do not forget it!'

'Yes, yes; I must.'

'No, *remember* it rather,' cried I; 'I could almost (putting up my hands as if praying) do thus; and then, like poor Mr. Hastings just now to the house, drop down on my knees to you, to call out "*Remember it.*" '

'Yes, yes,' cried he precipitately, 'how else shall I go on? I *must* forget that *He* is there, and that *you* are here.'

And then he hurried down to his Committee.

(DL III, 445: 13 February 1788)

A passage from eighteenth-century theatre: as Burney writes jubilantly to her correspondents, 'Was it not a most singular scene?'

Their argument at the trial is renewed two years later in April and May 1790. Hastings 'is so gentle-mannered, so intelligent, so unassuming, yet so full-minded', Burney declares, that had she been able to introduce them years earlier, Windham would have been convinced of his innocence. ' "I have understood that," he answered; "yet 'tis amazing how little unison there may be between manners and characters, and how softly gentle a man may appear without, whose nature within is all ferocity and cruelty. This is a part of mankind of which you cannot judge – of which, indeed, you can scarce form an idea." ' (*DL* IV 389: 20 May 1790). A gentleman's view of a lady's experience; but Burney probably knew – and certainly was to know – better.

In May 1790, she was able to spend three hours alone with her father, and took the opportunity to tell him just what her life at Court was like. Her account reduced him to tears (*DL* IV, 392). '[I]f you wish to resign – ', he apparently cries, sounding like a character in one of his daughter's novels, 'my house, my purse, my arms, shall be open to receive you back!' This is the permission Burney needs. She determines to present a petition to the Queen. But the Queen, 'gracious', 'benign', 'condescending', 'kind', as Burney repeatedly calls her, is obviously without an inkling of the demands of her courtiers' lives, and fear of royal surprise and displeasure inhibits her now desperately ailing attendant from broaching the subject. Finally Burney presents her resignation to Mrs Schwellenberg: 'How aghast she looked! – how inflamed with wrath! – how petrified with astonishment! It was truly a dreadful moment to me' (*DL* IV 443). A petition is one thing – getting out of her 'marriage', a process as painful as divorce, is another. It takes from December 1790 to July 1791 to extricate herself, months when Burney is repeatedly and seriously ill, with faintness, pains in the side, and other manifestations of acute nervous distress. When Windham sees her at the renewal of the Hastings trial in June 1791, she is so thin and sickly that he does not at first know her (*DL* IV, 464–8).

Released a month later, Burney went on holiday to the south-west of England, 'a Travelling Invalide' (*JL* I, 18). Hardly had her journey begun when she came across a party of French aristocrats, refugees from the Revolution, and was charmed by the manners of these 'poor Wanderers!' – an intimation of events to come. Burney remained loyal to the royals, filling in when she was needed, and concerned that her resignation not be misinterpreted by the Opposition enemies of the Court. Announcing herself as a '*democrate*' whenever she sees injustice perpetuated (*JL* I, 89), she finds herself at odds with the political leanings of her friends, and especially of James Burney, who, in common with many English liberals, sympathised with the French Revolution. She renews her visits to the Hastings trial (*JL* I, 118–25: February 1792). The encounters with Windham are now even more complicated since she is deeply indebted to Windham for persuading her father that she must get out of the Court. It is the '*compact*' they have forged to speak with a certain 'privileged sincerity' that underlies this almost final exchange as the trial reopens:

> Mr Hastings was just entered – I looked down at him, & saw his half motion to kneel, – I could not bear it, &, turning suddenly to my neighbour – 'O Mr Windham! I cried, – after all – 'tis indeed – a barbarous business! –'
>
> This was rather further than I meant to go, for I said it with serious earnestness: but it was surprised from me by the emotion always excited at sight of that unmerited humiliation.
>
> He looked full at me, upon this solemn attack, & with a look of chagrin amounting to displeasure; saying, 'It is a barbarous business *we* have had to go through!'
>
> I did not attempt to answer this, for, except through the medium of sport & raillery, I have certainly no claim upon his patience. But, in another moment, in a tone very flattering, he said, 'I do not understand, nor can any way imagine how YOU – can have been thus perverted?'
>
> 'No, no!' quoth I, 'it is *You* who are *perverted*!' (*JL* I, 124–5)

Burney records these interchanges with Windham with an attention to the intimacies of tone and gesture even more precise than usual: in her own way she is registering the fact that here matters of great political moment are in play. There is nothing fashionably affected about Miss Burney's sensibility, as Windham plainly knows. But here, as before, feeling and response, the interplay of subjects, are in the foreground: repartee is allowed to obscure or replace the real political matters that are its occasion.

Soon after, Burney's and the country's political sympathies turned decisively against 'the Fiends of France' (*JL* I, 228: September 1792). The prophecies of chaos and bloodshed in Burke's *Reflections* (1790) were being fulfilled. At the same time – alarmingly for persons of her persuasion – societies for the reform of the British parliament were springing up. It was not long before her sister Susan told her of a 'poor french Colony', the émigrés who had begun to arrive in her neighbourhood (*JL* I, 239), nor much longer before Fanny herself made the acquaintance of a set of alluring beings at Juniper Hall to whom she was drawn as much by their distress as by their royalism and their charm. Among them was the soldier Count Alexandre d'Arblay. The vicissitudes of their courtship (*JL* II, March to July 1793) are reported to Susan in a style employing all the diacritical assets of the literature of sensibility – italics, multiple dashes, multiple exclamation marks, words in capitals, words in capitals in italics – a perfect barrage of effects to simulate overwhelming excitement. The obstacles to their union were complex: they had nothing except a pension of £100 a year from the Queen, which Fanny might lose on alliance with a Frenchman; Dr Burney was 'cold and averse'.

Married in July, the d'Arblays began an 'entirely retired life' (*JL* II, 140) on Fanny's income. D'Arblay, now 'perfectly a private man' (*JL* III, 21), warned away from London, where an Aliens Bill was passed in January 1794, tried to grow vegetables, while Frances became the breadwinner through her writing. 'I had previously determined', she wrote in June 1795, 'when I *changed my state*, to set aside all my innate & original abhorrences, & regard & use as resources MYSELF' (*JL* III, 113). The main result was *Camilla*, published in five volumes in 1796. D'Arblay named their house 'Camilla Cottage' (*JL* III, 249): a rural 'Hermitage' built out of the profits of this novel. Fanny's celebrity and connections ensured the success of its subscription publication. The letters of the years of their retreat (1793–1801) are occupied by family affairs – the dreadful shock of the so-called 'elopement' of James and his half-sister (*JL* IV, 204–17), perpetual anxiety about her sister Susan's life in Ireland (usually expressed in a breathlessly agitated style), and their son Alexander's precociousness (with interesting descriptions of his inoculation for smallpox (*JL* III, 282–5; 288–91)). At the same time, Burney kept up her connections with the royal family. To Susan, she continued to write 'Court Journals', recounting each of her receptions in detail, with much gratitude for the Queen's 'sweet condescendsion' (*JL* IV, 182).

These years saw the rise of Napoleon Bonaparte. The d'Arblays, in their country cottage, happily away from the London world, were nevertheless readers of the newspapers, and watched developments in France with an anxious eye. Frances early formed a hatred of the 'man of blood', Bonaparte (*JL* IV, 368). When d'Arblay was 'erazed from the List of Emigrants' in 1800 (*JL* IV, 459), he seized the opportunity to recover what remained of his estate in France, travelling to Holland to begin the process. Soon the family moved to Paris, where the breakdown of the Peace of Amiens (1802) effectively trapped them. England and France were once again at war. In Paris, they lived perforce quietly, in 'the safety of deliberate prudence, or of retiring timidity': as in this later letter to an old friend, Mrs Waddington (*JL* VIII, 282–6), Burney can now command a spare, grim prose, adequate to characterise the psychological states of people living under 'Tyranny', where 'corporeal liberty could only be preserved by mental forebearance – ie. Subjection'.

Besides dialogue in these journals, Burney was mistress of two main modes – the expressive, dramatic, immediate style of sensibility, and the austere, concentrated, summary prose of Johnson, Hume and the later eighteenth century. These styles, when they work in combination, empower much of her later journalising, and perhaps most of all the account of her mastectomy in September 1811 in Paris, when she was fifty nine. Written as a letter to her sister Esther in England, the document was copied for safe keeping in France, a communication simultaneously recognised as a piece of history. It is the preeminent early example of the genre that has blossomed since the 1950s, the 'pathography' – the story of an illness or medical intervention from the patient's viewpoint. Like the modern pathography, Burney's is not merely an account of the patient's experience, but a critique of the medical context which determines it.

Though living an extremely retired life in Paris, the d'Arblays retained the good connections formed in England. It is to these that Burney owes the attendance of first-class surgeons – particularly Larrey and Dubois, the one famous for amputations on the battlefield and for the invention of the field ambulance, the other accoucheur to the Empress – and probably her life. As a famous novelist, a cultural treasure, Madame d'Arblay presents Larrey with an impossible challenge, for it is one thing to hack off the wounded limbs of soldiers temporarily anaesthetised by shock on the battlefield and another to perform radical surgery on a lady's breast without anaesthetic, in her own Parisian drawing room. And Burney is an eighteenth-century 'patron' patient: in England, at least, the doctor is still subservient to the patient, who calls the tune.

Her account of the mastectomy is therefore partly the story of a power struggle, in which we see in miniature a phase of cultural history enacted: the ceding, or transfer, of the patient's power to the medical profession. From the first Madame d'Arblay seeks to set the terms of the operation – to decide when it will be, the hour at which it will be performed, how it will be performed, to engage her own female attendants – and progressively she is stripped of these prerogatives, as she is ultimately stripped of her gown. The doctors attempt to make her anonymous, a mere female body whose inter-rogatory eyes can be hidden by a muslin handkerchief, which she calls her 'veil'. Yet a feature of this report is that Burney does not surrender her identity as a gentlewoman, that throughout the preliminaries and the opera-tion, while losing control, she retains authority.

Burney has suffered pains in the right breast for some time, and various doctors are consulted. The pains augment, and 'A formal consultation now was held, of Larrey, Ribe, & Moreau – &, in fine, I was formally condemned to an operation by all Three' (*JL* VI, 603) – condemned, despite her own 'dread & repugnance' (*JL* VI, 600). There are 'a thousand reasons *besides* the pain' for her reluctance – the transgression of gentility and the fear of death among them – and for a while Burney's 'faculties' are helplessly paralysed, a condition of what one might call 'terror fatigue', which she is to describe tellingly in other crises of her life. The doctors being equally averse to the performance of the operation, there is much consultation behind the scenes. Yet it is Burney, acting as the client, who takes the initiative: 'My heart beat fast: I saw all hope was over. I called upon them to speak' (*JL* VI, 604). Her 'doom' is 'pronounced' and the day of the operation fixed.

From this point on, medicine takes over, and Burney is left in ignorance. A young doctor arrives and makes arrangements. She requests time to make her own, but when the appointed hour comes, and all is ready, it is put off for two hours. 'This, indeed, was a dreadful interval.' She writes notes:

> These short billets I could only deposit safely, when the Cabriolets – one – two – three – four – succeeded rapidly to each other in stopping at the door . . . I rang for my Maid & Nurses, – but before I could speak to them, my room, without previous message, was entered by 7 Men in black, Dr. Larry, M. Dubois, Dr. Moreau, Dr. Aumont, Dr. Ribe, & a pupil of Dr. Larry, & another of M. Dubois. I was now awakened from my stupor – & by a sort of indignation – Why so many? & without leave? – But I could not utter a syllable. M. Dubois acted as Commander in Chief.   (*JL* VI, 609–10)

Madame d'Arblay has become the modern patient. But this is not the whole story, since the absence of anaesthetic changes everything. The patient cannot be obliterated by a muslin 'veil'. Burney does not cede her authority easily, and, throwing off the handkerchief, recalls the physicians to her existence as an agent. Burney depicts the nervousness of the physicians – Dubois tearing up a bit of paper, 'unconsciously, into a million of pieces', Larrey 'pale as ashes' (*JL* VI, 611) – reflections, or projections, too, of the terror of her own mind.

The '7 Men in black', 'the glitter of polished steel' above her, the 'fatal finger' of the surgeon describing the 'Cross' over the body have gothic, even cabalistic, overtones and perhaps transmit the unconscious fantasies of male violation which accompany surgery on the breast. Yet Burney's recounting of the operation itself is a matter of sustained consciousness. 'Again all description would be baffled – yet again all was not over, – Dr Larry rested but his own hand, & – Oh Heaven! – I then felt the Knife rackling against the breast bone – scraping it! – ' (*JL* VI, 612). The ejaculatory stylistics of sensibility do not merely plug the gap of the indescribable: they work in tandem with unnerving specificity.

Burney's next considerable narrative inaugurates the series of more formal journals that she was to write, in the aftermath of her husband's death, as commemorations of their shared life and love. D'Arblay had joined the royalist forces. After the final defeat of Napoleon at Waterloo in June 1815, Madame d'Arblay, learning that her husband was ill and wounded at Trèves, where he was stationed, more than a hundred miles to the southeast, set out to find him. From there they travelled back to England and Bath, formerly a place of high fashion but now a health resort popular with genteel folk of limited resources. It soon became evident that d'Arblay was in a serious condition. Burney's 'Narrative of the Last Illness and Death of General d'Arblay' (1820: *JL* X, 842–910), begun eighteen months after his death in May 1818, is another pathography, this time told, as are many modern pathographies, from the viewpoint of a relative, and (again like modern examples) as much concerned with the drama and heroism of the carer's role as it is with the patient's. D'Arblay knows that he is dying, and approaches death with the resignation traditionally enjoined by religious faith: his wife refuses to accept this truth, subscribing instead to the romantic ideology of resistance. The 'Narrative' is shaped by the drama of this pervasive, but largely tacit, conflict. Madame d'Arblay, refusing to give in, does battle on all fronts – with her husband, the priest and the doctors. D'Arblay's last months are told as a story of married love and the passionate devotion of his nurse – the culmination of their great romance.

Burney was writing narratives that dealt with extreme situations and events, her imagination now seemingly drawn towards pain and crisis. The Oxford edition of Burney's *Journals and Letters* prints her 'Waterloo Journal' and the narrative of her subsequent journey to Trèves according to the chronology of the events they record, and not in the order of their composition, which is to be regretted. These journals were in fact written in 1823 and 1825, after the death of d'Arblay, and are addressed to their son Alexander. They relate Burney's adventures during the 'Hundred days' (March–June 1815) in which Napoleon, escaped from Elba, marched upon Paris. These are records framed by lament for the past, the memorials of a lonely widow, writing now to recover the semblance of communication with a lost, loved object. From this point on, everything that Madame d'Arblay does, and everything that she writes, is shaped by the desire, one way or another, to be in contact with d'Arblay.

Written avowedly as the reminiscences of a private citizen – 'merely a narration of my own little history' (*JL* VIII, 429) – Burney's 'Waterloo' and 'Trèves' journals have, nevertheless, immense historical interest. For what she experienced was to be recounted over and over again by civilians caught up in the terrors of war. She was a refugee, a displaced person, a seeker after asylum before these terms were coined, and she records the vicissitudes – the fleeing with nothing but a small basket of possessions, the fear of betrayal, the need for disguise, the pleading encounters with brutal and hostile officials, the constant anxiety – that have become familiar in the memoirs of victims of the holocaust and many others forced to abandon everything in the face of an advancing enemy. Terror does not bring people together, but cracks the mould of genteel decorum, 'the whole Composition' of her friend Madame d'Hénin 'dislocated' into near madness (*JL* VIII, 362–5); and splits them apart, even when travelling in the same carriage: 'It was every way a frightful night. Misery both public & private oppressed us all, & the fear of pursuit & captivity had the gloomy effect of causing general taciturnity, so that no kind voice, nor social suggestion diverted the sense of danger, or excited one of Hope' (*JL* VIII, 375). The language is woodenly Augustan, but here as elsewhere in the later journals it succeeds in defining the psychological states of people in extreme situations, and Burney, as with the mastectomy, is a forerunner of modernity.

Perhaps this is an exaggeration. Madame d'Arblay was saved from the worst horrors – physical violence, starvation – by her gentility. She had good connections. She was able to escape from Paris with friends, the terrifying zig-zagging carriage journey towards safety was broken by acts of kindness performed by clandestine Royalists, and when they arrived in Brussels her life resumed its usual round of social visits. But her friends fled, fearing that Napoleon would conquer the city as he had conquered Paris. She chose not to leave, since only there could she receive letters from d'Arblay. In June she was a solitary private citizen, in a state of acute anxiety and suspense, fearing for days that the French had won the battle of Waterloo. Misinformed of their victory, she is overcome with horror. 'What a dreadful day did I pass! dreadful in the midst of its Glory!' (*JL* VIII, 440). There is no Glory in Burney's account of these days and the battle's aftermath: instead, a clear-eyed recognition, as the carts of wounded men roll into the city, of the cost of this famous victory.

The Trèves journal is equally remarkable. To reach d'Arblay meant travelling through a countryside ravaged by war and roamed by banditti; this

French territory was occupied by the victorious Prussian army, and it was necessary to show a passport for each stage of the journey by the public coach or 'diligence'. Because the coach direct to Trier had left for the week, Burney – driven by the need to reach her husband as speedily as possible – was forced to take a roundabout route through Cologne, Bonn and Koblenz, facing crises at every destination, surmounting them with a courage and effrontery that, she declares, is foreign to her shy retiring nature. The narrative is one of nearly excruciating suspense as impediments – the 'cruel' slowness of the coaches, the endless delays, the refusal of officials to grant her passports until she pulls a name out of a hat – pile up to be surmounted. She draws on her usual memorandums made at the time: there is no reason to think that any of it is invented.

One might think of the Trèves journal as the culmination or end-point of the eighteenth-century tradition of the picaresque, as the final ironic commentary on a narrative form now rendered obsolete by the emerging conditions of modernity. For the 'adventures' of the narrative, once comic or at least entertaining, are now made harrowing by anxiety, the landscape devastated by conflict, with 'scarcely a man unmaimed to be seen, in civil life' (*JL* VIII, 492). Burney compresses the expansive narrative of the picaro into six anguish-riven days: her encounters are with insolent authority, and her alleviations are not from inns, but from the melancholy charity of gentlefolk whose own lives and fortunes have been ruined by war. Lost in St James's Palace in 1787, Burney could turn her bewilderment into an amusing recital: now lost in Bonn, desperate to get back to the coach in time, Madame d'Arblay recreates a nightmare of paranoid bafflement that culminates in 'indeed, nearly, the most tortured crisis of misery I ever experienced!' (*JL* VIII, 504). But this traveller is indeed a female Quixote, in the sense that she is driven forward on her journey by dedication to her beloved, 'the sole object of my anxiety & my wishes' (*JL* VIII, 495).

Not the least of Burney's anxieties when she fled from the advance of Napoleon was that she was forced to leave behind in Paris a trunkful of manuscripts. These included masses of her father's papers, which she had undertaken to turn into a memoir or biography. Luckily, they survived and were transported back to England. In the event, disappointed at much of the material, since the records left by Charles Burney had little of the vivacity of his early *Tours*, and concerned about family affairs they would reveal to the public, it was many years before Burney was able to publish her *Memoirs of Doctor Burney* in 1832. '[R]esum[ing], though in trembling, her long-forsaken pen' (*Memoirs*, I, vi) the eighty-year-old Madame d'Arblay then produced a strangely or presciently heteroglossic narrative, melding together biography and implicit autobiography, in which Charles Burney's own records gradually give ground to hers. In effect, she drastically rewrote both her father's and her own material. The contrast between her early and late account of the actor David Garrick teasing a hairdresser and later mimicking Dr Johnson, for instance (*Memoirs*, I, 349–53: *EJL* II, 95–7), shows how she cut, amplified and embellished incidents which she had once recorded with careless youthful vivacity. Letters, such as one to Mr Crisp describing a memorable musical evening at the Burneys' (*Memoirs*, II, 11–19), are so altered from the original letters, in this case, from May 1775 (*EJL* II, 128–35), as to be effectively fakes.

But the retrospective character of the *Memoirs* is not all loss. It includes many portrait sketches in the manner of the seventeenth-century 'Character', and these condensed, generalised appraisals of celebrities of the time, such as those of the painter James Barry and the sister of Sir Joshua, 'Mrs' Frances Reynolds, often have a psychological acumen which is compelling. The account of a visit to Mrs Anna Williams is hard to correlate with any actual occasion recorded in the Journals, but it includes a perceptive account of Johnson's delicate attitude towards this blind and dependent gentlewoman. Madame d'Arblay's wariness about publishing material that might in any way reflect badly on her father and his family does not prevent her from writing a direct, unpompous and moving account of her reunion with him, after ten years, in 1812, and her shock at his decline: 'She found him – alas! how altered! in looks, strength, complexion, voice, and spirits! … his whole appearance manifesting a species of self-desertion' (*Memoirs*, III, 403). It is not at all certain, as is so often asserted, that Madame d'Arblay exaggerated Fanny's importance to her father or the depth of their relationship: they were, after all, kindred spirits.

This was a long and eventful life, recorded in great, sometimes even daily, detail. '[T]he superiority of the Diary to the Novels' as Austin Dobson put it, became axiomatic until the mid-twentieth century (*DL* VI, Postscript, xiii). Modern critics of Frances Burney, more alert to issues of genre, more interested in the politics of the fiction, would dispute such a judgment. Yet, painting in their first years a vivid portrait of family life among 'all the dear Burneys little and great',[3] following this with intimate glimpses of the elderly Johnson, then giving a full account of life at the Georgian Court, with all its terrible demands and awkward comedy, following this with the years of sequestration and suppression, and then the writing of pathographies of physical pain and mental anguish in a Europe overshadowed by Napoleonic ambition: these writings are extraordinarily vivid – and extraordinary in the variety of scenes and milieux they record so comprehensively. Whether they told the literal truth, we can never know, and it would be wisest to take the author's word for the purity of her intentions: 'all that I relate in Journalising is *strictly*, nay *plainly* Fact', she wrote to 'Daddy' Crisp in 1780, 'I never, in all my Life, have been a sayer of the Thing that is not' (*EJL* IV, 217).

It is one of the central paradoxes of Burney's nature that she was both withdrawn and charismatic, both modest and driven. The paradox of her journals is that, composed as the work of a lady, apparently for the family and its archive, they are at the same time aware of their importance, self-known contributions to history. Burney's later novels are, I think, more precursors of Balzac than of Austen. The journals similarly reveal a woman who, without ceasing to be genteel, was propelled by events to shake hands with modernity. 'Why so many? & without leave?' she had cried: privacy and privilege had been invaded by the forces of history.

NOTES

1. Thrale, *Anecdotes of the Late Samuel Johnson LL.D.* (London, 1786).
2. *Boswell's Life of Johnson*, ed. G. B. Hill and L. F. Powell (Oxford: Clarendon Press, 1934), I, 30.
3. *The Letters of Samuel Johnson*, ed. Bruce Redford (Princeton: Princeton University Press, 1992–4), IV, 437.

6

MARGARET ANNE DOODY

Burney and politics

Near the end of Burney's first published novel, *Evelina, or the History of a Young Lady's Entrance into the World* (1778), there is a farcical contretemps. Rough Captain Mirvan brings a monkey, 'full dressed, and extravagantly *à-la-mode*!', into the assembled company, chiefly to make fun of the snobbish fop Mr Lovel, who has been a plague to Evelina (399). Lovel, enraged at being confronted with what he is told is his likeness, strikes the monkey which then 'fastened his teeth to one of his ears'. Lovel, 'a dreadful object' with blood from his ear 'trickling down his cloaths', naturally objects to this treatment, but Mirvan is unapologetic:

> 'What argufies so many words?' said the unfeeling Captain, 'it is but a slit of the ear; it only looks as if you had been in the pillory.'
>
> 'Very true,' added Mrs. Selwyn, 'and who knows but it may acquire you the credit of being an anti-ministerial writer?' (401–2)

Mrs Selwyn is usually a woman of tough good sense; it may be a surprise to find her as 'unfeeling' as Mirvan. Her taunt carries the altercation into the overtly political realm. We could already have gathered, when hearing that Mrs Selwyn 'had business at a pamphlet-shop', that she likes to keep abreast of the news (318). Recalling punishments administered earlier in the century to dissident journalists and pamphleteers like Defoe, she ironically transforms Lovel into a writer protesting against the government in the era of the American War. Lovel would be undergoing a form of martyrdom for his principles and utterances which would gain him (in some liberal eyes at least) 'credit'. In fact, Lovel, an ignorant Member of Parliament and fashion's slave, utters little of note (save malicious digs at supposed inferiors), and would never be capable of going against any ministry in power in any matter. The whole object of his life is to fit in. Compelled to exhibit himself as occupying a superior position in relation to vulgarians, Lovel would find political protest not only abhorrent to him, but truly unimaginable. It is he and his class who have the right to pillory others, not to be subjected to violent political and social control.

In creating Mrs Selwyn, Burney shows that she can imagine (satirically) a woman with political interests. The Burney who wrote *Evelina* would have been surprised to hear that later she would write a pamphlet herself. Her *Brief Reflections Relative to the Emigrant French Clergy* (1793) is her only direct and non-fictional political intervention. It was bravely written, at a time when it was assumed by enemies and even some distressed friends that upon her marriage to a French émigré the author had forsaken her religion and even her own national identity.

Frances Burney's national identity was in fact mixed. Her father, Charles Burney, was a Scotsman from a poor family named 'Macburney'; Charles had dropped the Scottish 'Mac' from his name. Scots were often ridiculed; moreover they were seen as parasites on English wealth, or worse – as incorrigibly hostile, innately surly and ignorant enemies. The Jacobite rebellion of 1745–6, in which the forces led by Bonnie Prince Charlie were eventually defeated by the royal troops led by the Duke of Cumberland, took place only half-a-dozen years before Burney's birth. And her mother was even less 'English' than her father; Esther Sleepe Burney was French, and Burney's maternal grandmother (who had a share in her upbringing in her childhood after her mother died) was a French Roman Catholic. The French were popularly viewed as the permanent enemy (the way Captain Mirvan sees them); France was the political Satan stirring up rebel energies at home among the barbarous Scots while trying to take away English colonies abroad. England was at war with France for most of Burney's lifetime. Peace truly came only after the Battle of Waterloo in 1815; Burney, then in her sixties, was in Brussels at the time of that battle in which her husband was fighting.

With her French and Scottish background, and the lurking Catholicism to boot, Frances Burney knew from early youth what it meant to be on the outside or nearly on the outside. Charles Burney was a nobody, a self-made poor man who by charm, effort and literary as well as musical talent pushed himself into the rank of a 'gentleman' – if that term were generously used. (Hester Thrale on meeting Frances recognised that she was not 'a lady'.) Family politics were centrally concerned with the importance of the father, whose upward stride must not be interrupted. Charles always wanted support from his children; he was critical of them, and alienated himself from his three sons. Burney's personal life was early shaped by the need to please her father; there are signs that she herself at bottom distrusted both her own timidity and the need to please. She did one very daring thing when she published *Evelina* without her father's knowing anything about it.

Charles and his family were to do nothing irregular. They identified themselves as 'English' (and their religion as Anglican). Things were stitched up to look nice in all sorts of ways in the Burney family, hiding some less pleasing realities, including the fact that Charles and Esther were not married when their first child was born. This important circumstance Frances in youth may not consciously have known – though bastardy plays a large part in her first novels. But she must have been aware of it later when in the biography of her father she gently omits or fudges dates. The matter of ethnicity was stitched up too, though within the family the sutures were rather visible. Charles Burney's profession brought the family into close contact with foreigners, opera singers and musicians; these were often Roman Catholic and frequently spoke only French or only Italian. However proper Charles Burney might be, his home was in many eyes a Bohemian environment; foreign mixtures might pass muster there, but that was not the norm. A violent upheaval in English political life, like the Gordon Riots against the Catholics, could bring Burney's attention very sharply to the divisions within the country; seeing the destructive forces so easily let loose would inform her of her own vulnerable position. It is interesting that in 1797 she does not support Lord Moira and his plea for Catholic Emancipation in Ireland, despite or perhaps because of her own association with Catholics (*JL* IV, 44–5).

Burney's background was presumably a factor in turning the author's attention to the place and experience of 'outsiders', to what it means to be 'alien' or alienated. In *Evelina* and *The Wanderer* (her first and her last novels), mixed or multiple identities are embedded in the plot, and the alternative French language and multiple possible identities find representation. In all the novels, the heroine reaches some point of alienation, threatened by the group and without a secure bolt-hole. Only in *Evelina* does that situation remain (if precariously) on the simply comic level, a comedy sustainable because the heroine is not as aware as the reader of the implications of her initial legal state of bastardy.

Like other women of all classes of her time, Burney had no vote. She could be a member of no political party. Neither did she take direct and open part in political campaigns, unlike some of her contemporaries such as Hester Lynch Thrale, or Mrs Crewe. In the limited sense sometimes accorded to the word 'politics' Burney had none. The political life of Britain was used against her in a peculiar way when she was urged by Samuel Crisp to forget all hopes of a production of her play *The Witlings* (written in 1779), because these were bad times with the country at war with the American colonists and with France. Crisp does not however imagine (or wish to imagine) that his young friend and protégée would or could have any views different from his own pessimistic and conservative outlook. As a mature adult, in the period of the French Revolution, she was expected by unwary onlookers to share the views of her father Charles Burney, increasingly conservative as he aged. In the late 1790s, her father and Mrs Crewe urged Frances, now Madame d'Arblay, to write for the new *Anti-Jacobin*; Burney tactfully refused to contribute to what we would term a right-wing periodical (*JL* IV, 65–6).

Burney evaded the exploitation of her pen for a directly political cause. Yet Burney as a writer has a deeply political imagination, something that differentiates her from her most prominent contemporary, Jane Austen. Her fiction is at its heart political. In each of her novels, her world is presented in a different way, but the four novels all place the social world at the centre, and they share likewise a view of the social world as highly structured, very fierce and estranging. Through her fiction Burney constantly asks questions of the relation of the individual to community and to society in general – and these are not easy questions. While showing us abstract social structures, she uses the images of structures fairly constantly, displaying buildings as metaphors of social realities and social fictions, like Delvile Castle, in *Cecilia*, with its isolating drawbridge. *The Wanderer* is emblematically rich in real structures: Wilton, Arundel Castle and Stonehenge. Burney noticeably uses or even anticipates images and machinery destined to figure in 'Gothic' novels, while herself keeping clear of the gothic mode. Perhaps she distrusts the device which represents the evils of the present as if they were evils of the past – 'Gothic' fiction offers too much of an alibi. She deliberately praises a medieval edifice for exactly those virtues the Enlightenment would suppose it to lack: 'The beautiful Gothic structure before her, the latest and finest remains of ancient elegance, lightness, and taste' (*Wanderer*, 663). The author plays with the idea of structure, and of what is constructed, whether flimsy or heavy. Each individual character comes to us shaped (often not obtrusively) by social beliefs and systems – hence, almost every one of her characters has as an outer level of personality a set of clichés, which are ultimately modes of political operation employed primarily, if not only, for personal self-protection. In the complex character of Mrs Delvile in *Cecilia*, Burney digs deep. Mrs Delvile's charm, warmth and originality are evoked by the company of Cecilia, who feels she has penetrated beneath the superficial cold hauteur the lady displays to others. But the charm itself is just another outer layer – getting to know the woman more deeply, Cecilia, to her dismay, runs into all the stony fabrics in which the woman chooses to live in order to make sense of her life – the rigidities and deeply felt class clichés.

From *Cecilia* on, Burney seizes upon a central political paradox: the good society needs the good individual, but society is not good. It needs transformation. So then, how is the individual to achieve transformative goodness without questioning or even breaking away from the community in some way and at some time? The person who breaks away – especially the female person – is not called good nor recognised as such. Nor can breaking away be easy or complete. Without liberty, the individual will not be able to do much real good to her corrupt society. But the freedom of others, Burney shows us, is rarely, if ever, generally held to be desirable; conformity, often defined as common sense or necessity, serves to prevent the operation of liberty. The initial debate between Belfield and Mr Monckton in *Cecilia* sets out these issues more schematically than usual.

Liberty is a desideratum in Burney's novels. Yet it is difficult of realisation, being an energy, not a thing; and the impulse of liberty causes collisions with heavy structures and perverse obstacles not only in the outer world, but also within the person's self. A young woman, or a young man, both requires and imagines liberty; yet (s)he has an innate need for companionship, for being part of a group. And Cecilia is ready for sexual love, which ironically is her undoing, not in terms of conventional 'ruin' but in preventing her achievement of the liberty she had envisaged for herself. A woman's achievement of acceptable sexual expression (marriage) entails the legal and social loss of liberty and even identity. Loneliness cannot supply an answer. The free person is yet a social being. Cecilia is not really happy when in her pursuit of virtue she separates herself from her aimless extravagant companions, because she is not made for solitude. Within the group, however, Cecilia the 'heiress' has been brought to market, unwittingly made an object of exchange, 'sold' by Harrel and 'bought' (for real money) by his lewd friend Sir Robert Floyer. (Their exchange shows that slavery has reached every corner of the Empire, including home.)

A definition of virtue as consisting in purity of isolation is politically impossible. In *Cecilia*, the heroine and young Belfield, different as they are, both try this mode of virtuous isolation, and it does not answer. Albany, in his belligerent penitence and mad eccentricity, displays the defects of the hermetic ideal. Yet without some individual members getting away from the precepts and ideas of a depressed and corrupt community, change cannot happen. Burney in some ways poses Rousseauian questions about political life, but she never agrees with Rousseau's solutions. Indeed, she does not really offer 'solutions' at all. After *Evelina*, her novels end on ambiguous notes, the resolutions not totally satisfactory. The reader is meant to know that however well the heroine's affairs may have settled themselves (for the time being), the greater strife and social pain, the unresolved needs and questions, continue.

Burney's fiction does not assume the voice of someone possessing and anxious to disseminate philosophical or practical solutions or sets of answers to political questions. That reluctance to preach and teach differentiates her largely from radical writers such as William Godwin and Mary

Wollstonecraft – though not entirely, as these writers retain a capacity to question. At the same time, her restraint separates her from conservative Evangelicals like Hannah More, and also from Maria Edgeworth, whose father was only too anxious to spread abroad what he thought he had, namely liberal–progressive answers.

Instead, Burney makes the reader begin to question certain norms and practices, and most of all the conventional insistence on the 'naturalness' of certain forms of division or categorisation. She shows us the practical and immense effects of social divisions and categories. She never writes generally or abstractly on these issues – which include divisions according to gender, class, wealth and race. On race, Burney has less to say than would satisfy us; she wrote to congratulate William Wilberforce, whom she admired, on his efforts to end the British slave trade, but was willing that her husband should fight Toussaint L'Ouverture, leader of the Haitian slave revolt, for France. Yet in *The Wanderer*, Mrs Ireton's slave-owning is the ultimate manifestation of her sadistic love of tormenting inferiors, a pleasure that slavery immorally enshrines as permanent. In the comic play *A Busy Day*, various characters express disdain of 'the black' (an Indian servant), and the heroine's vulgar sister expresses a satirised horror of racial difference, saying she would be scared to go to India because of the people: 'Do they let 'em run about wild? ... La, nasty black things! I can't abide the Indins' (I.457–61). Burney clearly rejects such prejudices. Yet such rejection does not quite extend to questioning the colonial exploitation of India, the source of the heroine's wealth.

If Burney is not abstract, she may be subtly allegorical. Ideas do not meet us disembodied from characters, though she must persuade us that these characters are typical and thus general, and she follows an old custom in giving characters revealing names (Duval, Dubster), as well as some outrageously comic manufactured ones, like Branghton or Gwigg. Her characters are rooted in a believable world of custom, fashion and belief. The truly big question that Burney wants to deal with (if not to answer) is 'How are we all to get along with one another?' This is the question for a *polis*, whether considered as a society or a state. Aristotle's basic answer is that we unite in community seeking some kind of good (see the beginning of the *Politics*), but we have long argued as to what that good might be. Aristotle (like most other philosophers of the political) takes for granted distinction of privilege, gender and rank, while Burney, a female child of the Enlightenment, is less willing to do so. Before we look to the good we seek, we must first recognise each other, and thus are forced to return to that question 'How are we all to get along?' in the belief that everybody might have something to contribute to the answer. A desirable 'getting along' comprehends the recognition of difference as well as a recognition of a need for some degree of conformity (the degree to be under perpetual question). Liberty must be central to any response about how we are to live together, yet it is never enough. Ironically, as Burney shows in *Cecilia* and *Camilla* in particular, both liberty and conformity can lead to madness.

Individual liberty, even combined with recognition of difference, is little good without a compassion that is neither arbitrary or sentimental. Burney is not afraid to show that, in the present constitution of things, cruelty rather than compassion guides actual social responses. The young men in *Evelina* hold the race between two old women not primarily because they want fun, but to demonstrate and reaffirm their power over the cottager class. The two poor old women could not dare refuse to race, not only because of minor benefits, little gifts that will accrue to their families, but also because of the ill will their families would draw upon themselves from their landlords if the octogenarian females (unthinkably) refused. For all its superficial complacency and its great wealth, England in Burney's central political vision is a society held together by force and fear.

Burney the author constantly shows us members and groups who do not get along well in the present arrangement of things – and these persons and groups are in conflict with those of the privileged (or merely stupid) for whom the present state of things answers very well. The clash of cultures and groups and personal ideologies is a large source of her humour. Any intelligent and imaginative response to the simple question 'How can we get along well?' must comprehend an awareness of the most basic matter of class. In *Evelina*, Mrs Selwyn straightforwardly critiques Mrs Beaumont as a '*Court Calendar bigot*' (284), but Mrs Selwyn's satiric vision of the evils bred by the class system is too limited to extend to taking in the full horror of the race between the two aged peasant women. Even Lord Orville is worried only about the silly extravagance of the two gamblers, rather than the cruelty of the exploitation. Here Burney in 1778 is not far from Godwin in 1794, as Godwin in *Caleb Williams* traces the forms of unreasonable oppression used by Tyrell upon his tenants, Hawkins and his son; but then, Godwin had the advantage of reading Burney. And Burney takes, as her examples of the low on the scale, not sturdy males, embryonic republicans like Hawkins, but the most helpless and nugatory of persons, those overlooked by republicans and aristocrats alike – aged females of the lower orders.

Burney always notes the flux and flow of power. In the most minute conversational scenes in her novels, power is always flowing from one member of the group to another, and she sees that in 'polite society' serious systems of exploitation and control are in operation. She also notes where power resides and how it creates an ideal habitation, a total environment, to suit it. (Only Mr Harrel visibly fails to create a humbly literal habitation for his ideology; 'Violet Bank', the would-be villa built on the sandy soil of debt, will never be finished.) In *Cecilia*, Burney deliberately takes on these oppressive mental powers and their productions. The three guardians to whose destructive 'care' the orphaned Cecilia is left represent different aspects of the social structure and the three most important modes for displaying importance and power: Birth, Money and Fashion. The 'guardians' have all betrayed the *polis* – the insistent use of the word 'guardian' in the novel may hide a reference to Plato's theories on virtuous and corrupt rulers under its naturalism.

Burney tells this story not in first-person narration like *Evelina*, but in third-person omniscient voice, and the author's perceptions clearly outstrip those of the character. Young Cecilia has benevolence and good intentions, and a sense of humour. She sincerely tries to be helpful and compassionate to others, though there is a mixture of fantasy and uncertainty in her attempts. Her charity is not rewarded by sweet gratitude; compassion is not taken to be easy, arbitrary, nor sentimental. Cecilia herself is not privy to all the ironies of her situation; she never sees the entire social structure of display and exploitation that the reader is shown. Nor is she free to opt out of it, any more than any of us can truly opt out of our own society, so she endures the pressure of opposing forces upon her. In the climax, the contention between all these forces, which she has internalised, drives her momentarily out of herself, and she is labelled 'mad'. The treatment of Cecilia as a madwoman is one of the most effectively painful passages of the novel. Though she is in private care, we see the shadow of the institutionalised 'madhouse' for the restraint and discipline of the unhappy. If you show yourself as alienated, this is what you risk. Burney must have known something of the treatment accorded her father's friend Christopher Smart. The treatment of Cecilia influenced Mary Wollstonecraft (an admirer of Burney's novel), who set the opening sections of her *Wrongs of Woman* (1798) in a madhouse in which the heroine is wrongfully confined. The eventual 'happy' ending of *Cecilia* is touched with dubiety, for the heroine's marriage to Mortimer Delvile entails the sacrifice of her estate, with which she had hoped to do so much good, and the Delviles are never totally reconciled to their son's unamiable match with a relatively low-born woman now lacking wealth. Symbols matter more than people.

In *Cecilia*, civilised life is a matter not only of masking and masquerade but also of the utter importance of the realm of the symbolic. Capitalism and the feudal class structure, conventionally at odds, work well together in a symbiotic creation of imaginary values and important symbols, significant aerial endorsements both masking and supporting privilege. Edmund Burke objected to the mixed ending of the novel (*DL* II, 139), but the ending reflects Burney's view that really good things cannot happen unless there is a political reform of a most unlikely kind, occurring at a deep level. It may be that (as the vulgar miser Briggs hopes) rank will lose its charm, but some other chimera will take its place and hierarchies, exploitation and repressions will continue. This message is left to the reader; it has always been possible for some readers to enjoy the novel simply as the adventures of a beautiful orphan with comic or sinister guardians.

All of the four Burney novels, while hiding under the cloak of the courtship novel, are constructed around political questions or problems. The two later novels, arising in the turbulent period of the 1790s (when *Camilla* was written and published and *The Wanderer* begun), are more open in exhibiting their political nature, and seem even more insistent in showing the high price to be paid by those living under what is generally considered an acceptable and even desirable system of power. Both have an immense canvas of characters, and both take us to rural England and the littoral margin, rather than centring on London. Between *Cecilia* and *Camilla, or A Picture of Youth* (1796) fell the shadow of Burney's own experience of enforced incarceration and servitude at the Court of Queen Charlotte, which she entered reluctantly, feeling all the weight of the sacrifice to her father's enthusiasm and ambition, on 17 July 1786. Burney was to be a Keeper of the Robes to Queen Charlotte. She was an exalted servant, on call from early in the morning until late in the evening, and she was thrust day after day into the close society of the disagreeable and bossy Mrs Schwellenberg. The position was regarded as a great honour, and it brought some money with it; important families were vying to place unmarried daughters in such a position, and Burney was a mere nobody, a most common commoner. The King and Queen evidently felt they were making a gracious and modern gesture, and they were pleasing their well-born friend and protégée Mary Delany.

The incarceration at Court was soon rendered more hideous by the madness of George III and close confinement in the palace at Kew. In this period, Burney took to writing dramatic tragedies set in the Middle Ages, all of which have to do with the operation of unjust power, and the torment of a hapless heroine. Several of the dramas circle around invasion, conquest and occupation; on the psychological level they deal with repression and madness. Burney at last got out from a service that had become intolerable, under the plea of illness; she was recalled to life on 7 July 1791. She slowly recovered, her recovery enlivened by the courtship with the émigré Alexandre d'Arblay, whom she married in July 1793 (to a chorus of disapproval). Their son Alex was born in December 1794.

In marrying d'Arblay, Burney committed a political action. She united herself with a Roman Catholic and with a man whom some saw as a dangerous radical, for d'Arblay had been one of the French reformers, his position very like that of Lafayette. Charles Burney greatly disapproved of him as a *Constitutionnel* (a man who supported the writing of a new constitution for France). Burney remarks 'He [i.e. 'Dear Father'] is all aristocratic!' (*JL* II, 65). Charles Burney, born 'Macburney', who had come up from nothing and made himself into a 'gentleman' (if not one by everyone's standards), was by now ardently supportive of the aristocracy and all traditional hierarchy. Burney, adopting the new political language, herself said she felt *aristocrate* (i.e. of the aristocratic party) when she saw the power of the mob, but was *democrate* when she saw power being abused. For the first time she had a terminology available to describe complex positions, though characteristically she chooses both parties and thus, in a sense, neither. And she does not offer such political terms as solutions in the two later novels.

The first work published by Burney after her marriage was a pamphlet she wrote at the urging of Mrs Crewe's committee of ladies who were trying to help the destitute and dispossessed French clergy who had sought refuge in England. *Brief Reflections Relative to the Emigrant French Clergy: Earnestly Submitted to the Humane Consideration of the Ladies of Britain* (1793) was a pamphlet announced as 'By the Author of Evelina and Cecilia', thus ensuring sales. In her introductory 'Apology', Burney defends a woman's interference in public matters: women are not 'exempt from all public claims, or mere passive spectatresses of the moral as well as of the political œconomy of human life' (iii). This is a defining moment, as Burney rejects what had once been one of her own personal responses to familial pressures. Passivity is now condemned. She urges women to take action in the ongoing course of history, to get out of their British chauvinism and to use their imaginations in responding to others' afflictions. On entering personally and actively into the pamphlet arena, Burney knows that there will be sniggers, that her marriage evokes the laughter of some and the horror of others. Now she is perversely pleading for a pack of French Roman Catholic priests – in an England in which most of the French émigrés in general (as Alexandre d'Arblay knew first hand) were ignorantly feared as spies or loathed as firebrand radicals. Moreover, the Roman Catholic clergy were despised by stout Protestants, out of whose patriotic ranks Burney had publically stepped in her marriage.

Charles Burney did not support his daughter's marriage to d'Arblay; he gave cold consent but refused to come to the wedding. In her personal life Burney had been anxious to please and fearful of disobedience. Now she had taken her own way on three important matters: the publication of *Evelina*, the departure from Court, and her marriage. Her later works, both dramatic and novelistic, show a greater interest than ever in the politics of dissent. The turning moments of Burney's own life were moments of revolt or rebellion. Most of the later stories, novelistic or dramatic, have a central turning point consisting of a revolt or rebellion of some kind. This is most comically and (for the characters) successfully worked out in *The Woman-Hater* (c. 1801–2), when Joyce successfully rebels against her oppressively didactic 'Papa', Mr Wilmot, and the rules of ladylike behaviour.

> I won't be left to live with Papa, when he knows he i'n't Papa! read, read, reading! – I'd sooner be off with you, or … marry Bob! … I'll marry Bob! – I shall like that a great deal better than always studying Books; and sitting with my hands before me; and making courtsies; and never eating half as much as I like, – except in the Pantry! … the less money the less ceremony; and who cares for work, if it's followed by play? (V.xii.16–34)

Elinor Joddrel's revolt in *The Wanderer, or Female Difficulties* (1814) is a much more complex version of Joyce's rebellion, for family politics no longer stand in for (or veil) the larger social political life. In *The Woman-Hater*, Joyce's position as an innocent impostor foisted upon the wrong father is flipped so that we see the father as a kind of impostor, and she can question and throw off his authority. For both Joyce and Elinor, 'Papa' is revealed to be false – that is, the authority that has earlier been accorded obedience is perceived to be null and without sovereignty. Joyce is full of confidence, Elinor of hope and doubt. Elinor's capacity for analysis does not contribute to her success or happiness, and she is depressive, whereas Joyce, as her name indicates, is joyous.

Burney's plan for a novel in which a heroine (Cleora or Clorinda) goes wrong and repents was partly written and then scrapped in the mid-1790s. She then wrote *Camilla* which investigates not the wrong done by the heroine but the wrongs in her world. *Camilla* is painted on a wide canvas, with a large cast of characters differing in rank, age and occupation. The story moves about different areas of England. Again, Burney examines the governing assumptions about gender, and about rights and inheritance. In the anxious Edgar Mandlebert, orphan heir to Beech Park, we see the crippling effect forms of privilege may have on the supposed beneficiary. The advice given to Edgar by his powerful tutor Dr Marchmont is a mechanism by which love and spontaneity are cast out of a world transformed into calculation, generalisation and debased enterprise. Forms of calculation and the use of the abstracting intellect to gain inhuman mastery are visible throughout, from the anxious totting up of small sums to the comic lucubrations of the uninspiring and self-absorbed tutor Dr Orkborne engrossed by his own vast scholarly labour.

Early in the novel Burney makes a direct political point, against the holding of parties and balls to celebrate the arrival of the judges to the country town to hold the assize court, when poor prisoners will at last be sentenced, many to exile or death. She openly condemns this 'hardening of human feelings against human crimes and human miseries' (82). A man has been committed to prison for stealing a leg of mutton; the young Camilla endeavours to intervene to save the man and help his ragged family. That Burney meant her point to be heard and even acted upon by her readership is borne out by her statement that she had given the public 'a little hint against dancing around Thieves, Highwaymen, & poor wretches going to the Gallows' (*JL* IV, 134). The gallows has already shadowed *Cecilia*; the heroine steps into a side street in order to avoid the procession to Tyburn, and the Belfields occupy lodgings in Paddington, Blake's 'mournful, ever-weeping Paddington', mourning because it is the unhallowed perpetual site of recurrent legal killings.

Burney always notices the poor. We saw that in the two poor old women in the race in *Evelina*; we saw it again in *Cecilia* in the case of the carpenter's widow Mrs Hill, owed a substantial sum by Harrel, who feels no obligation to pay a debt to someone so unimportant. The Assize sequence in *Camilla* is one of the rare points at which Burney directly proposes a specific reform, though that reform would also mean a change of heart. A sober Lenten period during the time of sentencing and execution, mourning rather than rejoicing during the exercise of state power, might open hearts and minds to question the rugged and uneven law. Burney rarely makes specific suggestions, however. Her strength is rather in the deep analysis of the complexities of systems as they operate in and through real people, who are embedded in a social world they never made and proceeding through life with energies and desires. Energies and desires in Burney's world are always necessary – nay, vital – and almost always misdirected. And always at the bottom of the social pyramid that some adore, there is somebody who has to pay for the structure.

Stimulated by the Assize section of *Camilla* and that epistolary annotation, we see that 'dancing around ... the Gallows' is a powerful image of what Burney conceives English society to be doing. Looking at all the novels, we can see that each conceals near its centre an image of an instrument of societal control and licensed political cruelty. This image is sooner or later allowed to escape to the surface layer of narrative. In *Evelina*, where the characters frequently suffer humiliation and confusion, the figure of this instrument of social control proves, appropriately enough, to be the pillory, instrument of shame and embarrassment. In *Cecilia*, the finally revealed instrument of social control is the madhouse. *Camilla* early invokes the gallows, frank emblem and instrument of what power ultimately means, and on whose horrific phallic column the structure of society relies. Without it, the state feels it is nothing; with the sanction of death, it is confident. We have moved from the embarrassing to the confining, and thence to the starkly and absolutely lethal. The lethal continues to dominate in *The Wanderer*, where the phallic instrument of social control has become the guillotine.

In each of the four novels, Burney offers the reader a scene of festivity which plays a major part in the narrative. This scene of festivity is later to be supplemented by another festive scene, reflecting the earlier one, in which cruelty is made manifest. In *Cecilia*, for example, the primary festive scene is exemplified in the masquerade, the second by the mad party at Vauxhall at which Harrel shoots himself. Both are scenes of 'madness' and supplement and support the ultimate image of the madhouse. In *Camilla*, the first important festive scene is the first ball, at which the heroine encounters Mr Dubster, the retired wig-maker, and little Eugenia with her disability meets with derision. The second supplemental scene is the one in which the girls are left high and exposed in Dubster's unfinished house, the ladder (so necessary to the old-fashioned gallows) having been taken away. Eugenia is then publicly ridiculed by passers-by for her deformities, and sickeningly discovers the full range of her misfortune. To cure her melancholy, her father makes her and her sister stare at an unfortunate girl who is called 'an idiot' – despite the fact that his daughters do not wish to afflict the unhappy girl with their critical abstracting gaze as he drives home a 'lesson'. In *Camilla*, bodies in various states of disarray are perpetually subject to public inspection and commentary – culminating in the heroine's viewing of a dead body and then in her sense that her body is breaking into different parts with separate voices. Social relations have broken down to inspection of the body, a kind of universal autopsy. Characters are spying when they are not appraising; we repeatedly notice the control administered by what we have recently learned to call 'the gaze'. Edgar is taught that he must keep Camilla under observation, unceasing sceptical and moral observation – so he becomes a moral maniac, a kind of stalker.

Camilla demonstrates in different sets of relations that the world is ideologically run on the mistaken assumption of accessible perfect objectivity. Perfect possession of the perfected is thought to be not only obtainable but desirable. Hence, for the objective possessor, the ideal other must be an object, but a person who is completely an object and not a subject is a corpse. The novel suggests that England's political persona relies on metaphysical assumptions ineradicably political in nature. England's subjects are treated as objects. No grace is allowed for growth or change, for the necessary inconsistency of the maturing self, although, as the subtitle *A Picture of Youth* indicates, we are dealing with the young, who must inevitably develop and change. Religion is no help, for the two religious mentors, Edgar's tutor Marchmont and Camilla's father, both clergymen, give terrible advice urging their charges to engage in self-defeating masking and paranoid investigations.

In order to foil constant observation, people adopt disguise, making this a world where a wig-maker must become rich – society the while hypocritically declaring its preference for the simple and the natural. Burney certainly distrusts Rousseau, and the adulation of the 'natural'. For a start, as in *Emile* (1762), it means a return to an absolute hierarchical difference between men and women and their spheres. Young women will be adjured to 'act naturally', to be simply 'themselves', sincere, unstudied and undisguised – something impossible to anyone with a consciousness, especially once admonished to be natural. The world as it is, made out as a hard metallic ideal, like the Homeric shield of Achilles discussed by Orkborne and Marchmont, offers no place for deficiency, want, or need.

In *The Wanderer*, England's panicky desire for self-reassurance and its faking of stability has brought about a desiccated half-sullen dullness, barely masking the abusive power that must sustain the fantasy of English security and righteousness. *The Wanderer* is mapped around the figure of the guillotine, emblem of the political world's capacity literally to kill. The pistol that figured in *Evelina* (with Macartney's intended suicide or murder) and in *Cecilia* (instrument of Harrel's suicide) is not absent here, but it is supplemented by the knife with which Elinor threatens herself. It seems appropriate that things that cut and slice move towards the centre as images of death-dealing. The provincial and parochial English characters whom we meet take their own system for granted, and are blind to its destructive nature, even while they amuse themselves with thinking of the horrors of the Revolution, and the tyranny of Robespierre (though some of them cannot even pronounce his name). The enigmatic heroine has first-hand experience of the Revolution, but her knowledge is ignored while misinformation and ignorantly scandalised remarks are passed upon the greatest political movement of the century. Burney herself in her dedicatory epistle 'To Doctor Burney' says the Revolution is unignorable:

> To attempt to delineate, in whatever form, any picture of actual human life, without reference to the French Revolution, would be as little possible, as to give an idea of the English government without reference to our own: for not more unavoidably is the last blended with the history of our nation, than the first, with every intellectual survey of the present times.   (*Wanderer*, 6)

Burney, for the first time, directly says that in writing about the present she is writing historically and politically and that some political events are too pervasive to be ignored, even in fiction, which is here given status as a form of 'intellectual survey'. In the novel itself, she shows that while complacent remarks abound in a truly insular England, neither the French Revolution nor England's own political life since the 'Glorious Revolution' is truly understood. English society in its willed ignorance is not really equipped to handle the political. The bulk of the characters Juliet meets in Brighton and Lewes are single, well-to-do, self-centred persons. Some are aging, some are obviously sexually frustrated or inadequate, and all are very conscious of money and power, but any consideration of wider ideological moment irritates them. The coming of the mysterious 'Ellis' vexes their categories. Indeed, they make up her name themselves, by mistake, on hearing that she receives a letter addressed to 'L.S.' (We may wonder why Burney chose those initials, and note that they are the initials of conservative 'Letitia Sourby', a fictitious writer to the *Anti-Jacobin*, who complains about her liberal father; that squib is thought to be by Dr Charles Burney. 'Ellis' may be a sly riposte by his non-conservative daughter.)

The Wanderer perfectly illustrates how a society may school its members to be politically repressive while pretending not to be political. Good works and ladylike behaviour scarcely are equipped to meet the storm, or answer human need. The ladies' committee that patronises Ellis–Juliet degenerates into time-frittering occupations, and misuses money meant for her use in buying an unwanted costume that will mark her as inferior to the 'ladies'. If the women's little effort at political action is a failure, the men are not admirable either. High and low males have clubs or meetings where they repeat stale truisms. Albert Harleigh, though he is good and does fall in love with Juliet, is too fearful that she will lose caste by actual work to be a strong or admirable helpmate. He is a literary figure; a descendant of Mackenzie's Harley, the 'Man of Feeling' by way of the 'Augustus Harley' who is the object of the heroine's determined affections in Mary Hays's *The Memoirs of Emma Courtney*. Harleigh suffers likewise from the pursuit of Elinor, in a relationship which is not dissimilar to that of Bridgetina Botherim and Henry Sydney in Elizabeth Hamilton's conservative satire *Memoirs of Modern Philosophers*, in which the hero is pestered by unwanted attentions from a young woman who fancies herself liberated. Elinor, however, though she is witty in herself and does stupid things, is not a joke; modern readers may see her as serious and complex, while we may well fail to admire Harleigh. Burney's 'heroes' incidentally are usually very weak, not in their goodness of heart but in their subservience to convention; they are willing to take fewer risks than the women. None of Burney's heroes can really break through the wall of propriety, though Lord Orville, the most romantic, is willing to marry Evelina before her parentage is ascertained.

Albert Harleigh does so little to help Juliet that the role of heroic rescuer falls to her elderly and crippled admirer Sir Jaspar Herrington. The love of a man of seventy for a young and beautiful woman is an embarrassment that ought to be hidden; Sir Jaspar does not hide it, but masks it by a fantasy of sylphs and fairies – embarrassing devices which provide a means of over-coming the restrictions of convention, the normative law of custom. The invocation of the fantasy points to a deficiency in the ongoing order of things, a need for a supplement. The language is a means of evading the power structure; Sir Jaspar can put himself into subjection to something else, foregoing his power and privilege. The fiction is a repository not only for his sexual feelings but also for a sense of political unease. Herrington's fantasy language is an allegory of freedom at the same time as it is a sign of impotency.

Elinor Joddrel is singular in Burney's works not only in that she is pro-revolutionary but also in that she openly espouses and articulates a clear ideology. Here, at last, Burney has brought forward an overtly political character. Readers as well as other characters love to condemn her, but she is not totally condemned by her author. Like Burney, Elinor registers the political element of life as part of the first order of things, along with sex. Much of what she says seems true. She has understood much of Mary Astell and Mary Wollstonecraft, and is sometimes a very good speaker for women's rights. She is not, however, interested in their basic issue, the education of women in general, nor does she join them in considering economic realities. Elinor makes a common error not merely in confusing her own happiness with mankind's (or womankind's) but in valuing her own happiness far ahead of that of others. Elinor knows liberty, but is deficient and confused as to community. Longing for a happy ending for herself, she becomes perversely self-destructive. Undoubtedly, there is more than a touch of Mary Wollstonecraft's life about Elinor's; Burney must have read of Wollstonecraft's suicide attempts in Godwin's 1798 biography. Elinor's defect seems to rest not in her proto-feminist ideology in itself but in her persistent endeavour to apply liberation to herself alone. She thinks that since a new political day has dawned, she has a right to ask a man to marry her, but she will not consider that his equal and corresponding right under the new dispensation must be to say 'No'. Rather than trying to free other women, Elinor spends her energies on self-concern. Thus she has not really moved away from the self-centred habits of the dull and venal neighbours whom she (often reasonably) despises.

Ellis–Juliet, lacking Elinor's private income, has to struggle with earning a living, joining the working class and descending in social spheres; she is variously guest, humble companion, music teacher, performer, seamstress for a mantua maker, milliner, embroiderer and shopkeeper. When she flees her unwanted husband in the New Forest, she takes refuge with the hum-blest, living on a farm and teaching at a dame school. Elinor wants to be a solitary performer, surrounded by chosen spectators of her drama – Juliet is forced to participate in the humdrum strains of daily working life. Almost all the jobs available to women in the period are represented in *The Wanderer*. Burney was always interested in working women (the first act of *The Witlings* takes place in a milliner's shop) but her stint at Court apparently enlarged her insight into the pains of finding employment and the difficulties of work. To try to earn a living is a 'Female Difficulty' indeed. The political oppression of women, of which Elinor complains, cannot be remedied separately from their economic plight. Burney has a quick eye for exploitation; she notes how the milliner puts her prettiest girls in the window, to attract male shoppers. At the end, we may feel that although the heroine is rescued, England has learned nothing from the French Revolution; privilege, petty showing-off and gross, if largely hidden, exploitation go on as before.

Burney's public would have liked her novel better if she had spent all of it attacking the French and Napoleon. Instead, she disappointed them by turning a scornful gaze on English society, noting its petty tyrants like mean Mrs Maple or the evil-tempered slave-owning Mrs Ireton. She registers England's distressing inadequacy, its incapacity to respond to the issues raised so terribly through the French Revolution. It is not that she approved of or liked Napoleon's despotic rule. Burney made a very clear statement in a letter of 1815 to her friend Mary Anne Waddington (who had expressed admiration for Napoleon) regarding the ignoble and morally painful life under 'a Tyrant'.

> O had you spent, like me, 10 years within the control of his unlimited power, & under the iron rod of its dread, how would you change your language! ... the safety of deliberate prudence, or of retiring timidity, is not such as would satisfy a mind glowing for freedom like your's: it satisfies indeed NO *mind*, it merely suffices for *bodily* security ... PERSONALLY ... I was happy: but you know me, I am sure, better than to suppose me such an Egotist as to be really happy, or contented, where Corporal Liberty could only be preserved by Mental forbearance – i.e. subjection. (*JL* VIII, 282–3)

It satisfies indeed NO *mind* – here we get a clue to the base of Burney's political views. Essentially, hers is a vision of freedom. Dictatorship is abhorrent, the lack of freedom to speak and think is killing to the spirit. She knew this thoroughly from living in timidity and polite subjection at home with her father. Personal domestic happiness is never enough – we have seen this idea expressed throughout Burney's novels. Even her happiness with Alexandre d'Arblay and their son could not make her truly happy under a despotism. Personal and isolated solutions cannot meet our need for the good relations of the whole. Physical liberty is insufficient without

7

VIVIEN JONES

Burney and gender

The first of only two occasions on which Jane Austen sanctioned the appearance of her name in print was in the subscription list to Burney's *Camilla* – a significant tribute by the aspirant 'Miss J. Austen, Steventon' to the woman novelist whose work was, by 1796, widely acknowledged to be 'without a competitor' or, if comparisons were made, to equal that of Richardson and Henry Fielding.[1] When Austen paid tribute to Burney again, more famously, in her defence of novels in *Northanger Abbey*, she named *Cecilia* and *Camilla*, together with Maria Edgeworth's *Belinda* (1801), as examples of works 'in which the greatest powers of the mind are displayed, in which the most thorough knowledge of human nature, the happiest delineation of its varieties, the liveliest effusions of wit and humour, are conveyed to the world in the best chosen language' (I, ch. v). For modern readers, at least until twentieth-century feminist criticism rediscovered and properly reinstated women writers, Austen herself was the earliest female novelist to be allowed into the literary canon. But for contemporaries, it was Burney who first broke through the prejudices of gender and genre – her own, as well as those of her reviewers – to achieve unequivocal canonical status as a practitioner of the new form of the novel. Beginning with the acclaim which greeted the anonymous publication of *Evelina* in 1778, Burney's career and reputation and the emergent, but still fragile, respectability of the novel at the end of the eighteenth century are crucially interdependent. Indeed, Austen's assertive celebration of fiction not only as displaying 'the greatest powers of the mind', but also as a form whose greatest living exemplars are women, was possible largely because of the critical respect won by Burney.

This chapter examines the ways in which the reciprocal relationship between Burney's reputation and that of the novel itself is shaped by issues of gender. In spite of her notorious feminine diffidence, Burney boldly used the anonymous publication of *Evelina* to identify herself at the start of her career with a male rather than a female novel tradition, with Fielding, Richardson and Smollett rather than Lennox, Griffith and Brooke: in other words, with the writers widely accepted as setting the standard for contemporary fiction. And the critics followed her lead, describing *Evelina*, for example, as a performance that 'would have disgraced neither the head nor the heart of Richardson' and *Cecilia* as combining 'the dignity and pathos of Richardson' with 'the acuteness and ingenuity of Fielding'.[2] Burney's critical success was in part a discriminating acknowledgement by the reviewers of the quality and originality of her writing. But once her identity became known, this immediate response was importantly reinforced by Burney's carefully cultivated professional persona which was not only decorously feminine, but also supported by some of the most influential leaders of cultural opinion – both male and female. Burney's conservative mode of femininity, combined with her intellectual seriousness, fitted very well with the figure of the decorous woman of letters, which by 1778 carried considerable cultural power. As is well known, the success of *Evelina* (and a little help from her father) gained Burney entry into Hester Thrale's Streatham salon, which included Samuel Johnson, Joshua Reynolds and Edmund Burke; it also brought her positive notice from the leading Bluestockings, Elizabeth Montagu, Elizabeth Carter and Hester Chapone. In the Bluestocking circle particularly, women writers received active support. Burney was taken up by intellectual circles in which gender mattered, but where it was always in tension with an ostensibly ungendered standard of literary taste – and one based on conservative assumptions about genre which tended to devalue the novel. Her particular achievement was to attract respect as a female intellectual on the basis of works of fiction, a recognition which led, in turn, to her taking her place in the late eighteenth century's pantheon of major novelists, alongside the male writers of the mid-century. An understanding of the role played by gender across Burney's long career is thus inseparable from questions of genre, of literary sociability – and, as the novel and literary reputations changed in response to the political intensity of the 1790s, of patriotic feeling.

A young (female) novelist's entrance into public notice

Evelina was published at a low point in the history of the novel, but at a moment when the woman of letters was enjoying particularly high visibility and status. 1778 saw the appearance of only sixteen new novels, symptomatic of what the monumental bibliography, *The English Novel 1770–1829*, describes as 'a steep decline in novel production in the late 1770s'.[3] But it was also the year in which the publisher Joseph Johnson chose to include a print of Richard Samuel's *The Nine Living Muses of Great Britain* in *Johnson's Ladies New and Polite Pocket Memorandum for 1778*. Samuel's culturally significant group portrait celebrates female intellectual and artistic achieve-ments through its depiction of nine distinguished women: Elizabeth Montagu, the Bluestocking hostess and commentator on Shakespeare, is surrounded by six writers – Anna Letitia Barbauld (formerly Aikin), Elizabeth Carter, Elizabeth Griffith, Charlotte Lennox, Catharine Macaulay and Hannah More – as well as the singer Elizabeth Sheridan and the painter Angelica Kauffman. *The Nine Living Muses* is a contribution in visual form to a well-established tradition which sees the progress of women as a key measure of Britain's position at the forefront of civilisation. Many of the texts in this tradition make their case by naming individual women, and the effect is to establish a canon of female writers as well as conferring a kind of celebrity status on the particular individuals concerned. The classical scholar Elizabeth Carter, for example, who appears in Samuel's portrait, was old enough to have been included in John Duncombe's roll-call, in his poem *The Feminiad* of 1754, of the 'blooming, studious band' of those women writers whom he conside-red to be appropriately inspired by the 'modest Muse' (lines 56, 139). By the 1770s, in Mary Scott's words, 'the sentiments of all men of sense relative to female education are now more enlarged than they formerly were', and women began to construct their own lists of national treasures: Carter again, Barbauld, Griffith, Lennox, Macaulay, Montagu and More are among the many women named in *The Female Advocate*, Scott's 1774 update of Duncombe (vi). And in the same year, Hannah More added an epilogue to her pastoral drama, *The Search after Happiness*, in which she invokes a more select but similar group to counter what she presents as the outdated view that,

> How well soe'er these learned ladies *write*
> They seldom *act* the virtues they *recite*;
> ...
>
> But in our *chaster* times 'tis no offence,
> When female *virtue* joins with female *sense*;
> When moral CARTER breathes the strain divine,
> And AIKIN's *life* flows faultless as her *line*;
> When all-accomplish'd MONTAGUE can spread
> Fresh gather'd laurels round her SHAKESPEARE's head
> When *wit* and *worth* in polish'd BROOKES unite,
> And fair MACAULAY claims a LIVY's right. (43–4)

Anxiety about respectability is a striking, if predictable, refrain through-out these texts. It is explicit in Duncombe's moral distinction between a 'modest' and a 'wanton' muse, which leads him to exclude from his approved list Delarivier Manley, author of risqué *romans à clef*, Susanna Centlivre and Aphra Behn, 'notorious for the indecency of their plays', and the scandalous memoirists Teresia Constantia Phillips, Letitia Pilkington and Lady Frances Anne Vane;[4] but it is also implicit at a generic level in his poem's silent exclusion of all novelists. Of the popular female novelists who might have been named, Eliza Haywood was still known as the author of titillating romances, in spite of the publication of *The History of Miss Betsy Thoughtless* in 1751. But Sarah Fielding, whose *Adventures of David Simple* (1744) was much admired, and Charlotte Lennox, author of *The Female Quixote* (1752), ought surely to have passed Duncombe's respectability test – particularly Lennox, whose work was supported and promoted by Richardson, 'the sex's friend / And constant patron' (lines 15–16) and the leading figure in Duncombe's intellectual circle. For Duncombe in the 1750s, it would seem, only those women working in established genres rather than the still slightly disreputable novel can be a source of confident nationalist pride. Both Fielding and Lennox are celebrated by Mary Scott, however, together with Elizabeth Griffith, who appears with Lennox in Samuel's portrait. And in spite of Hannah More's mistrust of fiction, her select list includes Frances Brooke, who by 1774 had written two well-received novels, *The History of Lady Julia Mandeville* (1763) and *The History of Emily Montague* (1769).

By the mid-1770s, then, the pantheon of women writers to be accorded public approval, not simply through popularity but because they were deemed, as More put it, to combine '*wit* and *worth*', did include a small number who wrote fiction. Indeed, together with the reputation of the male mid-century novelists, the status and visibility of these individual women did much to boost the novel's growing, but still precarious, respectability. The influential reviews could be scathing about new fiction ('It is something, however, in a modern novel, to find *half* of it worth reading'), and particularly patronising towards anonymous novels written or claiming to have been written, 'By a Lady' ('If this piece of clumsy patch-work was put together by a fair sempstress, we wish her better success in the labours of her needle, to which we would advise her for the future to confine her ambition').[5] As the material made available by *The English Novel* demonstrates, however, reviewers were more discriminating than has sometimes been allowed. By the 1770s, they were eager to distinguish good writing, and the critical respect shown to a new novel by Griffith or Brooke is absolutely comparable with that shown to successful male writers such as Henry Mackenzie. It is nevertheless significant that none of the publicly celebrated female writers wrote only novels; nor were they necessarily best known for their fiction. In *The Female Advocate*, for example, Sarah Fielding is praised for her novelist's ability 'To trace the secret mazes of the Heart', but also as an educationist; Lennox's *Shakespeare Illustrated*, a play and a translation are cited alongside *The Female Quixote*; and Elizabeth Griffith is identified primarily as 'Frances', co-author with her husband of the autobiographical *A Series of Genuine Letters between Henry and Frances* (1757, 1766), and as a translator, poet and playwright, while her popular novels *The Delicate Distress* (1769) and *The History of Lady Barton* (1771) are not mentioned at all.[6] And when she featured in More's favoured list, Frances Brooke was known not just as a writer of fiction, but most immediately as a translator and playwright and as co-manager of the King's Theatre. An appropriately decorous woman who specialised in fiction had yet to make it into the public category of 'living muse' – or into the social circles which nurtured and promoted the visibility of the female intellectual.

It was against this background of real, if constrained, opportunity for the woman writer and of uncertainty about the future and status of the novel that Burney published *Evelina* and chose to do so anonymously. Like so many other aspects of Burney's professional self-presentation, this strategic anonymity intriguingly combines ambition with diffidence, independence with obligation – an ambiguity managed through the unobtrusive wit both of the preface and of the dedication 'To the Authors of the Monthly and Critical Reviews' which precedes it:

> Without name, without recommendation, and unknown alike to success and disgrace, to whom can I so properly apply for patronage, as to those who publicly profess themselves Inspectors of all literary performances?
>
> The extensive plan of your critical observations . . . encourages me to seek for your protection, since . . . it entitles me to your annotations. To resent, therefore, this offering, however insignificant, would ill become the universality of your undertaking, tho' not to despise it may, alas! be out of your power.
>
> . . . to appeal for your MERCY, were to solicit your dishonour; . . . – and though
> It droppeth like the gentle rain from heaven
> Upon the place beneath, –.
> I court it not! to your Justice alone I am entitled.   (5–6)

The full force of the teasing wit here can be appreciated only when we know that the writer is a woman. But at any level, this is an unusually deft example of a well-worked topos, as this unknown novelist turns the familiar appeal for critical indulgence into something close to a declaration of rights – certainly of equality. Uninhibited by 'recommendation . . . success [or] disgrace', s/he is free to challenge the reviewers to use their power responsibly, to demand the just hearing to which s/he is 'entitled'. The aim is to secure 'patronage' and 'protection', yet the claim to entitlement and the language of honour invoke a relationship between intellectual equals in which Portia's feminine 'quality of mercy' is rejected in favour of strict justice.[7] The writer's ambiguous anonymity ensures that this insistence on a fair and serious hearing is made on behalf of both genre and gender, as s/he defies the critics to treat her/his work with the kind of condescending critical indulgence often meted out to novels, and particularly to those suspected to be by women.

This tantalising play with gendered identity in defence of fiction continues in the preface which, by invoking male precursors, appears to suggest a male author:

> while in the annals of those few of our predecessors, to whom this species of writing is indebted for being saved from contempt, and rescued from depravity, we can trace such names as Rousseau, Johnson, Marivaux, Fielding, Richardson, and Smollet [sic], no man need blush at starting from the same post.   (9)

A little further on, however, any idea that the present writer might simply be imitating these male models is gently rejected: we are told that, in spite of 'feel[ing] myself enlightened' by their example, 'I yet presume not to attempt pursuing the same ground which they have tracked'. The language is modest and the writer eager to assure readers that doing things differently is 'not [to] be imputed to an opinion of my own originality' (10–11). A kind of originality is, nevertheless, what is claimed, as the debut novelist appeals to nature and 'sober Probability' in order to distance her/himself from 'Romance, where Fiction is coloured by all the gay hints of luxurious Imagination', and thus from 'the vulgar herd of authors' who are incapable of 'avoid[ing] what is common, without adopting what is unnatural' (10). To a contemporary audience, the 'vulgar herd' of novelists would consist largely of women, and romance was popularly seen as a dominantly female taste. To this extent, then, the suggestion of male authorship is maintained. But the alert, informed reader might nevertheless detect an alignment with an alternative female tradition: the best-known critique of romance was, after all, Charlotte Lennox's *The Female Quixote*. The identity of *Evelina*'s author remains enigmatic.

It is undoubtedly true that Burney's decision to publish anonymously was born of a mixture of inherent and learned timidity, her natural shyness reinforced by the conventions of female propriety and by a terror of public humiliation inculcated by her father's 'continual struggle, both social and financial'.[8] But it is true, too, that she put her anonymity to powerful strategic use in support of a professionalism and self-belief also, perhaps, learned from her father. These more assertive qualities are amply evident in the letter Burney wrote to her eventual publisher, Thomas Lowndes, accompanying the first volume of *Evelina*:

> The plan of the first Volume, is the Introduction of a well educated, but inexperienced young woman into public company, and a round of the most fashionable

Spring Diversions of London. I believe it has not before been executed, though it seems a fair field open for the Novelist, as it offers a fund inexhaustible for Conversation, observations, and probable Incidents.   (*EJL* II, 215)

The aim is to convince Lowndes to read an anonymous manuscript, but the hard sell of author to potential publisher simply makes fully explicit the confidence in *Evelina*'s originality, which is only partly masked in the preface by the requisite tropes of modesty: the claim that this is a work different from the novels of Richardson or Fielding, but which aspires to their standard. In spite of the respect in which Lennox, Griffith and Brooke were held, to have named them in the preface would have been to make a polemical gesture which effectively announced Burney's femaleness. Instead, anonymity allows Burney to transcend gender in the interests of securing an unbiased reading for subject-matter and a mode of realism 'not before executed'. The real coup, for women as for fiction, would be to reveal *Evelina*'s female author-ship only when critical success was assured.

Which is, of course, what happened. '[W]ithout recommendation', *Evelina* was nevertheless an immediate hit with both a general audience and the reviewers. Initially 'concluded ... to be the Work of a *man*!', as Burney noted of its enthusiastic readers in her cousin's household, it was 'spoken very highly of, & very much enquired after' by the members of circulating libraries, and greeted in the first reviews as 'one of the most sprightly, entertaining & agreeable productions of this kind that has late fallen under our Notice', with 'much more merit ... than is usually to be met with in modern Novels' (*EJL* III, 6, 13, 14–15). Burney's cousin Richard, still ignor-ant of its authorship, claimed to have 'read nothing like it, since Fielding's Novels' (*EJL* III, 10). The *Critical* assumed a male author and, as we have already seen, judged it to be worthy of Richardson, an accolade indeed from the review which the previous year had worried that '[t]he abuse of novel-writing is so great, that it has almost brought that species of entertain-ment into discredit ... and the manes of Richardson, Fielding, and Smollett have often been cruelly tortured by their imitators'.[9] But *Evelina*'s – and Burney's – moment of ungendered freedom, or at least of cross-dressing, was necessarily short-lived. Once her identity was known, Burney had to adjust her professional self-representation accordingly and had to define her parti-cular version of female authorship. And here, forms of literary sociability and the already-established status of the female writer play a significant role.

At least as important as *Evelina*'s popular and critical success for Burney's long-term reputation were the enthusiasm of Samuel Johnson, who per-suaded Hester Thrale that 'Harry Fielding never did any thing equal to the 2ᵈ Vol: of Evelina'; Burney's consequent introduction into Thrale's Streatham circle; and the attention she received from members of the Bluestockings as a result of Thrale's friendship.[10] Burney's gradual accommodation to 'the idea of Appearing as an *Authoress*' and her responses both to the triumph of her novel and to speculation about its authorship are entertainingly, and self-consciously, recorded in her journals and letters for 1778. Even before Burney met her, Hester Thrale emerges from this narrative as a touchstone, a model for Burney's aspirations and the repository of her projected anxieties. 'But, – Mrs. Thrale! – She, she is the Goddess of my Idolatry!' is Burney's flattered tribute on hearing that Thrale had declared *Evelina* to be '*very* clever ... writ by somebody that knows *the top & the bottom* – the *highest & lowest* of Mankind'. It is Thrale's praise, Burney suggests, which might tip her into the '*almost* irresistible' risk of another publication, even if that means raising 'Expectations which it could not answer'; and the idea that Thrale might herself be the author of *Evelina* is received as a measure of high esteem: 'There's Honour & Glory for You! – I'll assure you, I Grinned prodigiously' (*EJL* III, 63, 35 and n. 12, 36–7, 45). Most revealing, however, is the gendered language of Burney's reaction at the prospect of Thrale discovering who did write the novel: 'your wish of telling *her* quite *unmans* me – I *shook* so, when I read it, that, had any body been present, I must have betrayed myself'. Burney's immediate referent is this dangerous moment in which feminine sensibility (a key feature of her persona), makes her tremble with uncontrollable nerves. But a more permanent 'unmanning' of her authorship is also presaged here, as she contemplates public recognition as a woman. The mask of anonymity allowed for any aspects of her novel judged indecorous to be attributed to a male author and masculine experience. Revealed to the intellectually and socially respected hostess Mrs Thrale as the creator of 'the Branghtons, Mr Brown & some others', Burney fears she will fall short of the level of respectability she assumes is required by and of the public female intellectual: 'I am afraid she will conclude I must have an *innate vulgarity of ideas* to assist me with such coarse colouring for the objects of my Imagination ... I should certainly have been more finical' (*EJL* III, 50).

Burney need not have worried. Her own anxiously snobbish scruples, generated by social insecurity, were much more 'finical' than Thrale's. She was canny, however, both in recognising the role that propriety, both personal and intellectual, might play in securing public approval and support and in her sense that this was particularly true for the woman novelist, so readily identified with her subject matter. Her father, and particularly her mentor, Samuel ('Daddy') Crisp, were even more alert to the importance of image, as they tried hard to manage Burney's emergence as an 'Authoress'. Crisp, for example, stressed (in disturbingly eroticised terms) the strategic usefulness of Burney's proper femininity: 'Your coyness tends to enhance your Fame greatly in Public Opinion – "'Tis *Expectation makes the blessing dear*"'; and he saw immediately the value of *Evelina*'s authorship being made public by a woman such as Thrale: '*you* have not spread it, there can be no imputation of vanity fall to *your* share, & it cannot come out more to your Honour than through such a Channel as Mrs. Thrale' (*EJL* IV, 76; *EJL* III, 65).

Indeed, it was Thrale who stage-managed the introduction of the young female novelist to Elizabeth Montagu, 'our sex's Glory', as Burney described her, and 'Queen' of the Bluestockings (*EJL* III, 144). Burney's account of Thrale working to secure Montagu's approval for *Evelina* is worth quoting at some length:

> "'Tis a Novel; & an exceeding – but it does nothing good to praise too much, so I will say nothing more about it: only *this*, – that Mr. *Burke* sat up *all night* to read it.'
>
> 'Indeed? – well, I propose myself great pleasure from it; – & the more I am gratified by hearing it is written by a *woman*.'
>
> 'And Sir Joshua Reynolds, continued Mrs. Thrale, has been offering 50 pounds to know the Author.' ...
>
> 'And Mr. Johnson, Ma'am, added my kind *Puffer*, says *Fielding* never wrote so *well*, – never wrote *equal* to this Book; – he says it is a better picture of Life & manners than is to be found *any* where in Fielding.'
>
> 'Indeed? cried Mrs. Montagu, surprised, *that* I did not expect, for I have been informed it is the work of a Young lady, – & therefore, though I expected a very pretty Book, I imagined it to be a work of mere Imagination; – & the *Name* I thought attractive; – but Life & *manners* I never dreamt of finding.'
>
> (*EJL* III, 157–8)

The complexities of gender and literary sociability with which Burney had to contend and through which her reputation was established are brilliantly captured in this scene, in which Thrale skilfully negotiates Montagu's contradictory attitudes to women. One of the most striking features of Thrale's strategy (other than a desire to torment Burney in her extreme diffidence) is the way in which, in spite of being addressed to a female intellectual already 'gratified' that *Evelina* is by a woman, it replicates Burney's preface in its felt need to appeal to male authorities. Thrale mobilises her own familiarity with these influential men, as well as a shared enthusiasm for 'good Girls' writing 'clever Books', to both gratify and expose the conservatism of Montagu's attitudes to gender and genre. And, in so doing, she establishes herself as a rival leader of taste, more closely in touch than Montagu with the latest opinion, more open in her expectation of what a modern female-authored novel might achieve, and capable of cajoling Montagu into accepting her point of view. Equally striking is Burney's role in the drama: as actor, she embodies feminine modesty to an almost absurd degree; as writer,

she collusively orchestrates Thrale's gentle mockery of Montagu's suscep-
tibilities – yet another example of the tension between conformity and
critique, sensibility and satire, which characterises all Burney's work. The
mockery remains gentle, however: Montagu's influence was powerful and
her support was, after all, the object of the meeting. The professionalism
which Burney developed through her relationship with the Streatham circle
is perhaps nowhere more apparent than in this deliberate cultivation of
powerful advocates.

In the event, Montagu 'c[ould] not bear' *Evelina* and was 'amazed that so
delicate a Girl could write so *boisterous* a book'. But she did enjoy *Cecilia*
when it appeared in 1782, and she certainly approved of Burney, whose
social persona matched the 'very high degree of Reserve and Delicacy'
required by Montagu's 'Ideas of Female Excellence'.[11] Symptomatically,
indeed, Burney's good relations with Montagu were to last longer than her
friendship with Thrale, whom she famously, and ignobly, dropped when
Thrale followed private desires rather than public expectations and married
the Roman Catholic Italian singer, Gabriel Piozzi, in 1784. But in the early
days of her career, as she experienced an 'endlessly increasing expansion of
visits and acquaintance in London', Burney's private writings play sceptically
with becoming 'a *Bluestockinger*', as she jokily puts it, as if trying the identity
out for size. She is chatted up at Bath by a would-be dancing partner
who 'had no small reverence for us *Bluestockingers*'; and, told of Hester
Chapone's enthusiasm for *Evelina*, her response is flattered, but distanced:
'There's for you, – who would not be a blue stockin*ger* at this rate?'
(*Memoirs*, II, 218; *EJL* IV, 154, 93). In the public perception, however, the
association was quickly made. In June 1781, the following announcement
appeared in the *Morning Post*: 'Miss Burney, the sprightly writer of that
elegant Novel, *Evelina*, is domesticated with Mrs. Thrale, as Miss Moore is
with Mrs. Garrick, and Miss Carter with Mrs. Montague [sic]' (*EJL* IV,
354n.). This is the downside of female celebrity: literary sociability scurri-
lously represented as a distortion of domestic orthodoxy. (Interestingly,
Burney promised Thrale to 'take it *like a man*' (*EJL* IV, 355).) But it is yet
another measure, albeit in scandal-raking form, of the cultural fascination
with accomplished women, and particularly of the identification of Burney
in the public mind with Britain's 'living muses'.

It was an identification made not least because Burney in fact offered little
to the scandalmongers. Her success as a novelist was supported and con-
solidated by an unerringly decorous and thus unobtrusive femininity which
ensured the Bluestockings', as well as the public's, lasting admiration, and
which allowed for her work to be judged according to the highest literary
standards. In 1785, Elizabeth Carter paid tribute to Burney in terms which

make feminine virtues a desirable, but not a necessary, adjunct to ungendered 'genius': 'the Simplicity & Modesty of her Behaviour are worthy of so uncommon & great a Genius' (*EJL* IV, 161n). And a few years later, commenting on Charlotte Smith's *The Orphan of the Castle*, Montagu invoked Burney alongside Fielding and Richardson, just as the preface to *Evelina* had ideally envisaged: 'the characters have not those distinguishing features which you find in Miss Burney, Fielding, and Richardson's works'.[12]

In assigning Burney this canonical status, Montagu was reiterating what the publication of *Cecilia* had established as a critical commonplace. *Cecilia*, the *Monthly*'s reviewer suggests, combines the 'dignity and pathos of Richardson' with 'the acuteness and ingenuity of Fielding', a (feminine) 'purity of ... heart' with (masculine) 'understanding'.[13] This androgynous conjunction of heart with understanding replicates the kinds of terms in which the Blues themselves were described. In 1776, for example, in an article offering 'Observations on Female Literature in General', the *Westminster Magazine* praised Montagu for both her 'benevolent heart' and 'the solidity of her understanding', and commended Anna Letitia Barbauld's 'affability' as well as her formidable 'intellectual powers'.[14] Their femininity firmly established, the work of such women is accepted as potentially equal to that of men. Thus, Barbauld's poems are described as the products of 'Genius alone and the ear that Nature has harmonized'; and, according to the *Monthly* reviewer, Burney, similarly, 'doth not plead any privilege of her sex: she stands on firmer ground'.[15]

As well as being a judgment of *Cecilia*'s quality, this is literally true. Her identity known by the time she presented *Cecilia* to the public, Burney couldn't repeat the tantalisingly ungendered performance of the *Evelina* preface. But neither does she fall back in any obvious way on her femaleness. In the rambling draft introduction to *Cecilia*, which she ultimately abandoned, Burney plays very deliberately with feminine sensibility and the outsider status of the woman writer, categorising herself as one of 'the *Quakers* of Litterature': a modest, almost passive, nonconformist inspired by neither 'the wild effusions of Genius' nor 'the egregious folly of vanity', 'fearfully & feelingly awake to the perils wh · [sic] surround them, yet, urged by an impulse irresistable [sic]' (945). But when she came to publish the novel, Burney wisely decided against this anxious over-elaboration, offering it instead with a simple 'Advertisement': 'the precariousness of any power to give pleasure, suppresses all vanity of confidence, and [the writer] sends CECILIA into the world with scarce more hope, though far more encouragement, than attended her highly-honoured predecessor, EVELINA' (3). Modest femininity is certainly at work in the decorously overt 'suppression' of confidence here; but so is Burney's strategic professionalism, as she transcends gender to plead not the 'privilege of her sex', but the 'firmer ground' of an established critical reputation.

Cecilia was hugely successful in consolidating that reputation. By the time Burney published *Camilla* in 1796, *Evelina* had gone through eleven editions and *Cecilia* ten, and Burney had attracted 'a flock of imitators' – perhaps the most telling evidence of her status, and a significant feature of the novel's recovery during the 1780s.[16]

Fiction, femininity and politics

Burney's success is marked by her inclusion in two importantly different texts about British women writers which appeared in the last decades of the century: the anonymous *Dialogues concerning the Ladies* (1785) and Richard Polwhele's *The Unsex'd Females* (1798). The final section in *Dialogues* follows in the tradition of Duncombe or of Samuel's painting, praising several 'Ladies who have distinguished themselves by their Literary Talents', of whom Burney is the only one to have written nothing but novels. In a reiteration of what were becoming the standard terms of approval for her fiction, she is commended for the 'invention, the strong delineation of character, and the knowledge of life and manners' in her 'two excellent prose performances' (151). Though the text is explicit about the republican historian Catharine Macaulay's 'ardent love of liberty' (145) and about Anna Letitia Barbauld's dissenting background (147), the various writers named in *Dialogues* are celebrated regardless of their, in some cases incompatible, political views and they are imagined as an enlarged Bluestocking circle defined by its literariness: 'The English female authors of the present age are sufficiently numerous to form a very agreeable literary academy; ... Mrs. MONTAGUE, I think, would make a very proper president' (151–2). In *The Unsex'd Females*, Polwhele's notorious anti-Jacobin poem, however, political sympathy overrides literary merit as the primary criterion of acceptability. In the context of war against post-Revolutionary France, *The Unsex'd Females* reinterprets Duncombe's binary divide between a 'modest' and a 'wanton Muse' in order to mount a vicious attack on Mary Wollstonecraft whom, according to Polwhele, 'no decorum checks' in her Revolution-inspired call to women to 'Surpass their rivals in the powers of mind / And vindicate *the Rights of womankind*' (13, 15). The women writers, including Burney (and Montagu), of whom Polwhele approves gather this time round Hannah More who 'may justly be esteemed, as a character, in all points diametrically opposed to Miss Wollstonecraft' (35n.). In a 'voice seraphic', More urges women to 'clai[m] a nation's praise' by adopting her Christianised version of classical 'modest Virtue', which 'In silken fetters bound the obedient throng, / And soften'd despots by the power of song', a form of ambition in which proper patriotism and proper femininity are mutually defining (28, 30, 31). Burney, whom Polwhele places 'above all the Novel-writers that have existed, since the first invention of this delightful species of composition', precisely fits this vision of appropriate feminine influence: her novels 'mix with sparkling humour chaste / Delicious feelings and the purest taste' (34).

Polwhele's division, along crudely drawn political lines, of women writers who had previously been celebrated side by side is objectionable in all kinds of ways. But it is usefully symptomatic of a gradual but significant shift in cultural perceptions of the relationship between gender and reputation which intensified during the 1790s, and according to which, as Harriet Guest has suggested, 'patriotism becomes more prominent than learning'.[17] Typically, Polwhele condemns as 'unsex'd' women whose work he nevertheless admires because, like Charlotte Smith, they are 'infected with the Gallic mania' or, like Helen Maria Williams, they have 'become a politician' (19n., 18n.). In the intensely anti-French atmosphere of the 1790s, when any claims for (female) equality ran the risk of being interpreted as 'Gallic mania' and women's appropriate spheres of activity and subject matter were increasingly restricted, officially at least, to the private and domestic, female patriotism was measured precisely by not 'becom[ing] a politician', by women eschewing any overt involvement in the male world of politics.

This had always been the principle of the leading Bluestockings, and it was a principle explicitly endorsed by Burney in both public and private during the 1790s, in terms which identify her very closely with women's 'own distinctive brand of patriotism', as defined by Linda Colley and associated particularly with Hannah More. Burney's only overtly political work, *Brief Reflections Relative to the Emigrant French Clergy* (1793), exactly fits Colley's model of occasional, focused activism by women who have 'left their customary domesticity only in order to further the greater good'.[18] Prefaced by an anxious 'Apology' for this unwonted excursion beyond 'the allotted boundaries and appointed province of Females', *Brief Reflections* accepts the orthodoxy that the 'privacy ... of [women's] lives is the dictate of common sense', but looks forward to the public honour which will eventually accrue to the modestly anonymous women who join its charitable scheme of relief for refugee clergymen from Revolutionary France (a scheme Hannah More also supported): 'female tradition will not fail to hand down to posterity the formers and protectresses of a plan which, if successful, will exalt for ever the female annals of Great Britain' (iii–iv, 5–6). Predictably enough, the gender politics of *Brief Reflections* were welcomed by the anti-Jacobin *British Critic*, anticipating by some years Burney's appearance in Polwhele's 'female annals': 'The Rights of Women are set in a much more amiable light by this admired novelist, than by the *gentleman-like* Miss Woolstoncraft. She gives up the claim to public exertions in general, but asserts the right of benevolence as belonging more particularly to them.'[19]

As this reviewer recognises, Burney's reputation as a novelist lent weight to her pamphlet which, like *Camilla* three years later, was identified simply as 'By the Author of *Evelina* and *Cecilia*'. But central to Burney's novelistic principles – as well as to her identity as a celebrated woman of letters, schooled in literary circles which 'seemed to exclude the factionalisms of politics'[20] – was the conviction that politics was not the business of her fiction. Her diary from 1796 records a visit to the royal family at Windsor, including a telling exchange with the princesses in response to their excited anticipation of *Camilla*:

> 'There have been so many *bad* books published of that sort,' said Princess Mary, 'that every body should be glad of such a good one.' 'Yes,' said Princess Sophia, '& the Writers are all turned Democrats, they say.'
>
> I now explained that *Politics* were, *all ways*, left out: that ... they were not a *feminine* subject for discussion, & that I even believed, should the little work sufficiently succeed to be at all generally read, it would be a better office to general Readers to carry them wide of all politics, to their domestic fire sides, than to open new matter of endless debate.   (*JL* III, 185–6)

The feminine space of the 'domestic fire side' is presented here, somewhat disingenuously perhaps, as a politics-free zone, a claim which helps Burney defend her novel against two potential lines of attack: the perceived radicalism of much 1790s fiction ('all turned Democrats'); and the standard of novels in general ('so many *bad* books'). Both a particular political position and the quality and status of the novel itself are at stake. For Hannah More as, of course, for Edmund Burke in his anti-revolutionary *Reflections on the Revolution in France*, the domestic fireside, far from being apolitical, is the focus of family affections, of that love for 'the little platoon we belong to in society', which provides the 'first link' in developing the individual's patriotic allegiance to established political systems.[21] As More recognised, the effect is to make the domestic sphere a site of considerable political influence. Burney implicitly endorses More's politics, but her main focus here is the function of (women's) fiction: a concern both narrower and wider than More's Burkean traditionalism. The previous year, while writing *Camilla*, Burney had attempted to define her work: 'I own I do not like calling it a *Novel*: it gives so simply the notion of a mere love story, that I recoil a little from it. I mean it to be *sketches of Characters & morals, put in action*, not a Romance' (*JL* III, 117). Burney's conventionally feminine concern to 'carry [readers] wide of all politics' is, paradoxically, part of her ambition to redefine the novel itself by taking it beyond any narrowly feminine 'notion of a mere love story'.

Though the reviews of *Camilla* were more mixed than those which greeted Burney's previous novels, they confirmed that Burney 'appears without a competitor in the track that [she] has chosen to tread', a judgment which included, from the other side of the political divide, Wollstonecraft's review in the *Analytical*, which paid tribute to 'the sagacity and rectitude of the author's mind' and to a talent 'of the highest order'.[22] Wollstonecraft does comment, however, that 'The incidents, which are to mark out the errours of youth, are frequently only perplexities, forcibly brought forward merely to be disentangled' (465). Respectful of the established woman writer, Wollstonecraft also hints at her own more polemical agenda on behalf of women in the fictional sequel to *Vindication of the Rights of Woman*, which she was just beginning to write. In her unfinished experimental novel, *The Wrongs of Woman*, Wollstonecraft exposes 'matrimonial despotism', mobilising revolutionary language to describe the recalcitrant socio-political structures underpinning 'the wrongs of different classes of women, equally oppressive'.[23] Burney's exquisitely painful depiction of her heroine's 'perplexities' in *Camilla* highlights the oppressive double bind of female modesty and warns against relying too heavily on the flawed judgments of male mentors. But, as Wollstonecraft implies, Camilla's difficulties – like those of Cecilia and Evelina before her – are always susceptible to being 'disentangled' through the comic resolution of the courtship plot which shapes Burney's broad social canvas, confirming rather than disrupting paternalistic structures of authority.

Burney's subject, as she announces it in the opening paragraph of *Camilla*, is instead no less than 'the human heart in its feelings and its changes'; her method, that of the 'investigator of … that amazing assemblage of all possible contrarieties', compared with which the 'historian of human life finds less of difficulty and of intricacy to develop, in its accidents and adventures' (7). Her aim is to 'trace nature, yet blot out personality': to offer a disinterested account of contemporary character in which national or factional politics are ostensibly subsumed by the contrarieties of the human heart. An unobtrusive politics of gender is discernible here in the opposition between 'human life' and 'the human heart', between 'adventures' and 'feelings': Burney's claim for the superior complexity of what would come to be known as psychological realism over a fiction of incident is in effect a defence of skills traditionally associated with sensibility and the feminine, and which can be learned by 'the domestic fire side' – or by reading novels. But to make claims for fiction is, after all, entirely acceptable within the 'allotted boundaries and appointed province of Females', and by keeping gender firmly subordinate to the politics of genre, Burney enabled her 1790s novel to sidestep the politicised critical atmosphere of that decade.

In fact, as Margaret Doody has observed, Burney's 1790s novel is *The Wanderer*, published in 1814, rather than *Camilla*.[24] Not so much because *The Wanderer* is set in the '90s, 'During the dire reign of the terrific Robespierre' (*Wanderer*, 11); nor even because in the dedication to her father Burney notes the impossibility of 'attempt[ing] to delineate ... any picture of actual human life, without reference to the French Revolution'; but because of the way in which the novel announces gender politics, 'female difficulties', as its subject and, as Ellis–Juliet's narrative unravels, makes them central to an anti-revolutionary position (6). In the dedication, Burney once again claims to have eschewed partisan politics: 'I held political topics to be without my sphere, or beyond my skill'; again, she offers 'a composition upon general life, manners, and characters; without any species of personality ... or of national partiality'; and, again, her appropriately feminine hope is that her novel retains 'the power of interesting the affections' (5, 4, 9). But, though it is true that *The Wanderer* avoids 'political topics' in its narrowest definition, it is clearly influenced by the politicisation of gender which took place in the revolutionary atmosphere of the 1790s. Ellis's passionate cry against female dependency – 'how insufficient ... is a FEMALE to herself! How ... for ever fresh-springing are her DIFFICULTIES, when she would owe her existence to her own exertions!' (275) – restates the message of Mary Hays's radical novel *The Victim of Prejudice* (1799). The everywoman narrative of Ellis's doomed attempts to find sustained employment reads like a practical critique of Priscilla Wakefield's advice, in her *Reflections on the Present Condition of the Female Sex* (1798), on the kinds of work through which women at different social levels might become self-sufficient. And Ellis's situation is revealed to stem ultimately from despotism – though it is the despotism of the French Revolutionaries rather than of the *ancien regime*. As the depiction of the would-be radical Elinor Joddrel and the novel's final restoration of Ellis–Juliet to her aristocratic family also make clear, *The Wanderer* confirms Burney's social and political conservatism. But, unlike her earlier novels, it is explicit in its recognition that the personal and the political, gender politics and social structures, are inseparable. One of the most interesting aspects of Burney's career is its longevity. Her last novel suggests a further stage in the process of gender politicisation, whereby the female novelist lauded and nurtured by those earlier forms of sociability absorbs the explicit focus on 'female difficulties' in the work of 1790s radical women into her still essentially conservative vision.

At the time *The Wanderer* was published, Burney's position in the canon of English fiction seemed assured. *Evelina*, *Cecilia* and *Camilla* were all reprinted in Anna Letitia Barbauld's influential fifty-volume collection, *The British Novelists*, published in 1810. In her introduction to Burney's work, Barbauld reiterated the established view that: 'Scarcely any name, if any, stands higher in the list of novel-writers than that of Miss BURNEY', and praised Burney's achievement in terms which transcend gender: '[she] has observed human nature, both in high and low life, with the quick and penetrating eye of genius'.[25] The reviews of *The Wanderer* were far less complimentary, however. Burney was accused of being out of time, and particularly so in her representation of gender. Thus the *Monthly* complained that Burney seemed unaware that 'an alteration insensibly progressive has effected considerable change in our idea of the gentleman and the lady'; and the *Critical* objected to the old-fashioned 'prudish refinement of sentiment' which 'create[s] [its] own misery' for women: 'it is now time for the honour of one sex, that the other should be brought to believe what is absolutely true, that ... to betray unprotected youth and beauty, is not uniformly the first object of every man who happens to encounter them'.[26] Most damning was William Hazlitt, who used his review in the *Edinburgh* to write a political history of the novel in which Burney is acknowledged to hold 'a distinguished place', but as 'a mere common observer of manners, – and also a very woman'. Hazlitt believed that Burney's novels offer merely 'a kind of supplement and gloss' to the 'original text' of the great male novelists, and the 'difficulties in which she involves her heroines are indeed "Female Difficulties;" – they are difficulties created out of nothing'.[27] Hazlitt's gendered judgments are symptomatic of more than just his usual fraught misogyny. They demonstrate that, where the still fragile reputation of female novelists was concerned, attitudes to the politics of gender difference had changed little, in spite of the reviewers' claims to the contrary: as all these reviews confirm, Burney's overt focus on gender inequalities, signalled in *The Wanderer*'s subtitle, serves to undermine the decorous femininity which, in an earlier moment, had helped secure her canonical standing alongside Richardson, Fielding and Smollett.

The Wanderer's political and social belatedness and its consequent negative reception do not invalidate the status accorded to Burney in Austen's *Northanger Abbey* manifesto. But they do signal a shift in taste which has its roots in the patriotic anxieties of the 1790s and which is represented by the novels of Austen herself. Walter Scott admired *Evelina* and *Cecilia* as 'uncommonly fine compositions', but in his famous review of *Emma* he praised Austen's new realism, in which by 'keeping close to common incidents, and to such characters as occupy the ordinary walks of life, she has produced sketches of such spirit and originality, that we never miss the excitation which depends upon a narrative of uncommon events ... In this class she stands almost alone'.[28] Austen's deceptively decorous domestic realism, first conceived in the 1790s, inherits Burney's ambivalent gender politics: both her essential conservatism and her acute awareness of 'female difficulties'. But unlike Burney, and because of her, Austen was content to announce that her anonymous first novel was 'By a Lady' and to identify the best examples of contemporary fiction as being by women.

NOTES

1. Review of *Camilla, Critical Review* 18 (1796), 26.
2. Review of *Evelina, Critical Review* 46 (1778), 202; review of *Cecilia, Monthly Review* 67 (1782), 453.
3. Peter Garside, James Raven and Rainer Schöwerling, gen. eds., *The English Novel 1770–1829: A Bibliographical Survey of Prose Fiction Published in the British Isles*, 2 vols. (Oxford: Oxford University Press, 2000), I, 26–7. 16 novels in 1778 compares with 60 in 1771, the annual total rising again gradually through the 1780s to 80 in 1788.
4. Duncombe, *The Feminiad*, lines 142, 151 and p. 15nn.
5. Reviews of *The Unfortunate Union* (1778) and *The History of Melinda Harley, Yorkshire* (1777), in *The English Novel 1770–1820*, I, 269, 254.
6. Scott, *The Female Advocate*, line 258 and pp. 22n., 24–5nn.
7. Burney quotes from Shakespeare, *The Merchant of Venice*, IV.i.185–6.
8. Janice Farrar Thaddeus, *Frances Burney: A Literary Life* (Houndmills, Basingstoke: Macmillan, 2000), 30.
9. Review of *The History of Miss Temple. By a Young Lady* (1777), in *The English Novel 1770–1820*, I, 263.
10. *Thraliana: The Diary of Mrs. Hester Lynch Thrale (Later Mrs. Piozzi)*, ed. Katharine C. Balderston, 2 vols., 2nd edn (Oxford: Clarendon Press, 1951), I, 329.
11. *Thraliana*, I, 329n; *Early Journals*, IV, 293; letter to Elizabeth Montagu from W. W. Pepys, 22 July 1782, quoted in *Mrs. Montagu, 'Queen of the Blues': Her Letters and Friendships from 1762 to 1800*, ed. Reginald Blunt, 2 vols. (London: Constable, 1923), II, 121.
12. *Mrs. Montagu, 'Queen of the Blues'*, II, 222–3.
13. *Monthly Review* 67 (1782), 453.
14. 'Observations on Female Literature in General', *The Westminster Magazine* 4 (1776), 284, 285.
15. *Ibid.*, 285; *Monthly Review* 67 (1782), 456.
16. James Raven, 'Historical introduction: the novel comes of age' in *The English Novel 1770–1820*, I, 34–5.
17. Harriet Guest, *Small Change: Women, Learning, Patriotism, 1750–1810* (Chicago and London: University of Chicago Press, 2000), 175.
18. Linda Colley, *Britons: Forging the Nation 1707–1837* (London: Pimlico, 1992), 281, 280.
19. *British Critic* 2 (1793), 450.
20. Guest, 'Bluestocking feminism', *Huntington Library Quarterly* 65 (2002), 63.
21. Edmund Burke, *Reflections on the Revolution in France* (1790), ed. Conor Cruise O'Brien (Harmondsworth: Penguin, 1969), 135.

22. Reviews of *Camilla*: *Critical Review* 18 (1796), 26; [Mary Wollstonecraft], *Analytical Review* 24 (1796) in *The Works of Mary Wollstonecraft*, ed. Janet Todd and Marilyn Butler, 7 vols. (London: Pickering and Chatto, 1989), VII, 465, 467.
23. Wollstonecraft, *The Wrongs of Woman*, *Works*, I, 84.
24. Margaret Anne Doody, *Frances Burney: The Life in the Works* (Cambridge: Cambridge University Press, 1988), 318.
25. Rpt. in Anna Letitia Barbauld, *Selected Poetry and Prose*, ed. William McCarthy and Elizabeth Kraft (Peterborough, Ontario: Broadview Press, 2002), 443, 449.
26. Reviews of *The Wanderer*: *Monthly Review* 76 (1815), 412; *Critical Review* 4th ser. 5 (1814), 407, 408.
27. [William Hazlitt], review of *The Wanderer*, *Edinburgh Review* 24 (1815), 335, 336, 337.
28. Walter Scott to Matthew Weld Hartsonge, 18 July 1814, *The Letters of Sir Walter Scott*, ed. H. J. C. Grierson (London: Constable, 1932), III, 465; [Walter Scott], review of *Emma*, *Quarterly Review* 14 (1815), in *Jane Austen: The Critical Heritage*, ed. B. C. Southam (London: Routledge and Kegan Paul, 1968), 63–4.

8

BETTY RIZZO

Burney and society

The *cri du sang* or 'call of blood' topos is common in French drama of the seventeenth and eighteenth centuries and in the English novel of the second half of the eighteenth. It was a topos used by Burney in both *Evelina* (her instant sympathy for Macartney) and *The Wanderer* (the instant sympathy of Lady Aurora Granville and Lord Melville for Juliet). For use here I would suggest an even more common and corollary topos, the *cri de l'âme* or 'call of the soul', also commonly used by Burney, in which two superior spirits recognise one another in spite of confusing circumstances. In her novels, though obstacles may intervene, all of Burney's lovers enjoy this rapport. Both these topoi, but particularly the second, depend upon the new hegemonic standard dependent on merit rather than blood, a standard that could instantly propel an individual to equality with aristocrats, to superiority over them. In their lives some of the Burney family were familiar with this recognition. In many ways their careers hung on this new standard.

Apart from the class into which she was born – her father was just struggling to enter the situation of the middling sort – no ambitious young writer could hope to replicate the advantages of Burney's early life. From her first years she mixed with gifted adults of varying character and station. Garrick was a playmate. At Drury Lane she had free access to his box and, familiar with the repertory of plays, could mimic the actors in appropriate diction and style, and invent and enact their further adventures. Her acquaintance, she informed the Queen in 1787, had been very numerous and very mixed, taking in most stations in life and most political parties. She had the opportunity to observe the characteristics of every social class: the servants, her low city cousins, artists and musicians, professional men, and the provincial gentry of King's Lynn. She also glimpsed the fashionable world, who could be seen at the theatre, but she was able to note closely, without interacting with, this world at her father's Sunday-night concerts. Perhaps most important of all, she had her beloved sister Susan to whom she recounted and interpreted experience, moulded it into stories, and so readied it for future literary use.

As soon as she could use a pencil, she was composing on paper. An urge to write almost alone distinguished her from her quasi-twin Susan. Unable to read until she was eight, she resorted to remembering speech. Her ability to memorise an entire conversation, though not effortlessly acquired and though deliberately cultivated, became remarkable. In her journal of May 1768, after a family party to Greenwich, Burney confessed a failure of memory about the conversation, though she had wracked her brains. But in November of that year, after a three-hour tête-à-tête with Alexander Seton, she wrote a long record of the talk, noting, 'I am quite surprised to find how much of his Conversation I have remembered but as there was only him & myself, it was not very difficult' (*EJL* I, 44–9). The reproduction of conversation, with attention to the peculiarities of the speakers' delivery, was already an object. In this the stage was her model, and her intention to produce literary works was already making itself known. Constrained by gender, she had nevertheless female playwrights and novelists as models. Delicacy was already a family responsibility but she knew that her father was an indefatigable writer, as were many of his friends. Most respectable (male) writers, in fact, originated from his own station, that of the well-educated professional – clergymen, physicians, lawyers, travellers – who, in order to prosper, advertised their talents by instructing and codifying the volume of information that flooded the culture and demanded print for its dissemination. Johnson, Garrick, Hawkesworth, Arthur Young, Baretti and James "Abyssinia" Bruce all wrote, and even the aristocratic Fulke Greville and his wife Frances, who had taught the young Charles Burney how to live in the World, wrote. Dorothy Young, her step-mother's greatest friend, was a dedicated writer. Among all their other acquaintance, the Burney house was thronged by writers and was filled with their books.

Moreover, on her deathbed her mother had enjoined Esther, older than Frances by three years, to write notes to her in heaven. The desolated Frances may well have begun her writings in answer to this injunction. Her first novel (the destroyed 'History of Caroline Evelyn') and her second, *Evelina*, both deal essentially with the trials of a young maternally deprived girl. As the age of the heroines (Cecilia, Juliet) matures along with the author, there is the same persistent lack in their lives; even Camilla painfully misses her mother at the crucial period. From first to last, Burney's books may be viewed as, in a sense, letters to her mother.

Despite the family's catholic acquaintance, though, the class with which Burney was most familiar and most comfortable all her life was the gentry. Burney's gentry was composed of both the pseudo-gentry, partially refined and superiorly gifted men like her father, who lived genteelly but had not the resources to establish their children in the same comfort, and that portion of the true gentry who derived from no particularly distinguished stock and thus could not disdain the Burneys as Hester Thrale was wont to do. 'The Burneys are I believe', she wrote in 1779, 'a very low Race of Mortals'; and in 1786, on the announcement of Burney's Court appointment, she wrote, 'What a glorious Country is ours! where Talents & Conduct are sufficient to draw mean Birth & original Poverty out of the Shades of Life, & set their Merit to ripen in the Sun.' In 1780 she was aghast with horror at the threat of a romantic involvement between young Richard Burney and her daughter Susan:

> I shall if I don't look sharp, be prettily rewarded for fondling the Burneys so . . . my second Daughter Susan; (only ten Years old thank God;) declares it her *fixed* and *determinate* Resolution to marry the Doctor's Son Dick, as soon as She is one & twenty. chearful enough![1]

Thrale herself was always torn between her love and admiration for the Burneys and an almost involuntary contempt for their origins, for Charles Burney's father had been a musician/dancing master/portrait painter and Burney's mother had 'nothing to boast from parental dignity, parental opulence, nor – strange, and stranger yet to tell – parental worth' (*Memoirs*, I, 63).

What was distressing Hester Thrale, in fact, was the conflict between the old class system and the new meritocratic standard. She hung uncomfortably suspended between them. The old system was based on family and money, and she took excessive pride in her own bloodlines. Married to a commonly descended but very rich brewer and revered for her literary talents, Thrale was also attracted to the new meritocratic class system (explicitly delineated in *Pamela*, where the heroine is valued for her character instead of her birth) and under its standards, she could recognise Charles and Frances Burney as equals. Perforce espousing the new standard, the Burneys and their friends could quietly assume a superiority to the more useless members of 'the World', but they were dependent for their prosperity upon the patronage and the countenance of that World and, in order to succeed, were constrained to a purity of conduct not observed by their betters. Most of the close friends of the Burneys could make only a meritocratic claim to preeminence; Burney and her father, without money and birth, stood on the same ground as the lowly heroine of Samuel Richardson's *Pamela* and, like Pamela, had to exhibit moral virtues. Social virtues were also required, and Burney habitually assessed new male acquaintance by their exhibition of gentlemanly qualities.

Though Charles Burney dedicated so much of his rare leisure time to cultivating useful aristocrats and musicians, his truly disinterested friendship was for the professional men with whom he was most comfortable. And his second wife, Elizabeth Allen, proud of deriving from the provincial gentry of King's Lynn and self-confident in her fitness for society, but indelicate and often raucous, never attained the friendship of such men; at Streatham and at Samuel Crisp's home in Chessington alike she was barely tolerated, and she was never invited into the great World that welcomed, because of their achievements and, equally important, their cultivation, her husband and her stepdaughter. From early days, Burney witnessed her father in pursuit of lucrative patronage struggling to earn admission to the great World through a too obligingly facile charm and perfect manners, but, more importantly, through his distinguished writing. She judged the intensity of his desire by his dedicated and punishing application. Burney was to employ her charm more subtly, but to her writing she applied herself with his own compulsive fervour, thereby demonstrating a social ambition like his, derived from his, and imitative of his. Charles Burney had not come naturally by his delicately cultivated manner, but he had assumed it well and Burney was careful to replicate it. Both father and daughter were to profit by repetitive operations of the *cri de l'âme*.

Burney herself, while most impressed by the family's best-acclaimed visitors (another indication of her father's standard), demanded elegance, delicacy and conversational powers from them as well. She often denigrated those who fell short of these qualities. Though in 1775 Burney found her suitor Thomas Barlow to have an excellent character, her objection was that he '[seemed] to know but little of the World', and though worthy, his language was stiff and uncommon and he had 'no elegance of manners' (*EJL* II, 116). It is fairly clear that these are the reasons for her invincible distaste and the near terror with which she responded to family approval of his advances. The Burneys, ever desirous of improving their station in life, were naturally fearful of falling. From the start, Charles Burney and his family were involved in the struggle for upward mobility and sought to rise from modest origins to the elegance of the Grevilles.

Important early social models for Burney were therefore Garrick, who with his mimicry and fun, his ability to enact any social station, inspired and directed her, and Samuel Crisp, who had lived in the World and who could demonstrate to Burney a distinguishing elegance in both manner and writing. With good reason, Crisp contributed to the mentor-portrait in *Evelina* of Mr Villars, who, like Crisp, provided his young charge with a rhetorical model. A third important and less recognised touchstone was her father's early patron and friend, the tonish Fulke Greville, and his wife Frances, her godmother. These, during his youthful period as Greville's companion, were the crucial influences on Charles Burney, and from Charles Burney's experience, Frances knew them well. Though Frances characteristically refuted the notion that in her writing she ever made specific capital of anyone, the Grevilles appeared as Lord Orville and as the sarcastic Mrs Selwyn of *Evelina*, at a time when Charles Burney described Fulke as the first gentleman of the age. Later, when the Grevilles were no longer cynosures and in the process of separating, Frances, perhaps recalling how little her godmother Frances Greville had done for her, portrayed them as the proud Delviles of *Cecilia*.

Both Charles Burney and his wife were gregarious, and from the start the company, of all kinds, in the Burney household was almost dizzyingly constant: visitors in the morning (till dinner time) or for after-dinner tea; but these gradually varied as Burney's father slaved for recognition and exerted his formidable charms to attract useful acquaintance. The upgrading of the family acquaintance presented a model of social advancement. In 1769, at sixteen, Burney considered a party 'large and *brilliant*' that consisted of Greville, Hawkesworth and Crisp in company with her cousin Charles Rousseau Burney, 'two gentlemen named Vincent', the wife and daughter of the mayor of King's Lynn, and a King's Lynn attorney (*EJL* I, 62–3). The Sunday evening music parties added visitors, such as aristocratic music lovers Sir William Hamilton, Lord Sandwich, Lord and Lady Edgcumbe, and Lady Mary Duncan. Burney at nineteen labelled a concert in May 1772 a 'select party' to which Sir William Hamilton, William Beckford, Uvedale Price (author of *Essays on the Picturesque* in 1794), an old Poland Street neighbour and experimental scientist Keane Fitzgerald, John Bagnall, 'a learned and rich philosopher' and Dr John Glen King, a Norfolk vicar, came, but Burney, recognising her father's immense social talent, even then noted almost wistfully, 'If my Father was disposed to *cultivate* with the World, what a delightful Acquaintance he might have!' (*EJL* I, 217–20). He was precisely, of course, disposed to cultivate with the world and Burney, like her father, would carry a passport for moving freely among classes. But perhaps what at the moment she found lacking in their acquaintance were polite, aristocratic women, for these, including most emphatically Mrs Greville, eschewed her stepmother. Frances Greville, who had come once to meet the new Mrs Burney and never returned (*Memoirs*, I, 201), had perforce to drop her god-daughter's acquaintance. The lack of elegant female models was a serious drawback to the Burney daughters.

The publication of Charles Burney's discoveries during his French and Italian tour (1771) and his German tour (1773) led to a great many more delightful acquaintances, and the Burneys had, in October 1774, moved to St Martin's Street to a house formerly belonging to Isaac Newton; his observatory at the top of the house bestowed the cachet of meritocratic lineage on the family. A concert in November 1775 was attended by the Russian visitors

Prince Orloff, Baron Demidov and Catherine the Great's General Bauer, the Dean of Winchester, Lady Edgcumbe, Charles Boone, Mr and Mrs Brudenal, Anthony Chamier, Lord Bruce and James Harris of Salisbury – a combination of the most fashionable of music lovers and exalted of foreign visitors come to see the sights. So many had applied for admission that a second concert had to be given two weeks later and was attended by the Earl of Ashburnham, Lord and Lady Edgcumbe, Mr Brudenal, the French ambassador the Comte de Guines, the baron and baroness of Deiden, Lord Barrington and the Earl of Sandwich (*EJL* II, 180–90). In addition, that lion of lions, the Tahitian Omai, came to dinner (*EJL* II, 59–63).

Meanwhile, such relations as Charles Burney's mother Ann Cooper Burney and his two sisters Ann (Nanny) and Rebecca (Becky), who kept Gregg's coffee house in York Street, though privately loved and well visited, were publicly unacknowledged and did not mingle with the visitors in St Martin's Street. Neither did the unacknowledgeable, but loveable James Sleepe, Burney's mother's city brother, and his two daughters Esther and Frances, candidates for the models for the Branghton sisters in *Evelina*.

Circumstances changed. Charles Burney was concerned not only in the coffee house, but among other affairs in the fashionable Pantheon (1772) which provided him with privileged access to its musicians. The family kept up a good show of prosperity; the girls went about to the theatre, the opera and public amusements. They were taught music and dancing but not, to the frustration of Elizabeth Allen Burney, housekeeping. And the family subscribed to moral standards, to which in earlier days, when Charles Burney had to take his pupils where he could find them, they had scarcely applied. One of those earlier pupils had been Maria Susannah Sloper, the natural daughter of his old friend Susannah Cibber, with whom Esther Burney cultivated a friendship. A friend of the family of whom Burney herself was very fond was Sarah Ford Colman, the actress mistress of the playwright George Colman and, before she married him, mother of George Colman the Younger, his celebrated playwright son; her daughter by another lover, Harriet Ford, was also an early pupil and friend of the Burney girls (*EJL* I, 181, 40 and n. 145). The young actress Jenny Barsanti, also a pupil, became a favourite friend of Burney's until 1775, when Burney seriously reconsidered the intimacy, deciding at last she might continue to call since Barsanti was 'so good a Girl, living wholly with her mother & being almost always at Home' (*EJL* II, 81). Nor in early days was Burney unable to appreciate (as her father always did) and record a shady joke, especially when sanctioned by an aristocrat: again in 1775 when the stately parade of attendants that preceded the singer Gabrielli was described, Mr Brudenal inquired as to the disposition of a lover, Lord March, and Burney recorded, for Chessington's amusement, Lady Edgcumbe's reply, 'O, ... *he*, you know, is *Lord of the Bedchamber*' (*EJL* II, 184–5).

In time, though, it became clear that Charles Burney's growing access as music master to the daughters of great houses depended not only on his cultivated demeanour but on the impeccability of his life and acquaintance, and his daughter's reputation, once it had with *Evelina* become a matter of public interest, required the same care. It was, then, not a prudish disgust with the fallen that made Burney later turn (albeit reluctantly) from those entrancing friends with tarnished reputations. (Her sister Esther, after all, had been born a month before her parents' marriage.) But it was an association with such reputations that Burney and her father latterly feared and eschewed, and therefore latterly she too publicly resigned her connection with Mary Cholmondeley (to whom she owed much of the success of *Evelina*), Madame de Genlis and Madame de Staël (both of whom, like Cholmondeley, she loved), and the Bluestocking Mary Monckton, known for having seduced Lord Cork from his wife. Already in June 1775, approached in the park by an old friend, Miss Lalauze, now known to be a mistress with a keeper, Burney answered her coldly and Hetty turned from her abruptly, for 'It is ... impossible & improper to keep up acquaintance with a Female who has lost her character, however sincerely they may be objects of Pity' (*EJL* II, 153). The lost character was indeed the point. Burney was quite willing to countenance other women who had similarly erred but whose errors had been overlooked. These included Henry Thrale's sister Lady Lade, who was known to have had a child with Sir Philip Jennings Clerke, and the pleasure-loving Harriet Bannister North, a patroness of the Worcestershire Burneys and wife of the Bishop of Worcester, but a woman whom Thrale identified as a former mistress of the wicked Lord Lyttelton.[2] It was the family reputation, and thus its livelihood, that Burney had to guard, a necessity that drove the entire family to agonies of resourceful concealment over the too-often repeated peccadilloes of their own sons. The prosperity of the meritocratic professionals still depended entirely on the countenance of the aristocracy, and the aristocracy claimed the prerogative of enforcing on the acknowledged meritocrats a purity of life in no way similar to their own. Significantly, it was the same purity that they demanded of their domestic servants.

It was, then, in a tacit declaration of station to the world that Charles Burney refused to have his daughters brought up as notable housewives, despite his second wife's urging. As a result, Burney never did become a competent housekeeper. In a social way, the Burney girls attended a series of balls where they danced and flirted, and the balls were given by a variety of undistinguished hosts. In 1770, Burney attended a ball given for his pupils by

Charles Lalauze, a French dancer and dancing master, to which he invited his daughter and others of his acquaintance, including the Burneys. The girls went to balls hosted by the feckless Rev. Pugh and the careless Mrs Pringle and met an assortment of persons, most of whom are not heard of again. Her father's visitors were now often distinguished; the dancing partners of his daughters were not. Marriage was a serious arrangement and, as Thrale well knew, contact of marriageable sons with inappropriate young women was to be avoided.

In fact, one family problem was the seeming inability of the girls to marry well, a difficulty that lay behind the willingness to perceive the charms of Thomas Barlow. With no bloodlines and no money, despite their good looks, their wit and their affability, they offered very little towards a proper establishment, and the kind of genteel husband Esther, Frances and Susan desired proved remarkably elusive. (Susan appeared to have married one in Molesworth Phillips, but her lack of fortune was probably an important cause of her husband's subsequent cruelty.) Genteel candidates considered marriage with the daughters of Charles Burney as outré, if not beyond possibility. Again and again, Burney was viewed, because of her writing, almost as a member of an anomalous third sex, and due to her background, station and circumstance, she was considered impossible to marry. Instead of receiving respectful suitors, she encountered the attractive male who considered it appropriate to transgress the social boundaries with a novelist. 'Polite' young men raised improper subjects, as did the one who asked her if she had read *Les Liaisons Dangereuses*. Like George Cambridge, Captain Fuller at Brighton, Captain Boissier at Bath, Colonel Digby at court and Jeremiah Crutchley at Streatham, they paid her undue, sometimes comically fervent, attentions, often arousing expectations, but they never proposed, probably never having intended to in the first place. In the same manner, Alexander Seton broke Hetty's heart, but he had already demonstrated his conviction that the Burneys were beyond the social pale when he called and sat through a three-hour tête-à-tête with the sixteen-year-old Burney (*EJL* I, 44–9). His perception was validated by her not putting a proper end to his visit after twenty minutes, or rather by her having received him at all.

But the publication of *Evelina* seemed to have changed everything. Hester Thrale at once saw the advantage Burney might be to her. Her own situation was so complex. Of some royal bloodlines (as she always took pains to establish), she had been married to a rich but low-born brewer who, though he had made the grand tour with the high-born William Henry Lyttelton, later Baron Westcote, and was an MP, took her to live in a house next to his brewery in Southwark, not a place where fashionable ladies could visit.

The family had acquired a villa at Streatham in which they spent the summer months, and they also visited Brighton and Tunbridge where they mixed with a great deal of company, but Thrale could keep up social relations with fashionable women only in these watering places or when her husband rented a house in London for the season. And, in 1778, she had daughters to bring out; Queeney was already thirteen. Yet they could not move to London and leave the detestable brewery behind. Instead they brought company to Streatham, where there was the attraction of almost unheard-of luxury. Crisp wrote of a dinner in 1780,

> everything was most splendid and magnificent – two courses of 21 Dishes each, besides Removes; and after that a dessert of a piece with the Dinner – Pines and Fruits of all Sorts, Ices, Creams, &c., &c., &c., without end – everything in plate, of which such a profusion, and such a Side Board: I never saw such at any Nobleman's.[3]

At this table, Burney herself frequently ate only morsels of such provisions as bread and fruit and sipped only water, as though denying the seduction of such extravagance.

Henry Thrale's strategy in 1766 of bringing Johnson to live with him for half the week brought eminent (meritocratic) male company, but women did not often make the journey from town and the company were ordinarily not men of aristocratic birth. There was one parliamentary colleague, Sir Philip Jennings Clerke, and his old companion of the Grand Tour, William Henry Lyttelton, but the others were the connections of brewing companies, William Seward, Dr Peter Calvert, probably John Cator, a timber merchant with a business near the brewery, and authors such as Arthur Murphy. The company, in fact, was similar to the company at St Martin's Street. In 1773, one dinner party included Sir Joshua Reynolds and his sister Frances, Goldsmith, Giuseppe Baretti and James Beattie – all meritocrats.[4] In 1775, Sir Joshua Reynolds introduced Thrale to Elizabeth Montagu, who became a great friend (and rival). Montagu may, on her husband's account, have affected aristocracy, but she was also, on her own and her family's account, a meritocrat. So was Lucas Pepys, an affable doctor who had married the Countess of Rothes.

To make up a female constituency, Hester Thrale had used as guests and companions her distant cousin Margaret Owen (no wit), the lovely Sophia Streatfeild with whom Henry Thrale fell in love, and the lively young Fanny Browne, attractive to the males but of no intellectual weight, who in September 1779 removed herself through a feckless elopement. The portraits by Joshua Reynolds that lined the library walls at Streatham were of the favourite familiars: Lord Sandys, William Henry Lyttelton (in 1776 Lord

Westcote), Mrs Thrale and Queeney, Murphy, Goldsmith, Reynolds, Henry Thrale, Johnson's friend the Oxford jurist Robert Chambers, Garrick, Baretti, Charles Burney, Burke and Johnson – of these the first two were barons and the rest meritocrats. Burney might have met all of these in St Martin's Street. Though in joining the Thrales at Streatham, Burney was encountering undreamt-of luxury, she was entering the great World only to the extent that the great World eagerly sought and accepted her. That this was a huge change was observed by Samuel Crisp, who in 1779 thought that '*occasion'd by Change of Circumstance and Station*' he might hear less frequently from her *(EJL* III, 261).

Hester Thrale, probably stirred by the need soon to present Queeney and to marry her advantageously, needed seriously to mix in society with the ton in a manner more satisfactory than heretofore. But Thrale was never, despite her efforts, taken up by the aristocracy. In autumn 1778, with Queeney, she essayed Tunbridge, where she entered into her usual verbal jousting with Elizabeth Montagu and aroused the curiosity of the Duchess of Devonshire, who, Thrale reported, had requested to be introduced to her and considered following Thrale to Brighton.

> The Duchess of Devonshire, who has every thing that Heaven can give except Health and a Son, will absolutely try for Celebrity among the Wits, & to that Humour I am indebted for all her Civilities I suppose. She talked of coming here in a Week, and said She hoped to find *me* here.[5]

For her own part, the duchess wrote of Thrale, 'I have great curiosity to know her, her singularity will amuse me, & like our books one may draw something out of her', but in the end it did not do. The duchess reported, 'Mrs Thrale seems certainly very clever & she entertains me very much, her fault is having a vulgarity about her that seeks to be fine.'[6] So though Thrale apparently remained unaware that the acquaintance had been dropped, it was. Now with Burney, a public toast, in tow, she might more readily contrive the result she desired. But the word had gone out against her: in her determination to score as a wit, she had a showiness, a fine vulgarity, a vulgar fineness, and that remained that.

Burney was introduced at Streatham in July 1778. After her initial trepidation, she found that she did very well there. The society was very much a meritocracy, but one that demanded, beside achievement (and, even better, fame), moderate cultivation, but immoderate wit. Among these companions, Hester Thrale appeared to be, as Charlotte Burney observed in 1810, 'of her shining qualities ... unconscious, there is no arrogance, she is as artless, easy, & unaffected as if all her companions were her equals'.[7] With Johnson her prize lion and Murphy a prize cub, she could subscribe to the standard of meritocracy easily enough. Meritocracy had a further attraction for Thrale: she had a prevailing thirst for admiration and wonder that would never have been accorded her by the World, and she rarely admitted anyone to Streatham who did not, even in the presence of Johnson, administer to her thirst. Literary achievement was therefore an important measure of eminence at Streatham. Burney soon found, however, that the greatest meritocratic qualification at Streatham was wit, or 'flash'. The inner circle prized that quality above all. But such an intimate circle could not cannibalise and had an implicit need of butts to exercise their wit upon. These were thankfully plentiful. There were the neighbouring Pitches, Tattersalls and Rose Fuller, and more intimately there were John Cator, Merlin the inventor, Peggy Owen and a variety of others who, unconscious of ridicule, remained delighted with admission to the house and its table. These personages were vital to the exercise of wit and mimicry. A staple of Charles Burney's humour had been the benign ridicule of various butts, but in St Martin's Street these were not residents. Burney had now, therefore, to join in, to share meaningful glances at table while suppressing laughter, perforce later to use her powers of mimicry and to sharpen her mastery of such particular rhetorical peculiarities as Cator's, which were transferred literally to *Cecilia* into the character of Mr Hobson.

After 1778, every literate person in London wanted a look at the author of *Evelina*, and Burney was taken about to meet the Bluestockings. Significantly, this led to much respectful acquaintance but few lasting friendships. She apparently found the company affected. Elizabeth Montagu, who would always remain a privileged acquaintance, had attacked *Evelina* at Tunbridge in 1778, and it is quite unlikely that the ebullient Thrale had failed to tell Burney so – before the projection of *The Witlings*. *The Witlings*, in fact, was probably an enactment of Johnson's vigorous advice (which hardly makes sense otherwise): '*Down* with her, Burney! – *down* with her! – spare her not! attack her, fight her, & *down* with her at once!' (*EJL* III, 151). Burney never considered Elizabeth Vesey graced with any talent but that of bringing others comfortably together, and Vesey later became a butt, ridiculed at her own parties, by Burney and George Cambridge. The spirited Mary Monckton was later to be repudiated for her alleged affair with the 7th Earl of Cork before his wife's death, though he afterwards married her. From her contempt, Burney excepted the minor Bluestocking Mrs Ord, Elizabeth Carter, whom she revered, and Mary Delany, niece of Lord Lansdowne and intimate friend of the Duchess of Portland, who had, however, fallen on hard times – and who was to prove an unlucky intimate precisely because she *was* an aristocrat and a happy courtier.

Thrale's own feelings toward the aristocracy were made clear at Brighton in 1779 when Burney and Queeney saw her trick the Duchess of Ancaster out of the best seat at a ship launching and retain it, murmuring 'How comfortable it is to stand here at *one's own* Window!' despite the duchess's hints as she with her daughter peered round the interloper. 'I never give way to folks because they are people of Quality', she later explained. 'I never got any thing from *them*, so why should they from *me*?' (*EJL* III, 387–8). Though both were at Brighton at the time, the duchess clearly, then, did not 'know' Thrale.

Burney, well aware of the Duchess of Devonshire's advances at Tunbridge, had not understood Thrale's social limitations, writing on their arrival at Brighton in 1780, 'Since we came hither, I have seen nobody that I know, & Mr. & Mrs. T. very few, – but we are in the *way* to *know*, soon, all that we *see*' (*EJL* III, 359). True enough at Brighton they saw, but they did not mingle with, such tonish folk as the duchess, Topham Beauclerk and his wife Lady Di, her sister Lady Pembroke, and Lord and Lady Sefton. As everyone was eager to know Miss Burney and since she was already familiar with the music-loving Seftons, it is likely that the obstacle was an undesirable intimacy with Thrale, pronounced by the duchess as 'so finely vulgar'.

But in the dizzying months after the publication of *Evelina*, Burney met hundreds of fine acquaintance in intense confrontations. 'You are now at school – the great school of the World', Crisp wrote Burney at Bath in 1780, 'where swarms of New Ideas, & new Characters will continually present themselves before You' (*EJL* IV, 73). Still at Bath, Hester Thrale kept the small party of her husband, Queeney, Burney, and herself, somewhat to themselves, affecting a *chosen* choiceness and attending no balls till the last, visiting a limited set of acquaintances (that notably included Montagu) and her friend Mrs Byron, wife of the admiral 'Foul Weather' Jack, and a rather artistic set – the Bowdler family, Thomas Whalley, a dilettante writer, and as always, with Thrale's eye to her husband's ailments, a number of well-known, sometimes literary, physicians. Aware that Thrale had already made an acquaintance with her, Burney noted on 18 April that the Duchess of Devonshire had arrived at Bath, but no advances ensued; the duchess, though later in 1791 she courted Burney, had ruled and set her face against Thrale (*EJL* IV, 66; *JL* I, 45–61). Moreover, Thrale required of her set not only loyalty, but also subjugation. She snubbed Edward Jerningham, probably because, having played upon the harp and sung, he had awaited, unavailingly, adulation for himself; Jerningham demonstrated his aversion to this snub by publicly hanging upon Mrs Coke of Norfolk, instead of Thrale, who wrote, 'all *my* Worshippers wondered' (*EJL* IV, 82–3).[8] Christopher Anstey, famous author of the immensely popular *New Bath Guide* (1766), was rejected as dull and devoid of flash, but the very precious Thomas Whalley, who apparently did hang on Mrs Thrale, was accepted by her as a lifelong friend. In sum, the closest acquaintance Burney made at Bath would have been quite at home in St Martin's Street. Some of them were noted, but none of them were grand. The only difference now was that, in their adoption of her, she could no longer hang back silently observing.

Nevertheless, Burney had seen enough of the grand to use them liberally in her next novel, *Cecilia* (1782), which she had soon set about writing. Lady Louisa Larpent in *Evelina* may have been derived from ladies seen at the concerts at home or from the theatre. The aristocrats in her other three novels, after presumably she had encountered many, with some notable exceptions were either bored, vapid, and physically and mentally unoccupied or dedicated to frivolous or reprehensible pursuits. Burney did not like aristocrats. She preferred amusing people of more stringent morals, a more sincere Christianity and less antipathy to work.

And she had, by this time, grown increasingly expert at understanding social nuance. Thomas Lawrence's mother, the mistress of an inn, she found 'something above her station', whereas Margaret Riggs, a longtime Bath Bluestocking, like all who addressed Burney directly on the subject of *Evelina*, was portrayed as without delicacy (*EJL* IV, 25, 168–72). The lack or possession of good breeding is often worthy of her note (*EJL* III, 278; IV, 40, 161). She had, by 1780, adjudged the great World to be absurd, 'now bursting forth in impertinence, now in pomposity, now giggling in silliness, & now yawning in dullness' (*EJL* IV, 217). But, in a tacit collaboration with her delighted father, for the next five or six years she lived in it.

Thus her life progressed until 1786, her fame, if anything, increasing, her acquaintance widening; and thus it might have continued to progress. The most significant event of those years, apart from the publication of *Cecilia* (1782), was the affair of George Owen Cambridge, the young man who (like Esther's Seton) courted her but never spoke. Perhaps she had been too cautious, like Camilla in the next novel (1796). It might have been that Cambridge could not bring himself to marry her, with all the ensuing disadvantages, without her revealing an ardent preference. It might be that the disadvantageous blood lines and lack of fortune convinced him belatedly not to venture after all. Even more likely, because of her anomalous position as a lady author, he simply believed that the usual rules did not apply. He may have regarded and used her as something like a close male friend. When he did marry it was to beauty, blood and fortune; but he was afterwards to remain Burney's useful friend.

Charles Burney had enjoyed companionship to Fulke Greville and said it had made his fortune; he would not have eschewed companionship for his daughter, who was, however, much prouder than he. He had hoped, through his powerful friends, to obtain for himself some post to make his own life easier. And he believed that Mrs Delany, the adopted grandmother of the

King and Queen, had done as much for his daughter in 1786 when she had (doubtless) arranged Frances's invitation to employment at Court, which so much entranced him.

The five Court years punished Burney excruciatingly, not least by confining her almost exclusively to the company of courtiers – confirmed aristocrats with their own infuriating hegemony. Though she portrays herself as a great success among them, instead of prospering by emulating their sycophancy, protocol, greed and back-biting, she withered. Her confinement, her distaste and concealed contempt almost killed her. And she was used as no fine lady could have been used by the Queen, Mrs Schwellenberg, and finally by another jilt, Colonel Digby, who not only never proposed but who turned out to have proposed already to another more appropriate lady. She of course recognised that the stringencies of class had licensed him to behave as abusively as had Seton and Cambridge. No doubt, like Cambridge, he was enormously attracted to her company; but apparently without real embarrassment he married the lady of money and family.

Burney suffered enormous losses in 1784: Johnson and Crisp died; Thrale remarried in distressing circumstances; Streatham was lost, and Chessington all but lost. Luckily and seamlessly Burney had become intimate friends with the Locks of Norbury, a family of elegance, wealth and no particular birth. Mrs Delany wrote in 1788 of a visit to them:

> Their characters, their dwelling, their manner of living, and their extraordinary qualifications, want the pen of the author of Cecilia to do justice to; it is like entering into a new planet. Mr. Locke is esteemed one of the most perfect characters living. His lady's outward form and amiable disposition are truly angelical.[9]

The Locks embraced both Susan Burney Phillips and her family, who lived nearby in Mickleham, and also Burney herself, and were soon as intimate with her as ever Crisp or Thrale had been. They were ideally suited; deemed perfect themselves, possessed of money, beauty and manner, they never sought tonish society, and they most valued accomplished artists, or meritocrats. Lock himself was the natural son of a rich London merchant. His wife Frederica Augusta Schaub was the daughter of a Swiss diplomat and successful adventurer. Without bloodlines, both had been genteelly raised and had exquisite taste. Everyone Burney met at Norbury was enormously compatible.

In the autumn of 1792 William Lock aided a group of fleeing French constitutionalists to settle in Juniper Hall, near Norbury, and soon the Locks, the Phillipses and Burney herself were enchanted with the company. The Constitutionalists had been faithful to the King, but desiring to create a fairer society had recommended the abolition of church revenues, thus attracting the enmity of republicans and monarchists alike. They were aristocrats – the Comte de Narbonne and his mistress Madame de Staël, Lally Tolendal and the Princess d'Hénin, Talleyrand, and the Comte d'Arblay – but the enchanted Susan and Frances both thought them incontestably the best company and conversationalists they had ever met: 'There can be nothing imagined more charming, more fascinating than this Colony' (*JL* II, 18). The romance between Burney and d'Arblay was born entirely of these uniquely propitious circumstances. In France, d'Arblay would not have considered for a moment marrying an unmonied, unfamilied, non-Catholic professional author, and their love affair, if it had developed, would have resembled the Cambridge or Digby affairs. Perhaps d'Arblay loved her no more than the other two, and like the others he was fascinated by her grace, her intellect, her *breeding* and her conviviality. But penniless, an émigré, even his title now worthless, he valued the gift of their relationship and, more important, felt sufficiently liberated from all his former advantages to act on his desire.

The marriage produced another change of venue. The d'Arblays, protected by the Locks, retired to the countryside and for some years saw almost only their neighbours, the visitors to Norbury, and the members of the Burney family who came to Mickleham or who entertained them in London on brief visits. Burney was immensely appreciative of the kind Mrs Cooke of Bookham and her pastor husband – a pair that were butts of their cousins, Jane Austen's family. More intimate than ever were the royal family, King, Queen and princesses, with whom Burney, who depended on her pension from them, maintained a warm relationship and made regular visits. Otherwise, domesticity closed in. Some of Burney's old friends had dropped her on her marriage to a penniless Frenchman. Others forgot her when she faded from their London parties. And when her son Alex was born in 1794, Burney added to her acquaintance a new and almost totally engrossing person.

But the years in France (1802–15) that followed resulted in a long immersion in a milieu never reflected in Burney's fiction. She did not judge very astringently the aristocrats that befriended her family during those years – some of them the old Juniper Hall set (but never Madame de Staël against whom the Queen herself had warned her, though she was introduced everywhere by the Princess d'Hénin, who in England had been engaged in an equally culpable affair with Talleyrand). And in the long final years of widowhood, those years in which one salutes with a farewell those whom one once had so warmly greeted, Burney increasingly confined herself to her son, her siblings, and her nieces and nephews. Her final social world shrank to the approximate size of her first – her family and a set of interesting relatives and friends including George Cambridge, Dean of Ely, who assisted very much with the difficult-to-assist Alex.

An analysis of Burney's experience of social hegemony as expressed in her works would require a volume. But one important theme was the social suspension of her heroines, most notably Evelina and Juliet, who are, like Burney, uncomfortably poised in a world that can sense their fineness but cannot identify their entitlement to it. In both their cases, the worthy suitors are known by their recognition of the *cri de l'âme*, the call of the soul – the instinctive recognition without proof, even against contradictory evidence, of one superior soul by another. (Cecilia and young Delvile enjoy the same recognition; Edgar's recognition of Camilla is inherent but confused.) All her life, Burney was suspended in the same ambiguity of station. Burney and, even more importantly, Burney's lovers experienced the same recognition in their affairs. It was this recognition for which she longed, and her polite, witty and elegant work was a *cri de l'âme* addressed to those (her mother, ourselves) who could distinguish her true merit from her stubbornly static station.

NOTES

1. *Thraliana: The Diary of Mrs. Hester Lynch Thrale (Later Mrs. Piozzi)*, ed. Katharine C. Balderston, 2 vols., 2nd edn (Oxford: Clarendon Press, 1951), I, 243, 443, 368n.; II, 662.
2. *Thraliana*, I, 373; II, 935 and n.
3. *Burford Papers*, ed. William Holden Hutton (London: Constable, 1905), 49.
4. Mary Hyde, *The Thrales of Streatham Park* (Cambridge: Harvard University Press, 1977), 74.
5. *The Letters of Samuel Johnson*, ed. R. W. Chapman, 3 vols. (Oxford: Clarendon, 1952), II, 261–2.
6. Devonshire Collections, Chatsworth, Letters 225, 227.
7. Charlotte Burney to Charlotte Barrett, 21 May 1810, Barrett Collection, British Library.
8. *Letters of Johnson*, II, 346.
9. *Letters from Mrs. Delany (widow of Doctor Patrick Delany) to Mrs. Frances Hamilton*, 3rd edn (London, 1821), 103.

9

GEORGE JUSTICE

Burney and the literary marketplace

Burney's career as an author might be labelled a failure: although she published four celebrated, best-selling novels, the works of the latter part of her career were skewered by the periodical press and failed to reach successful multiple printings. She wrote more plays than she did novels, whether from artistic inclination or the wish to take advantage of a lucrative market, but only one of these was staged during her lifetime. When it was staged, for one performance only, it met with derision not only from the audience, but also from the actors. Burney's final work as a living author – the *Memoirs of Doctor Burney* (1832) – was attacked more than any other, and her posthumous success as a diarist failed to revive interest in her later novels. Her career ended as it began: Madame D'Arblay was still 'the Author of *Evelina*', as the running header of the 1905 edition of her *Diaries and Letters* insistently stated.

It is difficult to say whether Burney's 'failure', as I choose here to call it for rhetorical purposes, resulted from her miscalculations of the market or the difficulty, if not impossibility, of aligning artistic genius with popular taste. We can learn much about the history of the novel and its relationship to market forces, as well as about this particularly important late eighteenth- and early nineteenth-century novelist, from an account of her travails with the publishing industry and the critics. In this essay I briefly survey Burney's forays into the literary marketplace, tracing her highly self-conscious, but somewhat unplanned, authorial career.

Burney has been interpreted as representative of eighteenth-century women writers – and eighteenth-century authorship more generally. But, in fact, her experiences were anomalous in many ways for her gender and her historical period. In the first draft of her first letter to the bookseller Thomas Lowndes, who published *Evelina*, Burney discussed her 'singularity of situation' (*EJL* II, 291). We should retain a sense of this singularity when considering her career. Burney follows Alexander Pope as an eighteenth-century writer striving mightily to reconcile a professional author's attention to profit with an uncompromising drive to pursue her art at its highest level. She wrote novels to make money and, at the same time, wrote novels that refused to pander to the reading public.

As an artist, Burney strove for the 'independence' aimed at, but never achieved, by Belfield, a character in her second novel, *Cecilia*. Using words from Johnson's *Life of Pope* to describe Belfield's would-be career as an author, Burney's narrator lets us in on the gap between the aspirations of an author and the reality of daily life in late eighteenth-century England. Burney herself experienced 'independence' in tension with her relationships with others, as she lived with her family, in the literary coterie at Streatham and the royal family at Windsor, in married life, and finally in a widowhood that included deeply felt social connections. Like the protagonists of her novels, which place one central character in a network of social relations, Burney was embedded in a literary world of family, friends and business connections.

When Burney turned fifteen, she burned all of her papers, including 'The History of Caroline Evelyn', the ancestor of her bestselling *Evelina*. This must have been a highly considered act of destruction; subsequent to this 'grand Firework of destruction' Burney kept all of her manuscripts, 'all the works, begun, *middled*, or done', along with her father's memoirs, her deceased sister's papers, and her own letters and journals, in one place, shielding them from accidental destruction with great care (*JL* VIII, 279). Destroying her manuscripts at fifteen was perhaps the most effective way of preventing interaction with the literary marketplace: after all, a bookseller could not commission a printing from non-existent copy. The cause of the young Burney's decision to burn her writing may have been primarily psychological: she saw her 'scribbling' as a compulsive obsession with an attached component of immorality. As she wrote of herself, late in life, in the third person, she feared that 'what she scribbled, if seen, would but expose her to ridicule, that her pen, though her greatest, was only her clandestine delight' (*Memoirs*, II, 124).

Wherever her sense of shame came from, it shaped her authorial career, and although Burney never again burned her writings en masse, she withdrew them from the stage or altered them for publication with that sense of shame in mind. Burney could not stop writing, and she could not stop herself from seeking an audience for her writing. At the same time, she seems to have experienced the process of publication as potentially humiliating and compromising exposure. She struggled throughout her career to bring to terms her intensely private life with her public role as a literary celebrity.

Conventional arrangements for publishing work in the eighteenth century varied according to gender and class. Male authors could bargain with booksellers with relative power or powerlessness depending on their previous reputation and the genre of the work they were trying to sell. Copyrights, even after the 1710 statute and the affirmation of limited copyright in 1774, were typically sold outright to the publishing booksellers. Women writers typically acted either from experience with the theatre or with booksellers (and were therefore knowledgeable, if disempowered) and often published anonymously. Burney's experience as an assistant to her father gave her knowledge and ambition, but her psychological make up and profound ambition complicated her dealings with the marketplace from the beginning of her career to its end.

We have (at least) three perspectives on Burney's first foray into the world of publishing: the ordinary documents that might herald any new book, including the paratexts of the work itself; Burney's contemporary journal; and the *Memoirs of Doctor Burney*, containing her retrospective analysis of the effort. Documents such as a newspaper advertisement in *The Daily Advertiser* tell us that *Evelina, or a Young Lady's Entrance into the World* was published 'this day' on 30 January 1778 by the bookseller Thomas Lowndes in three volumes, either sewn (for seven shillings and sixpence) or bound (for nine shillings). Lowndes was not a particularly eminent publisher, and the advertisement would not seem to launch the twenty-five year old Burney's first novel as a significant contribution. Nor would the look and price of the volumes themselves. Even the book's title – referring to an eponymous heroine with a romantic name – would seem to mark it out as a conventional novel poised to find a home in a circulating library.

The work itself stakes a different claim, with ambitious prefatory material and an assured style that quickly captured attention. The contest between the modest claims that a 'mere' novel could make on culture and Burney's great ambitions shape the composition, publication, and even reception of all of her works. Burney's fusion of propriety and ambition helped pave the way for the novel's increased respectability in the nineteenth century. None of Burney's predecessors, whether male or female, could be accused of the acute modesty that played an integral role in her literary career.

How should we interpret Burney's 'singularity of situation'? Burney's anomalous status resulted not simply from the fact that she was a publishing woman writer, since there were many of those, particularly women who wrote novels. It was not that she was uniquely ambitious – as her journal records reading the novels of other ambitious women writers, such as Frances Brooke. Rather the relationship between Burney and her family – which gave rise to her own conflicting feelings about social class, gender roles and literary ambition – made her *believe* she was in a singular situation. The letter Burney sent to Lowndes was in a feigned hand, and it asked him to send an answer to 'Mr King' at the Orange Coffee House. As her father's amanuensis, Burney feared that the booksellers might know her handwriting. Her brother acted as her agent, disguising himself to carry out the transaction. Feigned hands and dress-up sound more like a childish prank than the work of a serious literary artist, but like Pope, who manipulated the sleazy bookseller Edmund Curll in order to enable the publication of his *Correspondence* against the prevailing mores of the culture, Burney was doing something new. Instead of a 'lady author', she would be a writer who happened to be a woman. Far from the androgyny claimed by some female authors, Burney's laborious attempt never to scandalise herself actually worked to create an authorship untainted by her society's expectations for women and women writers.

In her Journal for 1777, Burney describes the pains she took to copy the manuscript, staying up nights because her days were otherwise occupied. She told her father her plan to publish, and he 'promised to guard my secret as cautiously as I could wish' without actually knowing the title or contents of his daughter's literary work (*EJL* II, 233). The retrospective account in the *Memoirs of Doctor Burney* claims that an initial offer of twenty pounds for the manuscript 'was accepted with alacrity, and boundless surprise at its magnificence!!' (*Memoirs*, II, 132). In truth, the inexperienced but confident Burney strove to get what she felt she deserved. Her letter of 11 November 1777 to Lowndes attempted to bargain up to thirty guineas the twenty that Lowndes had offered. She even threatened to withdraw the manuscript if an unnamed expert she proffered as an unbiased judge of the novel's value happened to give a higher value than Lowndes was willing to pay. Lowndes did not budge, and the novel was published. Sheepishly, Lowndes presented Dr Burney with an additional ten pounds on the second printing of *Evelina*. The poor payment for *Evelina* was just the first example of Burney being outfoxed by her publishers.

Burney had asked her father for permission to pursue her 'scheme in regard to Mr Lowndes' but wished that she might '[manage her] affairs without any disturbance to himself' (*EJL* II, 233). Dr Burney 'made no sort of objection to my having my own way in total secresy & silence to all the World' (*EJL* II, 233, 235). Her dealings with Lowndes and relationship with her father reflect themselves in the anonymity with which the book appeared: neither Dr Burney, nor bookseller, nor public knew anything about the author of the novel, even when it achieved popular acclaim. The more prestigious publisher Robert Dodsley had refused to consider the manuscript of the novel for publication because the author refused to reveal her identity: anonymity, especially in relation to the transaction of business prior to publication, was the preserve of the mighty, even the titled. Burney was neither a sleazy anonymous pamphleteer nor of a noble name. As she styled herself in her diary, she was 'Nobody' (*EJL* I, 2).

Burney channelled this self-arrogation of authority into the fabric of the novel in the form of a bold mock dedication 'to the Authors of the Monthly and Critical Reviews' and a preface that placed *Evelina* in the genre's rapidly developing tradition. In effect, she was covering the past and present of the contemporary market for fiction and acknowledging that the market for books was much more limited in time and space than the idealised market of ideas. The tradition of novelists described by Burney – including Rousseau, Johnson, Marivaux, Fielding, Richardson and Smollett – differed from the more abstract literary lineage evoked by the epic poet Milton in *Paradise Lost*. *Evelina* had to compete with books by the authors mentioned in its preface not only as a literary composition, but also as a physical object jostling for space in booksellers' shops, circulating libraries and readers' collections. For Burney, the 'burden of the past' was also the 'burden of the backlist'.

Looking at *Evelina* as a commodity, we can see that it was formed perfectly for the market. Unknowingly, Burney was following the advice Alexander Pope had given Samuel Richardson before the publication of the second part of *Pamela*. She developed a Pamela-like heroine whose situation in life produced pathos, but whose sharp wit could afford a fresh look at the follies and foibles of modern urban life. Added to the novel's depiction of the triumph of virtue and wit was a dash of physical humour that could rival Smollett's and a brilliance of characterisation created particularly by the author's skill at dialogue. Reviews were positive, even glowing. The *Critical Review* declared that the novel 'would have disgraced neither the head nor the heart of Richardson'.[1] Considering the harsh reviews typically heaped on anonymous first novels, this was high praise, and it contributed to a 'media event' that saw *Evelina* capturing popular interest in the way that Richardson's, Fielding's and Sterne's works had once done.

Lowndes's initial printing of 500 copies was followed by another of 500 and then a third and fourth edition, the latter with illustrations, of 1,500.[2] There were also two editions printed in Dublin. Lowndes wrote to Burney's father that the great expense of commissioning illustrations and preparing engravings had been done 'as a Compliment to the Lady-Author. The Plates cost me Seventy-three Pounds' (*DL* II, 482). It gives us insight into the contempt with which booksellers treated novelists generally that Lowndes could see it as a 'Compliment' to a 'Lady' that he paid more to illustrate the novel than he ever paid to the writer. The 'Author of *Evelina*' had secured lasting fame but no fortune. Spurred on by ambition and economic necessity, Burney would attempt to squeeze more out of her career without endangering the high critical and popular reputation she had already earned.

Soon after Burney's authorship became known, Dr Charles Burney showed his daughter off to his prominent friends. From these introductions, Burney embarked on a public career that took her into two prominent families. From both of the coteries she entered, Burney acquired social and intellectual capital that could have made her first among living authors in profit as well as fame. *Cecilia* and *Camilla* were written for a large reading public in the context of coterie literary production. Burney, like many writers before her, relied upon the literary, financial and emotional support of small circles whose members could understand and encourage her artistic ambition.

In 1778, Burney first entered the orbit of Hester Lynch Thrale at Streatham, where Samuel Johnson and other literary figures gathered for respite and conversation. '[A] *play* will be something *worth* your Time, it is the Road both to Honour & Profit, – & *why* should you have it in your power to gain these rewards & not do it?' (*EJL* III, 133). Hester Thrale, in speaking these words, was among the first who encouraged Burney to try playwriting. It was obvious to Mrs Thrale and to others that Burney, whose literary sensibility was shaped by the London stage, had talent as a comic dramatist. Although 'honour' was certainly at stake (as it was with all of Burney's forays into publication and production), 'profit' remained at the forefront. The conversation with Mrs Thrale – recorded by Burney in a letter to her sister – continued: 'Hannah More, added she, got near 400 pounds for her foolish play', *Percy* (*EJL* III, 133).

Burney's experience with Lowndes had taught her that booksellers were scoundrels. She could stand to make much more money from a successful play, especially with encouragement from Arthur Murphy, Richard Brinsley Sheridan and other prominent members of literary and dramatic society. In addition to the sale of the copy for publication (if a play were particularly successful), the theatres allocated proceeds from the third, sixth and, if performed, ninth performances of a play to the author's benefit. On the whole, Hannah More had been better paid than most dramatists, including almost all women playwrights. For example, in the season of 1778–9, Elizabeth Richardson's *Double Deception* earned nothing for the author, and in 1779–80 Elizabeth Griffith's estimated net take from performance and print for *The Times* was £180.[3] It seems likely that on the heels of her great success with *Evelina* Burney would have earned at least £300, £50 more than she ended up getting from the much more laboriously composed and written *Cecilia*.

The Witlings, with its satire on female wits and other would-be literati, stemmed directly from Burney's experience at Streatham. The play was written in the first part of 1779. On August 3, Susan Burney reported to her sister that she, her father's friend Samuel Crisp (whom she referred to as 'Daddy' in respect for their close relationship), and Dr Burney all enjoyed reading through the play. Her letters ten days later to her father and Crisp reveal what really happened: Crisp felt the satire on Bluestockings in the play would give offence to their powerful leader, Elizabeth Montagu, and harm Dr Burney's literary career.

Burney agreed to give up the play, prompting a crisis of sorts. Here again was a conflict among the crucial aspects of Burney's professional identity: family, class and gender interacting with her demonstrated talents as a playwright. It would go too far to claim that her inability to get *The Witlings* produced pushed Burney fully into a career as a novelist, as she made later efforts to get plays produced. Yet the mediation provided by the chain of circumstances from author to book seemed to provide a psychological comfort that enabled Burney to remain a profit-making writer. As her father had written to her, 'In the Novel Way, there is no danger.'[4] After each of her unsuccessful attempts to earn money from the stage, she turned back to the 'Novel Way'.

Cecilia represents Burney's full immersion into the life of a professional author and resulted in the 'honour & glory' trumpeted by Hester Thrale. Burney began writing *Cecilia* as early as January 1781, fearful that her new novel would not be as well received as her first. The work of composition was feverish, as she was 'never letting [her] Brains rest even when [her] *Corporeal Machine* was *succumbent*' (*EJL* IV, 266).

Burney returned to Streatham on April 11 after Mr Thrale's death and then left again in July. In May, she had been associated too closely (for her comfort) with the literary coterie of Hester Thrale, appearing not as a literary lion but as the somewhat impoverished object of the widow's charity. A newspaper reported, to Burney's dismay, that 'Miss Burney, the sprightly Writer of the elegant Novel Evelina, is now domesticated with Mrs. Thrale in the same manner that Miss More is with Mrs. Garrick, & Mrs. Carter with Mrs. Montague' (*EJL* IV, 354). Authorship was Burney's path to independence, and yet, like other prominent women writers, she was at the same time 'domesticated' with a wealthy benefactor.

Another frustration emerged when Burney's closest friends refused to understand the work involved in writing. Samuel Crisp marvelled at his own picture of the author cogitating alone, conjuring money from nothing but mere thought.

> If she can coin gold at such a Rate, as to sit by a warm Fire, and in 3 or 4 months (for the real time she has stuck to it closely, putting it all together, will not amount to more, tho' there have been long Intervals, between) gain £250 by

scribbling the Inventions of her own Brain – only putting down in black and white whatever comes into her own head, without labour drawing singly from her own Fountain, she need not want money.[5]

In reality, *Cecilia* was painfully wrought by the author's hands and created with the fear of failure always in mind. The work was hard:

> for *labour* it is to me to take up a pen, because one way or other my Hand scarce rests an Hour in the whole day. Whenever this work is done – if ever that Day arrives, I believe I shall not write another word for 3 years! However, I really believe I must still publish it *in part*, for I begin to grow horribly tired, & yet am by no means *near* any thing *bordering* upon an end. And the dismal fagging of my mind & Brains does really much mischief to my Health.   (*EJL* IV, 288)

So much for Crisp's hallucination that his young friend scribbled 'without labour'.

In February 1782, Burney was still working hard, being pushed by her 'people' to get it 'produced' in a 'hurry' (*DL* II, 58). Even without revision, she complained to her sister, the copying of the manuscript for the press would take at least ten weeks! Her father was offering her the carrot of his strong approval of the first volume, which had already been prepared for the printers. In May, she defended a scene in the novel that had evidently disturbed Crisp: her confidence here contrasts with the tentative nature of the defence she made of *The Witlings* and the quick way she succumbed to Crisp and her father in that case.

Cecilia was published by Thomas Cadell and Thomas Payne, who together paid £250 for the copyright to the novel. They paid £200 in advance, with the promise of £50 upon the printing of a second edition. Lowndes was disappointed that the Burneys had excluded him, writing a letter to Dr Burney that Frances Burney answered. In this chilly letter she writes that 'She is certainly neither under Engagement or Obligation to *any* Bookseller whatever, and is to no one, therefore, responsible for chusing and changing as she pleases' (*DL* II, 482). Yet she was not happy with her new booksellers, either. Cadell and Payne printed a first edition of 2,000, four times the ordinary printing of a new work of this nature, thus delaying the subsequent payment. Indeed, Cadell tried to avoid paying her his half share of the initial sum. The £50, in her own words, had been '*jockeyed* out of me by surprise' (16 August 1782). Johnson estimated for his young friend that the book-sellers had turned a profit of £500 for the first printing, which sold out in three months. According to Burney, Payne was going to ask her for a new chapter in order to print a revised second edition, for which he and Cadell would offer additional money, but 'I fancy Mr. Cadell has dissuaded him' (15 October 1782). Burney relies on 'fancy' when she is essentially in the dark regarding the middlemen thrust upon her in order to bring her work to the public.

The reviews matched the popular reception, and both the *Critical* and the *Monthly* praised the book as uncommonly successful. The *Critical* implicitly compares *Cecilia* to the novels of Fielding and Smollett by suggesting that 'no improper scenes [are] presented to the reader; a fault which may be too often discovered in the most celebrated novel-writers',[6] and the *Monthly*, noting that the novel is 'universally read', explicitly states, 'We see much of the dignity and pathos of Richardson; and much of the acuteness and ingenuity of Fielding.'[7] The second and third editions of the novel were published in 1783, as was a first Dublin edition. A fourth edition was published in 1784 and a fifth in 1786. The sixth edition appeared in 1791 and the seventh in 1796, the final year of the statutory length of the copyright. Multiple editions were published in Dublin and in Germany, France and America. The book was an international phenomenon, but with each subsequent printing, Burney's share of the profit as a percentage dwindled, as her cultural capital continued to accrue. Burney even refused to aid the booksellers in their prosecutions for pirate editions within the reach of British law. She told her sister in 1786 that she returned a letter to Payne's lawyer declaring that she 'had wholly done with the book' and that she 'wished them well through a business that was entirely their own' (*DL* III, 128).

Burney was at the top of the literary world. At the same time, in 1786, she was an unmarried woman, 33 years old. *Cecilia* had, she told potential suitor George Cambridge, provided her merely with 'pin money' (post 14 January 1786). Cambridge declined to propose to Burney. He was not afraid of sharing his opinions with her, suggesting in one conversation that she should write a play to increase her earnings. The Queen, present at the time, hoped that Burney would *not* write a play, saying that though 'Miss Burney's *name* is *every where* ... her Character is as delicate as if it were *no where*; – & I should be sorry to have her write for so *public a thing* as the Stage' (post 14 January 1786).

Soon the Queen's opinion was to matter. Burney accepted an offer of a place at Court and entered the service of the Queen as a Keeper of the Robes on 17 July 1786. Her entrance into the world of the Court might be seen as a repudiation of the literary marketplace, or at least a rejection of the financial and social opportunities it could provide for a young woman of little independent needs but with social and artistic aspirations. She did not stop writing, however. First and foremost, she continued writing letters, especially to her sister. The privacy of these letters would seem to represent a disengagement from the literary marketplace, but in the context of a culture increasingly interested in private correspondence, especially that of authors, Burney's labours here were an advance effort on her posthumous success as a diarist and letter writer.

And she continued to write plays. She turned from the comedy she had pursued in *The Witlings* and pursued a tragic mode that ran against the grain of success for most female playwrights, who generally specialised in comic offerings. Beginning in 1788, Burney wrote (in order) the tragedies *Edwy and Elgiva* (1788–95), *Hubert De Vere* (1790–7), *The Siege of Pevensey* (1790–1) and *Elberta* (1791–1814). That she continued working on all of these, save *The Siege of Pevensey*, after her release from Court service suggests that they were more to her than psychological responses to a troubled personal situation, even though she admitted shortly after she left Court that she never could have written them 'in the present composed & happy state of [her] mind' (*JL* I, 74).

Regaining command over her time and her place proved in all ways beneficial for Burney. In 1791, she was able to convince her family that the toll the position was taking on her physical and emotional health was not worth any amount of prestige. The Queen favoured her with a £100 yearly pension, the kind of sinecure that enabled the life of writing for many eighteenth-century authors. (Burney's annual income came with fewer strings attached than, for example, Samuel Johnson's annual pension of £300, first awarded in 1762, which became grist for the mill of his political opponents.) In 1792 Burney met Alexandre d'Arblay, an exiled French officer who had been a constitutionalist during the early years of the French Revolution; they married in July of 1793.

Now 'Madame d'Arblay', she began work immediately on getting her plays produced. She re-emerged in public (albeit without profit) with her pamphlet *Brief Reflections Relative to the Emigrant French Clergy* in 1793, and in that same year, John Philip Kemble accepted *Hubert De Vere* for production at Drury Lane Theatre. Burney withdrew that play before Kemble could show it to his partner Sheridan in favour of *Edwy and Elgiva*. (She did continue to consider publishing *Hubert De Vere* as a closet drama, another opportunity she for one reason or another did not pursue beyond giving thought to it.) *Edwy and Elgiva* was performed only once, on 21 March 1795. Luckily for Burney, the theatres had imposed a new system in late 1794 for remunerating playwrights, and we can assume that she would have received the standard £33 6s 8d playwrights received for each of the first nine performances.[8]

The pension from the Queen was not insignificant, but with a husband who could not work in England and a child on the way, Burney turned back to her work as a novelist. The copyright to *Camilla* was initially designed to be a legacy left to her son. 'This is hard & strange!' she wrote after she realised her dream was not going to come to fruition. 'I thought my *Brain* work as much fair & individual property, as any other possession in either art or nature' (*JL* III, 130).

In the account of the publication of *Evelina* in the *Memoirs of Doctor Burney*, Burney suggested of herself in the third person that 'Writing, indeed, was far more difficult to her than composing', differentiating between the intellectual work of literary composition and the physical labour of putting pen to paper (*Memoirs*, II, 126). In so doing, she supported the theoretical basis behind intellectual property (recognising the intellectual labour of composition) while emphasising the struggle to write. In the subscription element of the publication of her third novel *Camilla*, Burney attempted to retain property in her '*Brain* work' while succumbing to the realities of the world of print publication. She planned initially to cut the booksellers out by entering the literary marketplace on her own as author and proprietor. She would print the novel 'for herself', meaning that she would assume all of the risk, and take up all of the profit after paying the printers and booksellers for the novel's production and distribution. When that proved to be too difficult, or at least too risky, Burney turned to a plan that had first been floated some years before by her admirer, Edmund Burke: she would produce her 'grand work' by subscription.

Publication by subscription had developed as a way for authors of printed books to reap rewards from personal connections. The work would be advertised, and subscribers could order (and, usually, pay for) copies of books before they were printed. In exchange, these patrons would see their names printed in a subscription list at the head of the publication. Pope, Burney's authorial model in so many ways, had perfected this model of publication in his translations of Homer. Burney had turned away from the public exposure of subscription in the past, but now she embraced the opportunity to capitalise on her reputation as a writer. Advertisements were taken in the newspapers, and Burney enlisted the aid of gentlewomen who would take in subscriptions. In this way, and in the public support she received, Burney profited from her years of propriety, including the miserable years spent at Windsor with the Queen. The vast and fascinating list of subscribers fuelled sales of non-subscription copies of the novel, and the five-volume *Camilla*, published in 1796, became an instant bestseller.

Her long-term aspirations for the novel failed, though, as Burney ended up selling the copyright in the conventional way to a group of booksellers chosen partly in deference to family connections rather than, as she had hoped, auctioned off to the highest bidder. Publisher Thomas Payne's daughter had married Burney's brother James, and so Thomas Payne the younger, who had inherited his father's business, was included in a deal along with

Thomas Cadell and others. The deal was brokered by Burney's brother Charles, who acted as her agent. The arrangements angered Dr Burney, who was distressed that his own publisher Robinson was left out of the deal. Burney was paid £1,000 for the copyright. She also retained the profits of the subscription, approximately £1,000 pounds.

The first edition of *Camilla* consisted of a massive printing of 4,000 copies, and Burney marvelled in a letter that only 500 copies remained after just a few months. The book received respectful but mixed reviews. Sales slowed, whether because of the reviews or because everyone who wanted a copy of the 'work' (as Burney insisted on referring to *Camilla*) had purchased it already. It took years for those 500 remaining copies to sell. They were eventually advertised as a 'second edition' (with a new title page) in 1800, long after Burney had begun revising the novel. The 'new edition' was published in 1802, edited and rewritten to meet objections made by some of the reviews and to reflect Burney's developing aesthetic sensibility. Burney continued working on the novel, but it never saw another edition in her lifetime.

Burney sought to capitalise on the initial popular success of *Camilla* with another play. In 1799, *Love and Fashion* was accepted for the stage by Thomas Harris, manager of the Covent Garden theatre. According to Burney, Harris offered £400 for the manuscript (*Plays*, I, 105). Roughly £300 would have been for the first nine performances, and the remaining amount for publication rights. The two-pronged approach – making a grand re-entrance into the literary marketplace with *Camilla* and following it up with a work in a different genre but with a built-in appeal for Burney – mirrors what she had tried with *The Witlings* after the great success of *Evelina*. Dr Burney again argued against the theatrical and financial ambitions of his daughter. The death of her sister induced Burney to withdraw the play in 1800. She hoped for a production in the following year, but it did not come to pass. Although Burney wrote two other comedies – *The Woman-Hater* and *A Busy Day* – no play of hers would be produced again until late in the twentieth century.

The next set of incidents in Burney's life matched her years at Court in providing material for the posthumous success of her *Diary and Letters*. Burney and her son joined d'Arblay in France in 1802. When war resumed with Great Britain in 1803, the d'Arblays were stranded. In 1811 she underwent a mastectomy; the description of that event in a formal letter to her sister Esther Burney has become one of the 'best-selling' pieces of her writing, excerpted in anthologies otherwise unrelated to Burney or the eighteenth century. When peace was declared in 1812, Burney returned to England with her trunk of manuscripts and set out to finish her fourth novel, *The Wanderer* (1814).

As she had with *Evelina* and *Camilla*, Burney employed her brother Charles as an agent to negotiate with the booksellers for her long-anticipated return to the literary marketplace. Burney again hoped to put the work '*to Auction*' (*JL* VII, 103). Using her husband's supposed demands as an excuse, she directed her brother to offer the manuscript successively to a number of the top booksellers, imploring patience so 'That we may not hear of some man who would have given £100 more than the rest, when it shall be too late' (*JL* VII, 104).

Ultimately, Burney rejected a flat-out offer of £2,000 for the copyright to *The Wanderer*, preferring a deal from Longman, Hurst, Rees, Orme and Brown. She did not play it safe: 'The real win, therefore, is dependent upon success' (*JL* VII, 195). The first £1,500 would be paid in instalments: £500 upon delivery, and then £500 more six months after publication and £500 six months after that. According to the agreement, she would receive £500 for the second edition, and £250 for each of the third through sixth editions. Her experience with *Cecilia* in mind, she contracted for a specified size of each printing, which included a large first printing of 3,000 copies followed by editions of 1,000. Burney was gambling that she would receive £3,000 by selling 8,000 copies of the novel. On a per-copy basis, this would have been less than she earned for the subscription and sale of the copyright to *Camilla*, but as a percentage of the publishers' gross take, it would have come to a respectable 18 per cent, or 7s. 6d. per copy sold, exactly the amount for which Lowndes had sold sewn copies of *Evelina*. Longman and Co., of course, would have made out very well: they hoped to recoup £500 immediately by the sale of a spare set of sheets to the New York businessman (and friend of Washington Irving), Henry Brevoort. At the same time, Longman was trying to sell rights to a French translation, which Burney herself would undertake. There was no international copyright agreement, but foreign firms might have found it worth their while to pay the copyright holder for a complete set of sheets prior to publication.

Writing *The Wanderer* had been as physically painful for Burney as writing her other novels. She felt neither elation nor joy at finishing the manuscript. In a letter to her brother Charles of 21 August 1813 she wrote: 'tired I am of my Pen! Oh tired! tired! oh! should it tire others in the same proportion – alas for poor Messrs. Longman & Rees! – & alas for poorer ME!' (*JL* VII, 163). The novel was published on 28 March 1814. The first edition sold out two or three days before publication; Burney wrote to her brother on 2 April that the booksellers had asked her to begin preparing her second edition. The second edition of *The Wanderer* did not sell as quickly, and twelve years later Burney was still accounting for the copies of the second edition, 535 of which she calculated to have remained.

There were three parties to blame for *The Wanderer*'s failure: the book-sellers, her brother, acting as 'agent', and the reviewers. According to Burney, the publishers had 'Printed for the whole 5 Editions', greedily believing that even at the 'rapacious' price of two guineas the book would continue to sell (*JL* XII, 640). In fact, as evidenced by the draft of a letter from Longman and Co. to Burney, the 'second 3000 Copies printed were divided into three editions of 1000 each'. The 'fourth and half of the third editions were wasted with the concurrence of Dr Burney' (here Charles Burney the younger).[9] Burney later wrote that she understood (or hoped) that the printed copies would not actually have been destroyed, but might be available to her. However, the *Oxford English Dictionary* quotes the *Fortnightly Review* later in the century on the word: 'Many unsaleable books ... are "wasted", that is, are sent to the mill, ground up, pulped down, and made again into paper.'[10] If the book were out of print (unavailable to purchasers), then, she wrote, she should be entitled to the entire sum of £3,000. By their original agreement, in this case the publishers would have to return to Burney the copyright '& *every remaining* sett, unless they re-print it themselves' (*JL* XII, 639, 640). Her brother Charles was to blame for whatever role he played in advising the publishers on what to do with the remaining copies of the novel: 'My Brother's agency ceased solely from the moment the Agreement was signed by *All Parties*' (*JL* XII, 640). We do not have a copy of Longman's response to Burney's emotional letter, although d'Arblay's diary records having received one on 4 February 1826. Given Longman's letter in 1817, it seems unlikely that it contained good news for her. With her last novel, Burney had gambled that she could create an instant best-seller with staying power in the market. The publication of *The Wanderer* was a 'media event', but one that passed quickly.

The negative critical response to the novel could not have aided its longevity. John Wilson Croker's notice in the *Quarterly Review* appeared the month after publication and mocked Burney's career, her writing style and her physical appearance in the guise of talking about the novel as if it were itself a woman in old age, *Evelina* in advanced years. Burney was reduced by the critical world she had approached as an unknown, genderless author in *Evelina* to a withered female whose works were seen as the mere reflection of her descent into the decrepitude of Johnsonian affectation.

Dr Burney died in 1814, shortly after the publication of *The Wanderer*. Burney went back to France and became caught up in Napoleon's escape from Elba. In 1818, her husband died. The final published work of her career would be a narrative *Memoirs of Doctor Burney*, published in lieu of his own composition (which she had not thought worthy of him) and his correspondence, which she had initially saved but had begun burning after rereading.

Burney had received notice that biographies of her father were in the works. (The genre of literary biography had caught on, given the perennial sales of Johnson's *Lives of the Poets* and the mammoth *Life of Johnson* published by James Boswell. Burney's father, part of that circle of London writers, would have been a prime subject for such a biography.) If Burney did not publish, someone else would. Because changes in the law meant that publishing the letters her father had received from others would have violated their intellectual property rights, and because she had destroyed so many of her father's own manuscript notes toward his *Memoirs*, Burney was forced to construct an awkwardly third-person narrative form for the *Memoirs*. Thus she became a main character herself, the 'author of *Evelina*', who assumed a large role in the whole. Published in 1832, the *Memoirs of Doctor Burney* might have provided her with £1,000, according to Joyce Hemlow, with an equal sum paid to Esther Burney's heirs (*JL* XII, 785n. 1). £2,000 was good pay even in 1832, and the money and attention (albeit again largely negative) that the *Memoirs* received testify to Burney's continuing strength in the literary marketplace. She had become the backlist against which she had rebelled in the beginnings of her career.

Burney's beloved son Alexander predeceased her, dying of influenza in 1837 at the age of 43. Burney was left with her memories – and her papers. She contemplated burning them, but she could not do for herself what she had done for her father. She willed the journals she had kept for her whole life to her niece, Charlotte Francis Barrett. Burney died in 1840 at the age of 87. Two years later, her *Diary and Letters*, edited by Barrett, began to appear. And although John Wilson Croker savaged these, as he had *The Wanderer* and the *Memoirs of Doctor Burney*, they sold well and were reprinted throughout the late nineteenth and early twentieth centuries.

Adding up Burney's earnings from her publications and lone play production, we might conclude that, all things considered, she did well in her lifetime. One should include in any accounting of her earnings the pension she received from the Queen, since without her literary celebrity, it was unlikely she would have received the offer to serve at Court. Much of her writing, however, produced through physical pain, earned her nothing and entertained only those family members and close friends privileged to read her work in manuscript. Her novels were read widely by the patrons of circulating libraries, whose payment to rent her novels would profit only the proprietors of those libraries. All of Burney's works have earned much more for their publishers and distributors than their author. Mixed success in the market, nevertheless, coexisted with happiness in Burney's life. Unlike some of her female contemporaries and near-contemporaries, including writers such as Charlotte Lennox and Charlotte Smith, Burney never had to appeal for financial support directly to her audience or to a body such as the Literary Fund. Her career as an author did not match her promise as a writer, but she had the privilege of retaining the 'singularity' that shaped her vision – and her profession – as an artist.

NOTES

1. *Critical Review* 46 (September 1778), 202.
2. See Lowndes to Dr Charles Burney, 5 September 1782 (*DL* II, 481–2); see also Vivien Jones's 'Note on the Text' in her and Edward A. Bloom's Oxford World Classics Edition of *Evelina* (Oxford, 2002). Bloom followed a letter from Burney to her father on 14 October 1796 giving the figure of 800 for the first printing. Hemlow's note to this letter quotes from a letter from Lowndes to Dr Burney in 1779 providing a figure of 1,500 sets of sheets to be printed for the third and fourth editions. I surmise that 500 of these sheets would have been used for the third edition, feeding an immediate need, while the other 1,000 would be reserved for use in the illustrated fourth edition.
3. Judith Milhous and Robert D. Hume, 'Playwrights' Remuneration in Eighteenth-Century London', *Harvard Library Bulletin* n.s. 10, no. 2–3 (1999), 65.
4. *The Letters of Dr Charles Burney*, ed. Alvaro Ribeiro (Oxford: Clarendon Press, 1991), I, 281.
5. *Burford Papers*, ed. William Holden Hutton (London: Constable, 1905), 74.
6. *Critical Review* 54 (December 1782), 420.
7. *Monthly Review* 67 (December 1782), 453.
8. Milhous and Hume, 'Playwrights' Remuneration', 6–7.
9. *Longman Archives*, Longman I, 100, no. 133 (draft).
10. *Oxford English Dictionary*, 'to waste'.

IO

LORNA CLARK

The afterlife and further reading

Early criticism

The afterlife of Frances Burney is a story as varied and exciting as the tale of one of her heroines, stepping tremblingly out on the stage of the world. The evolution of her reputation since her death in 1840 can be plotted as an upward trajectory of early vicissitudes crowned with eventual triumph. The reception history has the added twist that while she wrote in several genres, it has taken time for her whole oeuvre to emerge in reliable editions. With basic material still lacking, a full appreciation of her power as a writer has not yet been achieved.

Burney's posthumous reputation was a story which she tried to control herself, both through the voluminous material provided and the considerable amount destroyed, putting the evidence forever beyond reach. The legacy she would leave was very much on her mind during the last decades of her life when she worked on the 'myriads of hoards of MSS' (*JL* XII, 954) collected over seventy years – selecting, annotating and censoring her own papers in preparation for their possible future publication. In her will, she left them to her niece, Charlotte Barrett, who lost no time in contacting a publisher eager to capitalise on her aunt's reputation. Guided by the preselection of material, Mrs Barrett culled out seven volumes' worth of highlights, the first five appearing in 1842, the last two in 1846. Beginning in 1778 with the publication of *Evelina*, the first five volumes cover the years of literary fame, of royal service, of courtship and marriage, up until 1793. The last two volumes curtail drastically the last fifty years of Burney's life.

A brief memoir introduces the first volume, the first and only biography written by a family member (in marked contrast to Jane Austen, every one of whose 'major biographers ... for more than one hundred years after her death' was a family member).[1] Charlotte Barrett hoped that sharing her aunt's private thoughts and papers would edify the reader with the 'simplicity of her ingenuous confidence'.[2] The reviewers' response may not have been quite what was expected. Mme d'Arblay had by then become a classic, whose literary career had begun more than sixty years before. There was curiosity about the society of an earlier era, and appreciation for the skill of the pen which brought these brilliant assemblies to life: the variety of characters, lively dialogues and minute observation helped to give 'fresh colours to the pale and faded portraits of past ages'.[3] But there was criticism for the perceived egotism, for the curious discrepancy between Burney's professed modesty and her eager avidity for recording extravagant compliments so exhaustively. With the exaggerated sensibility of a sentimental heroine, Burney seemed obsessed with her fame as an authoress. Her excessive self-consciousness was read as pride and hypocrisy. The exposure of this foible injured her reputation.

Worse was yet to come. In June 1842, John Wilson Croker weighed in with a review in *The Quarterly*.[4] No admirer of Burney's later works, he had already taken her to task for improbabilities of plot in *The Wanderer* and for the grandiloquence of her style in *The Memoirs of Doctor Burney*. He had also accused her of embellishing the truth, even suppressing the facts about her age at the time she wrote *Evelina* (her supposed youthfulness having made part of its fame). Croker goes so far as to suggest that the success of her early novels was founded on a lie, which is why the later ones failed to measure up; the 'strange pomposity'[5] of her later style, he claims, shows her desperately striving to compensate for talents that she never had. His views on the trajectory of deterioration in her style (downhill all the way from *Evelina*) were influential.

But it was Croker's attack on the *Diary and Letters* which was devastating in its acrimony and effect; Burney's reputation would hardly recover for a century. In his review, he took Burney to task for 'affectation and vanity'. With demolishing sarcasm, he claimed that all the 'eminent and illustrious personages' of the day became, in her narrative, a 'wearisome congregation' of flatterers, intent on glorifying 'that great luminary of the age, the *author of "Evelina"* ' (244–5). He ridiculed the pretence that it was 'her duty, as a mere historian' to record all the compliments, meanwhile bewailing 'the intolerable torture' of having to endure them. The *Diary* displays 'the most *horse-leech* egotism that literature or Bedlam has yet exhibited' (251–2). Noting that Burney's accounts are highly coloured, he also questioned her veracity. The faults exposed in the *Diary* highlighted similar defects in the novels, their use of hyperbole and exaggeration: 'Her innate propensity was to *make mountains of mole-hills*' (271). Her plots were built on a tissue of 'trifling annoyances and imaginary difficulties'. With natural tendencies towards 'artifice and manoeuvering' (255–6), Burney was guilty of '*treachery*' (259) in secretly recording, circulating and preserving for posterity the private conversations of trusting friends. Finally, in Croker's eyes, Burney had no sense of perspective: the 'most trifling incident – ... if it concerns her own important self, is treated with all the pomp of history' (256). He ridiculed the pettiness of her grievances in the Queen's household, and the small-mindedness and triviality of the whole. In sum, he dismissed the *Diary* as 'nearly the most worthless' book ever written (287).

Burney's character and reputation could hardly have survived such an attack, as Croker's accusations gained currency. Five years later, a reviewer lamented that Burney's 'rapidly acquired' fame was 'subsequently deeply impaired by herself, and in the end injured'; he marvels that an 'excellent' writer had evolved into the 'very worst'.[6] To defend Burney against some of these charges, a champion did step forth: Thomas Babington Macaulay. He had declined an appeal by the family to vindicate Burney's character against Croker's 'Defamation', maintaining his independence as a reviewer.[7] Nevertheless, in a judicious review, he lashed Croker (whom he despised) for his meanness and malignity ('to twit a lady with having concealed her age')[8] and gave a sympathetic account of Burney's life and career. He had his own axes to grind, however, and agreed with the notion of deterioration in her style, which he attributed to the pernicious influence (even direct aid) of Johnson, and the long residence on the continent. In *Camilla*, he averred, there was 'a perceptible falling off', and *The Wanderer* merited 'oblivion' (558). *The Memoirs* also 'deserved its doom'; it was written in 'the worst style that has ever been known among men' (524). In assessing Burney's contribution, Macaulay praised her as a skilful 'character-monger' (559); she excelled at comedy, depicting 'humours' characters with exaggerated traits, an art which falls short of the highest rank. Finally, Burney was the first woman writer of note and prepared the way for Jane Austen and Maria Edgeworth, both of whom (he judged) surpassed her.

The early reference to Austen, and the appreciation of Burney as her precursor is worth noting, as is the comparison made between Burney's crude satire and Austen's more subtle effects. Ironically, Austen, too, has suffered from a similar 'myth of limitation' for the same fundamental reasons. 'Lady novelists' did not do well at the hands of male reviewers, who tended to label their preoccupations (by definition) as trivial (e.g. Burney is 'an admirable painter of the surface of society ... in how narrow a sphere she moves, how little of general humanity she displays, and how much the realities of life are overlooked "in her philosophy"').[9] Like Austen, Burney was accused of ignoring the big issues (like Sex, Death and War),[10] presumably because her shallow mind did not stretch to the more intellectually vigorous preoccupations of the male novelists. The issue was essentially one of gender: 'Her female and microscopic views of society' were to blame.[11]

Although many thought that Croker had overdone his criticisms, the gist of them remained; reiterations of the main points appear throughout the Victorian period. While *Evelina* and *Cecilia* might be tolerated as quaint relics of a bygone era, her later work was consigned to the dustbin of literary history, in which Burney's place was not a very elevated one. In a survey of English novelists published in 1858, she was denied 'a second-rate, or even a third-rate, place'.[12] She may have been 'the first woman novelist ... with a distinct vein of her own',[13] but it was a vein that was thought to be soon exhausted.

Occasionally there were those who differed from Macaulay's ranking of the relative merits of Burney and Austen and who preferred the 'grasp and vigor and broad humorous lifelikeness' of *Evelina*.[14] The *Diary*, in particular, attracted admirers; it was judged to be Burney's 'most important and most permanent contribution to literature'.[15] In an age addicted to realism, the diary had the advantage of apparently being true; it was appreciated for bringing the past to life so vividly and was thought to rival Boswell as a record of Johnsoniana. But for the most part, in the process of canon-formation that took place in the early twentieth century, Burney was firmly relegated to her niche as a minor woman writer, an inferior precursor to Jane Austen, whose admiration for her was somewhat mystifying.

Burney's fame as diarist increased in 1889 with Annie Raine Ellis's edition of *The Early Diary of Frances Burney*, which printed unpublished material from the decade prior to 1778, the starting point of the Barrett edition, so that a sampling of the full range was available. (So often, the story of Burney's reputation follows the history of new editions of her work.) Ellis treated the material with care, providing knowledgeable notes and an extensive introduction. A further boost was given when an expanded edition of the entire *Diary and Letters* came out, edited by Austen Dobson (1904–5) which would remain standard, until recently. Even more important, Dobson wrote a life of Burney (1903) for the 'English Men of Letters' series in which (as Peter Sabor points out) Burney appeared as an honorary man, preceded by George Eliot (1902) and followed by Maria Edgeworth (1904) and Jane Austen (1913). Although Dobson was 'offensively patronising'[16] in his attitude to the novels, he was convinced of the superiority of the *Diary* which he believed 'deserves to rank with the great diaries of literature',[17] a view of Burney's achievement that he helped cement. With the first scholarly editions of her writing and the first full-length biography, Burney moved closer to full recognition.

Other works of a biographical bent quickly appeared. A trilogy of books was written by Constance Hill – placing Burney within the context of her family (in *The House in St. Martin's Street* (1907)), in the royal household (in *Fanny Burney at the Court of Queen Charlotte* (1914)), and in associa-tion with the French émigrés (in *Juniper Hall* (1904)).[18] *Fanny Burney and the Burneys* (1926) by R. Brimley Johnson included excerpts from the writ-ings of various family members. The interest deflected from Burney to her family can be accounted for by the material she herself provides. Her private writings take as their subject the life around her, conveyed with such authen-ticity that the reader feels a part of the inner circle, privileged to call her 'Fanny' (a nickname actually used by very few). She also makes the first attempt at putting such biographical material together: *The Memoirs of Doctor Burney* is at least partly autobiographical, so insistent is her view-point and so prominent her role. It could be argued that even Burney's fame as a novelist owes its preservation to the publication of the *Diary*, that *Evelina* and *Cecilia* are not as remarkable as the vivid account of the sensa-tion they caused.

In the *Dictionary of National Biography* (1885), Burney merited eight columns, written by Sir Leslie Stephen himself, compared to the six devoted to her father Charles. In F. R. Leavis's *The Great Tradition* (1948), she appears briefly, commended as the conduit between Richardson and Jane Austen. David Cecil's *Poets and Storytellers* (1949) credits Burney with inventing the courtship novel and feminising social satire. In Ian Watt's *The Rise of the Novel* (1957), she is seen as a figure who combines the two divergent strands of English fiction: the presentation of minute particulars inherited from Richardson, and the comic detachment and objectivity char-acteristic of Fielding. Together with Austen and Eliot, she is said to have brought the 'feminine point of view' (340) to the novel.

It is in the company of other women writers and those critics who treat them seriously (often themselves female) that Burney begins to find a more favourable reception. She plays a significant role in J. M. S. Tompkins's study of *The Popular Novel in England 1770–1800* (1932). Burney's journals inspired two insightful essays by Virginia Woolf, and she is praised in Joyce Horner's *The English Women Novelists and Their Connection with the Feminist Movement* (1929–30) as a woman with 'natural gifts' (65) who succeeded despite a lack of formal education. Bridget G. MacCarthy in *The Female Pen* (1947) claims that she was 'the first writer to show us real life through a woman's eyes'; in *Evelina*, she created a 'convincing heroine' from the inside (102–3), instead of as a male projection, a feat later improved upon by Jane Austen. It is as a precursor to Jane Austen that Burney is often positioned or, alternatively, as a transmitter of the Richardson–Fielding tradition, as suggested by the title of Utter and Needham's study *Pamela's Daughters* (1936). An article celebrating the bicentenary of Burney's birth in 1952 summed up the main outlines of her reputation to date: 'Fanny

Burney is one of our greatest diarists ... [she] showed that a woman could bring new and sprightly charm to a domestic chronicle.'[19]

Criticism 1950 to 1990

The resuscitation of Burney's reputation began with Joyce Hemlow and her biography, *The History of Fanny Burney* (1958), which drew on her encyclopaedic knowledge of the vast archive of Burney manuscripts. In *A Catalogue of the Burney Family Correspondence 1749–1878* (1971), she would list some ten thousand letters. Later, she would edit twelve volumes of the journals and letters of Burney's later years, those most truncated in the Barrett edition (1791–1840). The fruits of her work are seen, in the decade to follow, in a handful of books based on the life (as the diary still exerted its pull) and a study by Eugene White on Burney's novelistic technique. Even more significant was a Twayne volume by Michael Adelstein (1968), aimed primarily at students, which gives a sensitive reading of the novels (valued for their 'satirical panorama' of society (149) and for their exploration of a new genre). Adelstein also examines the plays (like Hemlow, dismissing the tragedies and praising the comedies) and values the diaries for their vivacity but notes their 'limitations' (152) – reserve, prudery, egotism, dishonesty. In summary, Burney is accorded a place as 'a minor writer of lasting though limited significance' (153). The limitation is often made explicitly through comparison with Jane Austen. A still cited critique from the 1960s is Ronald Paulson's *Satire and the Novel in Eighteenth-Century England* (1967), in which *Evelina* is considered as a 'transitional' novel (283) pointing forward to *Pride and Prejudice*. Paulson praises Burney's protagonist for providing satiric commentary but also for developing as a character, a pattern important to Austen.

Certainly, as Jane Austen came into her own, she managed to pull others after her, though they were firmly relegated to her coat-tails. Typical is Frank Bradbrook's *Jane Austen and her Predecessors* (1966) in which Austen is said to inherit the conventions of the novel from Burney and to improve on them at every turn. The importance of *Evelina*, *Cecilia*, and *Camilla* is that, despite their 'absurdities and limitations' they 'established a tradition' for Austen to follow. Elements of Burney's fiction are traced in Austen's work to show the latter's 'greater refinement and subtlety' (94). Burney is relegated to a place among the host of predecessors whose 'inferior work' Austen transcends (104). Similarly, Hazel Mews's *Frail Vessels* (1969) sees Burney as providing the basic plot situation (courtship) that Austen brought to perfection.

It was in the 1970s that Burney began to step out of Austen's shadow. The first modern scholarly edition of *Evelina* was published by Oxford

University Press in 1968, edited by Edward Bloom, followed by an edition of *Camilla* in 1972 (by Edward and Lillian Bloom). Developing their editorial work, in 'Fanny Burney's Novels: The Retreat from Wonder', the Blooms write about the pattern of the Cinderella myth that underlies all of Burney's fiction. In 'Money in the Novels of Fanny Burney', Edward Copeland also identifies a unifying theme, the financial, felt by women writers of the late eighteenth century, whose motivation as well as subject is economic, presented from 'a hitherto unvoiced female point of view' (24). Offering solutions different from those of Austen, Burney's fiction shows that 'The middle-class woman had indeed begun to write – about herself'; she helped define 'a major shift in woman's consciousness' (36).

Feminist critics in the 1970s aimed to recover the rich heritage of forgotten women writers, excluded from the male-created and male-dominated canon. The late eighteenth century, with its abundance of female writers and readers, offered fertile grounds to explore. Of crucial importance in reviving Burney's fortunes was the work of feminist scholars like Patricia Meyer Spacks. In *The Female Imagination* (1975), Spacks identifies the underlying pattern in Burney's novels as that of a young girl 'being curbed and tamed' (130) as she grows up. The action of the novel represents the process of socialisation into a patriarchal world. The education of the heroine represents not growth, but a regression into childhood. Extending these insights in *Imagining a Self* (1976), Spacks presents 'fear of negative judgment' (160) as the underlying force shaping both Burney's self-presentation and that of her heroines: the yearning for freedom conflicts with the need for security. Burney's novels portray the female condition as a state of 'anxiety' (176), as heroines 'aspire to the negative condition of blamelessness' (178). Evelina 'chooses dependency and fear' (179); Cecilia and Camilla suffer the psychic costs of 'diminishment' (181). The protest is stronger in Burney's last novel, in which the heroine is forced to act although urged to be passive; 'like her creator, Juliet is dominated by terror of public wrongdoing' (186). There can be no resolution to the conflicts attending a woman's search for identity; Burney's novels 'betray her anger at the female condition' (189). Later feminist critics objected to some of this interpretation (the 'dynamics of fear'), preferring to see Burney as a courageous writer. Janice Thaddeus would identify Spacks's essay as the first of three stages of reinterpretation of Burney, moving towards envisioning her as a feminist writer.[20] But Spacks's critique was influential; her focus on Burney's depiction of the female condition, the emotional cost of conformity, and the submerged aggression and anger, would resonate.

Other critics were taking a fresh look at Burney's fiction. Susan Staves, in '*Evelina*; or, Female Difficulties', stresses the 'acute anxiety' of the heroine

(368) created by the threat of violence both physical and psychological. The array of comic characters who offend her delicacy function as projections of her own anxieties. The female difficulties of the novel, labelled trivial by early male critics, are essentially physical and psychological limitations which curb effective resistance. Judith Newton, in 'Evelina: or, The History of a Young Lady's Entrance into the Marriage Market', also notes the presence of violence; women are on display, and men seem licensed to abuse them. The only possible protection is marriage, but with it, a woman gives up her autonomy. Newton believes that while Burney perceives the oppressive conditions under which women suffer, she does not explicitly protest them, so that while a feminist reading of Burney is possible, Burney herself is not a feminist writer. This perception would change, as later critics would not be shy of using the label, and the sublimated protest in Burney's novels would increasingly be identified as violent and real.

The shift is already evident in Rose Marie Cutting's 'Defiant Women', which aligns Burney with the 'romantic rebels' of the day in 'dramatizing the difficulties and struggles of her sex'. Reversing the conventional view of deterioration in Burney's writing, Cutting finds instead a progression, a 'growing rebellion against the restrictions imposed upon women' (519–20). Rebel characters, strong-willed women who refuse to conform, appear in all the novels; they are presented with sympathy, although not fully endorsed. The 'most defiant and most "liberated"' of these is Elinor, a 'true feminist' (525–6) whose eloquent articulation of the wrongs of women is illustrated concretely by the struggles of the heroine. The theme of 'the suffering caused by the dependency of women' is present in all Burney's novels, but 'dominates' the last, which can be read, Cutting suggests, as Burney's 'demand for a change' (528–30).

The next decade deepened and extended the feminist revisioning of Burney's work. In Women, Power, and Subversion (1981), Judith Newton described a shift in feminist discourse: from being seen as victims of oppression, women were viewed rather as agents of social change. Burney's fiction, then, becomes 'the site of protest' (11); she subverts her depiction of male domination by emphasising female power and ability. While appearing to defer to male patriarchy, she asserts female autonomy. Kristina Straub articulated more fully this 'dividedness of the text' in Divided Fictions (1986). Writing during the second wave of feminist social reform, she points out that Evelina is a text 'that tries to go in two directions at once' (1). However, the 'apparently self-contradictory nature' of Burney's fiction is not necessarily problematic if aesthetic unity is not the criterion: the 'textual disruptions' (2) signal a survival strategy; they embody 'the ideological rifts implicit in female identity' (6) and show Burney trying to reconcile her conflicting roles as woman and writer. The later novels suggest increasingly the psychic cost of these divisions, as the heroines are driven to madness. Burney expresses the 'ideological tensions inherent in the lives of eighteenth-century middle-class women – and the strain of writing them into conscious-ness' (22).

Julia Epstein takes a similar approach in *The Iron Pen* (1989). She too finds Burney conflicted, but uncovers a darker side, exploring Burney's 'obsession with violence and hostility' and 'reservoirs of rage' (5). The tension between Burney's compulsion to write and 'social prescriptions for feminine conduct' (requiring modesty, submissiveness and silence) produced 'repositories of anger, defiance, and self-conscious authorship' (24). To interpret Burney's journals as 'transcripts of actual life' is to miss the 'split between defiance and compulsion' (27) in her writing, for which the perfect metaphor is Camilla's grasping of the iron pen which yet leaves no mark. Epstein focuses on the 'moments of tension, danger, or violence' (16) in the journals (Burney's near-drowning at Ilfracombe, her mastectomy, the death of her husband), to show how Burney 'channels her intense and volatile emotions into narrative control' (31), which served a cathartic function. To write about her experiences is to achieve objectivity and detachment. Burney's 'retrospective memorialization of herself at moments of trauma' (41) provided 'a kind of psychotherapy' (38); it helped to mediate reality. The urge to write was a compulsion, whose purpose was to control violence and pain.

Both of these critics helped to rehabilitate Burney's reputation, but it was Margaret Doody's *Frances Burney: The Life in the Works* (1988) that ushered in the third and final stage of Burney criticism.[21] Doody's biography was all-encompassing, reading Burney's work within the context of her life, revealing its 'pain and self-division' (5). Doody's Burney is a complex writer; her novels are 'violent and disturbing' (2). Revising the image of the 'cheerful little Augustan chatterbox' (387), Doody replaces the 'patronizing' nick-name, 'Fanny', with her proper name, 'Frances' (6). (In North American criticism, at least, this name change has remained.) Taking a psychoanalytical approach, Doody analyses Burney's relationship with her father, contextua-lised within eighteenth-century notions of 'filial piety' (24). She looks beyond realism to interpret Burney's work. *Evelina* features 'grotesque characters', 'violent farcical actions' and scenes of real cruelty (48). *Cecilia* is a 'much more daring novel' (101), which exposes English society as predatory. But it is *Camilla*, that 'long and "multifarious" novel' (238), which is transformed from an unreadable failure into a rich and innovative work in Doody's reading. Progressing beyond the omniscient narrator, *Camilla* is 'multi-voiced'; with its 'superimpositions and transformations', the whole novel is an image of disconnection (256, 258). The climax (as for Epstein) is the iron pen scene, which would remain *de rigueur* for critics thereafter. Doody's *Camilla* is a dark and brooding novel that 'marks a new departure in fiction'. With its 'affinity for "magic realism" ... the mythic and the violent' (273), it can be read as a surreal or postmodern text. In *The Wanderer*, Doody sees the culmination of issues that recur in Burney's fiction. The 'Female Difficulties' that so perplexed the early reviewers are presented sympathetically and *The Wanderer* is interpreted as an explicitly feminist text.

Doody also critiques the plays. The tragedies written at Windsor she reads 'as psychological documents' fraught with unhappiness at a time when (Doody believes) Burney feared going mad. She notes recurring patterns (good and bad father-figures, absent mothers, ineffectual lovers and suffering heroines) and their 'therapeutic' value (178–9). The Court years left 'an enduring mark' on Burney, giving her the 'vision of the depths' reflected in her later work (197–8). As for the comedies, Doody sees *The Witlings* as a new departure; she interprets the 'frustration, incompleteness, and anticlimax' (79) of Burney's first attempt at play-writing as a deliberate, 'brilliantly devised' strategy. *The Witlings* is an early example of 'theater of the absurd' (91) and the later three, *Love and Fashion*, *A Busy Day* and *The Woman-Hater*, are full of 'Chekhovian possibilities' (293). In *The Woman-Hater*, Burney digs deep into her psyche to create the character of Joyce, who is joyfully liberated from her father and free to embrace life. Thus, in her last play and her last novel, Burney is seen finally creating a feminist heroine.

Reversing the notion of deterioration posited by early male reviewers, feminist critics present Burney's work as a progression of increased radicalisation of ideas, with *The Wanderer* as the culmination. Doody confirmed this view by re-editing the novel (together with Robert Mack and Peter Sabor) in 1991 for Oxford World's Classics; Sabor and Doody also collaborated on an edition of *Cecilia* in 1988.[22] With the Blooms' editions of both *Evelina* and *Camilla* appearing in paperback in the early 1980s, all four novels could now be read in modern editions. Still more editions of *Evelina* would appear: a Penguin edited by Doody (1994); a Bedford Cultural Edition prepared by Straub (1997); a Norton edition by Stewart Cooke (1998); and a Broadview edited by Susan Howard (2000).[23] Nor were these the only developments in Burney studies in the 1980s, with narrowly focused studies (such as Tracy Edgar Daugherty's *Narrative Techniques in the Novels of Fanny Burney* (1989)) joining slim introductory volumes, like D. D. Devlin's *The Novels and Journals of Fanny Burney* (1987) and Judy Simons's *Fanny Burney* (1987). An indication that Burney had 'arrived' is the publication of an anthology, a volume of Modern Critical Interpretations on *Evelina*, edited by the master-canoniser Harold Bloom (1988).

Books on women writers include chapters on Burney that emphasise her achievement. Eva Figes's *Sex & Subterfuge* (1982) claims on the cover that the publication of *Evelina* in 1778 'was a landmark for women's writing' while Dale Spender in *Mothers of the Novel* (1986) suggests that Burney and Edgeworth represent the 'height of achievement' for women writers (270). In Jane Spencer's *The Rise of the Woman Novelist* (1986), Burney's fame is said to have lifted the prestige of women novelists, a point reinforced in Janet Todd's study, *The Sign of Angellica* (1989), which concludes with Burney because she 'most clearly represents the future of culturally approved fiction by women' (287). She also appears in influential studies such as Katharine Rogers's *Feminism in Eighteenth-Century England* (1982), Terry Castle's *Masquerade and Civilization* (1986) and Mary Poovey's *The Proper Lady and the Woman Writer* (1984).

Burney articles in the 1980s cover a variety of topics and approaches. The father–daughter relationship in *Evelina* comes under scrutiny in Mary Poovey's 'Fathers and Daughters' and Irene Fizer's 'The Name of the Daughter'. Katharine Rogers discusses the self-image projected in Burney's journals as similar to the ultra-sensitive sentimental heroines described in her novels, in 'Fanny Burney: The Private Self and the Published Self'. A reaction against feminist readings is contained in Martha Brown's 'Fanny Burney's "Feminism": Gender or Genre?' which claims that those elements interpreted as a form of protest are traceable instead to the romance tradition. Juliet McMaster disagrees, in 'The Silent Angel', pointing out that while her heroines must suffer in silence, Burney insists on her right to speak. John Richetti expands on this point in 'Voice and Gender in Eighteenth-Century Fiction', where he notes that 'Burney fashions a unique narrative voice out of the requirements and restrictions of female speaking' (271).

Criticism since 1990

In 1991, *Eighteenth-Century Fiction* ran a special issue devoted to *Evelina* alone. All four essays focus on the quest for identity and acceptance in Burney's first novel. As respondent to the essays in the volume, after noting their similarities, Margaret Doody calls for a more inclusive approach that would move 'Beyond *Evelina*', and contextualise Burney within a broader sweep of history and literature. Three full-length critiques suggest the wide range of views in this decade. Katharine Rogers in *Frances Burney: The World of 'Female Difficulties'* (1990) emphasises the conventional side of Burney whom she labels a 'thoughtful conservative' (165) whose expression of protest is neither conscious, clear-cut, nor consistent. While Burney does depict the 'painful ambivalence' of women (5), she does not wholeheartedly challenge the patriarchy, but is constrained within the limits of the genre in which she writes. Although Burney depicts female powerlessness and guilt, Rogers believes that her criticism is contained within comedy (admittedly rather grim) and that she endorses the status quo. By contrast, Barbara Zonitch's *Familiar Violence* (1997) highlights the rage and erupting violence in Burney's novels and asks why these 'scenes of disorder' (13) occur so frequently. She argues that Burney was writing at a time of ideological conflict in which women were increasingly subjected to 'the escalating violence of the modern world' (14). Meanwhile, Joanne Cutting-Gray in *Woman as 'Nobody' and the Novels of Fanny Burney* (1992) explores the problem of female namelessness in Burney, placing her view of Woman alongside that of French contemporary theorists such as Julia Kristeva and Luce Irigaray. She gives a postmodern reading of the novels, focusing on the points of crisis when speech fails the heroine to suggest that 'namelessness is the silent condition of individual women'. *The Wanderer*, who refuses to be named, suggests that 'the very process of naming itself becomes a phenomenality' (84).

Several studies of women writers published in the 1990s include a chapter on Burney. The address 'To Nobody' of the *Early Diary* is quoted by Catherine Gallagher to explore the nothingness that 'economic exchange, "woman," and literary representation ... had in common'. In *Nobody's Story* (1994), the namelessness of Evelina, the social insecurity of the Burneys, the suppression of *The Witlings*, and the increasing indebtedness of Cecilia are all cited to show how 'disembodiment, dispossession, and debt' were the common themes of women writers in the period (327). In *Unbecoming Women* (1993) Susan Fraiman offers a 'postmodernization of the *Bildungsroman*' by emphasising the 'counternarratives' in *Evelina* (xi), the disruption of the masculine teleological narrative with a female discourse of multiplicity. Burney's novel embodies the conflict, simultaneously presenting 'an account of courtship as successful education', with an 'antiromantic narrative of female development' (34) that, with a circular motion, leaves Evelina back where she began. The subversive underplot 'is a satiric and sadistic rewriting of the fairy tale' (36) which offers two contrasting images of female destiny, a triumphant wedding, or abandonment in a ditch. Familiar aspects of *Evelina* are highlighted in Huang Mei's *Transforming the Cinderella Dream* (1990): the motif of fear, the scenes of violence and the presence of a rebellious female character who functions as a fairy godmother. Like the early critics, Mei identifies Burney's greatest contribution as that of gender consciousness.

Evelina is used in Ruth Yeazell's *Fictions of Modesty* (1991) to show how the English courtship novel, focusing on 'the period between coming of age and marriage', relies on the heroine's modesty to delay narrative closure. The 'scenes of embarrassment and confusion' (122) suggest that a young woman entering the world is uncomfortably 'exposed to the gaze of the Other'. In cloaking her own aggressive impulses under a demure demeanour, Evelina 'enacts the fantasy of the modest heroine's triumph' (133) and 'doubles as a satirist' (142). Katherine Sobba Green's *The Courtship Novel 1740–1820* (1991) also looks at 'heroine-centred novels of courtship' that feature women who are 'no longer merely unwilling victims', but rather heroines with possibilities of choice and action (2). This time *Cecilia* is featured, notably the masquerade scene and the ending, which suggest that 'patriarchal authority, if not quite overturned, has definitely been unsettled' (90).

The masquerade scene in *Cecilia* is discussed by Catherine Craft-Fairchild in *Masquerade and Gender* (1993), in which she disagrees with Terry Castle's earlier contention that it represents a moment of liberation from patriarchal structures; rather, Cecilia remains very much imprisoned. The 'masquerade of femininity' (143) also appears in *The Wanderer*, with its insistence on namelessness and the use of disguise. Juliet and Elinor are doubles: Juliet's impulse for 'concealment and repression' becomes so habitual that 'the masquerade becomes her reality' (138–9) and Elinor with her theatrical gestures objectifies herself as spectacle. In the end, both are subsumed into the roles defined for them by the patriarchy.

Not everyone takes a view of Burney as feminist. In *The Excellence of Falsehood* (1991), Deborah Ross takes issue with those critics who see a rebellious sub-text in Burney's novels. Ross does not see her as a 'repressed radical' (114) and prefers 'to treat Burney and her texts as complex unities' (116), although Ross acknowledges that there are 'unresolved problems' (130) in the novels which make the happy endings problematic. Similarly, Claudia Johnson in *Equivocal Beings* (1995) believes that revisionist views of Burney tend to 'overstate Burney's confidence as a social critic' (144), and that she does not challenge the system. *Camilla*, written during 'an intensely repressive period of political reaction' (142), is essentially a conservative novel which upholds cultural institutions, though somewhat equivocally. Johnson glances briefly at Burney's overt political involvement in her pamphlet in support of the French clergy (1793), and describes *The Wanderer*, though published in 1814, as a belated novel of the 1790s, committed to reactionary politics and the related culture of sentimentality. In effect, Burney is seen sharing the same misogyny that prompted her early critics and 'upholding traditional notions of gender even as her own novel protests them' (188).

Scholarly articles and essays on Burney total more than one hundred since 1990. Such a dramatic increase in attention paid to a once-neglected figure is remarkable in itself; so too is the abundance and variety of viewpoints and methodologies represented. All four of Burney's novels take place in the domestic sphere and centre on courtship, so a focus on marriage and the family has always seemed apt. Julie Shaffer discusses the marriage plot and its challenges to patriarchy in 'Not Subordinate'; Elisabeth Rose Gruner explores sibling relationships in 'The Bullfinch and the Brother'; Susan Greenfield uses *Evelina* in her study of the cultural construction of mothers in *Mothering Daughters* (2002). The role of the father and education of the daughter receive attention in Mary Severance's 'An Unerring Rule'. Comedy, long a central issue in Burney's works, is explored by Audrey Bilger in her book on *Laughing Feminism* (2002), which highlights the subversive potential of comedy 'as a coping strategy and an outlet for revolt', when employed by women in a male-dominated society (57). Bilger shows how Burney used laughter to channel her aggression and anger.

Like Austen, Burney raises questions about class and money. D. Grant Campbell sees in her novels a reflection of the new consumerism in 'Fashionable Suicide'; Miranda Burgess writes on 'Courting Ruin'; and James Thompson points out, in *Models of Value* (1996), that all of Burney's novels 'eroticize ... the spending of money' (164), a point cited by Andrea Henderson in 'Commerce and Masochistic Desire in the 1790s'. Market conditions for women writers are explored by Jan Fergus and Janice Thaddeus in 'Women, Publishers, and Money, 1790–1820'. The professionalism of Burney's early career is discussed in Betty Schellenberg's 'From Propensity to Profession'. The overlap between literature and medicine is explored in three articles by John Wiltshire; closely related is Justine Crump's study of madness, in 'Turning the World Upside Down'.

Criticism of the novels tends to coalesce around one in particular. *Evelina* still gets the lion's share of attention, sparking numerous articles with a diversity of approaches: through epistolarity in Irene Tucker, 'Writing Home'; through theatricality in Emily Allen, 'Staging Identity'; through Christianity in Sharon Long Damoff, 'The Unaverted Eye'; through nationalism in Leanne Maunu, 'Quelling the French Threat'. *Cecilia* has been all but overlooked, meriting only the occasional article (although it does figure in Antoinette Marie Sol's *Textual Promiscuities* (2002)); *Camilla* was reinvented in the 1980s, but it is *The Wanderer*, that much maligned novel, which finally came into its own in the 1990s. A dozen articles address topics like Gothic motifs, nationalism and social criticism in the novel; moreover, it is the subject of a full-length monograph, *Frances Burney and the Female Bildungsroman* (2003), by Mascha Gemmeke, which seeks to explain the novel's puzzling complexities by providing a historical context.

As well as the novels, Burney's journals and diaries, long the cornerstone of her reputation, continue to attract interest, though as self-conscious literary constructs, rather than biographical documents. Judy Simons advocates this approach in several articles; Lorna Clark analyses Burney's narrative strategies in 'The Diarist as Novelist', while Linda Lang-Peralta discusses her 'Clandestine Delight' in writing.

The critical attention complements editorial activity which aims to bring all of Burney's writing into the public domain. The monumental edition of the *Journals and Letters* published from McGill University's Burney Centre is working towards bridging the gap to Hemlow's starting-point, re-editing the earlier material up to 1791 (with Lars Troide overseeing the *Early Journals* and Peter Sabor responsible for the *Court Journals*). Eight (of a total of twenty-four) volumes of material are still to come, which will finally give a full picture of Burney's achievement as a diarist and correspondent. There are also three collections of excerpts, selected by Hemlow (1987), Sabor and Troide (2001), and Justine Crump (2002).

A remarkable development has been the recent interest in Burney as a dramatist. Other than a single night's performance of one tragedy (*Edwy and Elgiva*, first printed in 1957), the four comedies and four tragedies that Burney wrote existed only in manuscript for two hundred years. Hemlow's landmark article, 'Fanny Burney: Playwright' in 1950, inspired Tara Ghoshal Wallace's edition of *A Busy Day* (1984), followed by Clayton Delery's of *The Witlings* (1995); these in turn have prompted premiere performances in private theatres and university auditoriums. But it was not until Sabor's two-volume edition of *The Complete Plays of Frances Burney* (1995) that the full scope of Burney's theatrical ambitions was realised (the subject is addressed in Sabor's 'The Rediscovery of Frances Burney's Plays'). With their combination of satire and sentiment, her plays might well have influenced the development of the English stage, had they been performed when written. However, these 'golden dreams' were not to be, with the result that one dimension of Burney's accomplishment as a writer has remained virtually unknown until the 1990s.

Critics have not been slow to take up the work of interpretation, with the first full-length appraisal of *Frances Burney, Dramatist* published in 1997; in it, Barbara Darby uses feminist and performance theory to explore gender issues in Burney's plays, and finds the tragedies especially powerful in their rendition of male power and female suffering. In her drama, with its questioning of social institutions, Burney appears to have a more radical and political agenda than was previously imagined. Other critics have begun to interpret the comedies, with *The Witlings* and *A Busy Day* attracting the most attention. No doubt the separate publication (by Pickering & Chatto in

1997 and Broadview in 2002), of *The Witlings* and *The Woman-Hater*, co-edited by Sabor and Geoffrey Sill, will stimulate further studies. (The plays have even sparked interest in Italy, with Francesca Saggini's *La messinscena dell'identità* (2005), which studies dramatic elements in Burney's writing within their cultural context.)

Recent attention has brought Burney criticism back to its roots. No fewer than five biographies have been published in the last decade, some of which are aimed towards the general reader. Just as play-goers in the West End are being exposed to Burney's wit, so a wider audience is being introduced to Burney's writing. Kate Chisholm's *Fanny Burney* (1998) combines a serious approach with an accessible style. Claire Harman's *Fanny Burney* (2000) is edgier, a testimony, perhaps, to the resilience of the Croker school of thought. Hester Davenport's *Faithful Handmaid* (2000) vividly evokes the court years, while Nigel Nicolson's brief *Fanny Burney* (2002) is geared for popular consumption. Janice Thaddeus's *Frances Burney: A Literary Life* (2000) manages to bring the tripartite image of Burney ('the one who fears to do wrong, the one who represses her rage, and the one who unleashes her rage' (6)) into focus in one figure.

University students, who once would scarcely have heard her name, may now encounter Burney in courses on women's studies, eighteenth-century literature, or the development of the novel. Paperback editions of her novels and plays are readily available. Burney has been the topic of conference papers and panels, even whole conferences. A Burney society has been formed with its own newsletter and journal. Her canonical status is confirmed by a memorial window in Westminster Abbey and a plaque by her gravesite in Bath. Her name has appeared in lights in London's West End; her life and fiction have been dramatised. Can a popular revival, led by a television series or Hollywood film, be far behind?

NOTES

1. Bruce Stovel, 'Further Reading', *The Cambridge Companion to Jane Austen*, ed. Edward Copeland and Juliet McMaster (Cambridge: Cambridge University Press, 1997), 227.
2. *Diary and Letters of Madame d'Arblay*, ed. Charlotte Barrett, 7 vols. (London: Henry Colburn, 1842–6), I, 22.
3. *Gentleman's Magazine* NS 18 (1842), 582.
4. John Wilson Croker, Review of *Diary and Letters of Madame d'Arblay*, ed. by her Niece [Charlotte Barrett], *Quarterly Review* 70 (1842), 243–87.
5. John Wilson Croker, Review of *Memoirs of Doctor Burney*, *Quarterly Review* 49 (1833), 111.
6. *Gentleman's Magazine* NS 27 (1847), 3, 5.
7. *Journals and Letters*, XII, 969. Macaulay's letter is reprinted in the note.

8. Thomas Babington Macaulay, Review of *Diary and Letters of Madame D'Arblay*, ed. by her Niece [Charlotte Barrett], *Edinburgh Review* 76 (1843), 523–70, 537.

9. Review of *Diary and Letters of Madame D'Arblay*, *The Athenæum*, 756 (23 April 1842), 355–8.

10. The words ('death or sex, hunger or war, guilt or God') are from Dorothy van Ghent's critique of Austen in *The English Novel: Form and Function* (New York: Holt, Rinehart and Winston, 1953), 99.

11. *Athenæum*, 756 (23 April 1842), 356.

12. J. Cordy Jeaffreson, *Novels and Novelists from Elizabeth to Victoria* (London: Hurst & Blackett, 1848), I, 312–39, cited in Joseph A. Grau, *Fanny Burney: An Annotated Bibliography* (New York & London: Garland, 1981), 104.

13. William Minto, *The Literature of the Georgian Era* (New York: Harper & Brothers, 1895), 119–24, cited in Grau, *Annotated Bibliography*, 120.

14. *Harper's New Monthly Magazine* 61 (Aug. 1880), 471–2, cited in Grau, *Annotated Bibliography*, 37.

15. *Nation* 81 (28 Dec. 1905), 526–7, cited in Grau, *Annotated Bibliography*, 40.

16. Peter Sabor, 'Annie Raine Ellis, Austin Dobson, and the Rise of Burney Studies', *The Burney Journal* 1 (1998), 25–45, 35.

17. Austin Dobson, *Fanny Burney* (London: Macmillan, 1903), 205–6.

18. For full citations of this and other works on Burney mentioned here, see Further Reading.

19. D. Hudson, 'Miss Burney Runs Away', *Spectator* 188 (13 June 1952), 771–2 cited in Grau, *Annotated Bibliography*, 103.

20. Janice Thaddeus, *Frances Burney: A Literary Life* (Houndmills, Basingstoke: Macmillan, 2000), 4–5.

21. Thaddeus, *Frances Burney*, 5.

22. These scholarly editions by Oxford World's Classics were an improvement over reprint editions, by Pandora of *The Wanderer* in 1988 and by Virago of *Cecilia* in 1986.

23. The latter three editions of *Evelina* (those of Bedford, Norton and Broadview presses) are each based on a different edition as copy text, all published within Burney's lifetime.

FURTHER READING

Bibliography

Grau, Joseph A., *Fanny Burney: An Annotated Bibliography*. New York & London: Garland, 1981.

Biographies

Barrett, Charlotte, 'Editor's Introduction', *Diary and Letters of Madame D'Arblay*, 7 vols. London: Henry Colburn, 1842–4, I, iii–xxii.

Chisholm, Kate, *Fanny Burney: Her Life 1752–1840*. London: Chatto & Windus, 1998.

Davenport, Hester, *Faithful Handmaid: Fanny Burney at the Court of King George III*. Stroud, Gloucestershire: Sutton Publishing, 2000.

Dobson, Austin, *Fanny Burney*. London: Macmillan, 1903.

Doody, Margaret Anne, *Frances Burney: The Life in the Works*. Cambridge: Cambridge University Press, 1988.

Harman, Claire, *Fanny Burney: A Biography*. London: HarperCollins, 2000.

Hemlow, Joyce, *The History of Fanny Burney*. Oxford: Clarendon Press, 1958.

Nicolson, Nigel, *Fanny Burney: The Mother of English Fiction*. London: Short Books, 2002.

Thaddeus, Janice Farrar, *Frances Burney: A Literary Life*. Houndmills, Basingstoke: Macmillan, 2000.

Early Criticism

Cecil, David, *Poets and Storytellers*. London: Constable, 1949.

Croker, John Wilson, Review of *Memoirs of Doctor Burney*, by Mme d'Arblay, *Quarterly Review* 49 (1833), 97–125.

Review of *Diary and Letters of Madame d'Arblay*, ed. by her Niece [Charlotte Barrett], *Quarterly Review* 70 (1842), 243–87.

Hill, Constance, *Fanny Burney at the Court of Queen Charlotte*. London: John Lane, 1912.

The House in St. Martin's Street: being Chronicles of the Burney Family. London: John Lane, 1907.

Juniper Hall. London: John Lane, 1904.

Horner, Joyce, *The English Women Novelists and Their Connection with the Feminist Movement (1688–1797)*. Smith College Studies in Modern Languages, XI (1929–30).

Johnson, R. Brimley, *Fanny Burney and the Burneys*. London: Stanley Paul, 1926.

Leavis, F. R., *The Great Tradition*. London: Chatto & Windus, 1948.

MacCarthy, Bridget G., *The Later Women Novelists 1744–1818: The Female Pen*. Oxford: B. H. Blackwell; Dublin: Cork University Press, 1947.

Macaulay, Thomas Babington, Review of *Diary and Letters of Madame D'Arblay*, ed. by her Niece [Charlotte Barrett], *Edinburgh Review* 76 (1843), 523–70.

Tompkins, J. M. S., *The Popular Novel in England 1770–1800*. London: Constable, 1932.

Utter, Robert P., and Gwendolyn B. Needham, *Pamela's Daughters*. New York: Macmillan, 1936.

Woolf, Virginia, *The Second Common Reader*. New York and London: Harcourt, Brace & World, 1932.

Criticism 1950 to 1990

Adelstein, Michael E., *Fanny Burney*. New York: Twayne, 1968.

Bloom, Harold, ed., *Fanny Burney's* Evelina, Modern Critical Interpretations. New York: Chelsea House Publishers, 1988.

Bloom, Lillian D. and Edward A., 'Fanny Burney's Novels: The Retreat from Wonder', *Novel: A Forum on Fiction* 12 (1979), 215–35.

Bradbrook, Frank W., *Jane Austen and Her Predecessors*. Cambridge: Cambridge University Press, 1966.

Brown, Martha G., 'Fanny Burney's "Feminism": Gender or Genre?' in *Fetter'd or Free? British Women Novelists, 1670–1815*, ed. Mary Anne Schofield and Cecilia Macheski. Athens: Ohio University Press, 1986, 29–39.

Castle, Terry, *Masquerade and Civilization: The Carnivalesque in Eighteenth-Century English Culture and Fiction*. Stanford: Stanford University Press, 1986.

Copeland, Edward W., 'Money in the Novels of Fanny Burney', *Studies in the Novel* 8 (1976), 24–37.

Cutting, Rose Marie, 'Defiant Women: The Growth of Feminism in Fanny Burney's Novels', *Studies in English Literature, 1500–1900* 17.3 (1977), 519–30.

Daugherty, Tracy Edgar, *Narrative Techniques in the Novels of Fanny Burney*. New York: Peter Lang, 1989.

Devlin, D. D., *The Novels and Journals of Fanny Burney*. New York: St. Martin's Press, 1987.

Epstein, Julia L., *The Iron Pen: Frances Burney and the Politics of Women's Writing*. Bristol: Bristol Classical Press, 1989.

'Writing the Unspeakable: Fanny Burney's Mastectomy and the Fictive Body', *Representations* 16 (1986), 131–66.

Fergus, Jan, and Janice Farrar Thaddeus, 'Women, Publishers, and Money, 1790–1820', *Studies in Eighteenth-Century Culture* 17 (1987), 191–207.

Figes, Eva, *Sex and Subterfuge: Women Novelists to 1850*. London: Macmillan, 1982.

Fizer, Irene, 'The Name of the Daughter: Identity and Incest in *Evelina*', in *Refiguring the Father: New Feminist Readings of Patriarchy*, ed. Patricia Yaeger, Beth

Kowaleski-Wallace, and Nancy Miller. Carbondale: University of Illinois Press, 1989, 78–107.

Graham, Kenneth W., 'Cinderella or Bluebeard: The Double Plot of *Evelina*', *L'Homme et la nature/Man and Nature*, ed. E. T. Annandale and Richard A. Lebrun, Vol. 5, Edmonton: Academic Printing & Publishing, 1986, 85–98.

Hemlow, Joyce, with Jeanne M. Burgess and Althea Douglas, *A Catalogue of the Burney Family Correspondence 1749–1878*. New York: New York Public Library, 1971.

'Fanny Burney and the Courtesy Books', PMLA 65 (1950), 732–61.

'Fanny Burney: Playwright', *University of Toronto Quarterly* 19 (1950), 170–89.

McMaster, Juliet, 'The Silent Angel: Impediments to Female Expression in Frances Burney's Novels', *Studies in the Novel* 21.3 (1989), 235–52.

Mews, Hazel, *Frail Vessels: Woman's Role in Women's Novels from Fanny Burney to George Eliot*. London: Athlone Press, 1969.

Moers, Ellen, *Literary Women*. New York: Doubleday, 1976.

Newton, Judith Lowder, '*Evelina*: or, The History of a Young Lady's Entrance into the Marriage Market', *Modern Language Studies* 6.1 (1976), 48–56.

Women, Power, and Subversion: Social Strategies in British Fiction, 1778–1860. Athens: Georgia, University of Georgia Press, 1981.

Paulson, Ronald, *Satire and the Novel in Eighteenth-Century England*. New Haven & London: Yale University Press, 1967.

Poovey, Mary, 'Fathers and Daughters: The Trauma of Growing Up Female', *Women and Literature* 2 (1982), 39–58.

The Proper Lady and the Woman Writer: Ideology as Style in the Works of Mary Wollstonecraft, Mary Shelley, and Jane Austen. Chicago: University of Chicago Press, 1984.

Richetti, John J., 'Voice and Gender in Eighteenth-Century Fiction: Haywood to Burney', *Studies in the Novel* 19.3 (1987), 263–72.

Rogers, Katharine M., 'Fanny Burney: The Private Self and the Published Self', *International Journal of Women's Studies* 7.2 (1984), 110–17.

Feminism in Eighteenth-Century England. Urbana: University of Illinois Press, 1982.

Showalter, Elaine, *A Literature of their Own British Women Novelists From Brontë to Lessing*. Princeton: Princeton University Press, 1977.

Simons, Judy, *Fanny Burney*. Houndmills, Basingstoke, Hampshire: Macmillan, 1987.

Spacks, Patricia Meyer, ' "Ev'ry Woman is at Heart a Rake" ', *Eighteenth-Century Studies* 8.1 (1974–5), 27–46.

The Female Imagination. New York: Alfred A. Knopf, 1975.

Imagining a Self: Autobiography and Novel in Eighteenth-Century England. Cambridge, Mass.: Harvard University Press, 1976.

Spencer, Jane, *The Rise of the Woman Novelist: From Aphra Behn to Jane Austen*. Oxford: Basil Blackwell, 1986.

Spender, Dale, *Mothers of the Novel: 100 Good Women Writers before Jane Austen*. London and New York: Pandora, 1986.

Staves, Susan, '*Evelina*; or, Female Difficulties', *Modern Philology* 73.4 (1975–6), 368–81.

Straub, Kristina, *Divided Fictions: Fanny Burney and Feminine Strategy*. Lexington: University Press of Kentucky, 1987.

'Fanny Burney's *Evelina* and the "Gulphs, Pits, and Precipices" of Eighteenth-Century Female Life', *The Eighteenth Century: Theory and Interpretation* 27.3 (1986), 230–46.

Todd, Janet, *The Sign of Angellica: Women, Writing, and Fiction 1660–1800*. London: Virago, 1989.

van Ghent, Dorothy, *The English Novel: Form and function*. New York: Holt, Rinehart, 1953.

Watt, Ian, *The Rise of the Novel: Studies in Defoe, Richardson, and Fielding*. London: Chatto & Windus, 1957.

White, Eugene, *Fanny Burney, Novelist: A Study in Technique*. Hamden, Conn.: Shoe String Press, 1960.

Criticism Since 1990

Books

Bilger, Audrey, *Laughing Feminism: Subversive Comedy in Frances Burney, Maria Edgeworth, and Jane Austen*. Detroit: Wayne State University Press, 1998.

Copeland, Edward, *Women Writing About Money: Women's Fiction in England, 1790–1820*. Cambridge: Cambridge University Press, 1995.

Craft-Fairchild, Catherine, *Masquerade and Gender: Disguise and Female Identity in Eighteenth-Century Fictions by Women*. University Park: Pennsylvania State University Press, 1993.

Cutting-Gray, Joanne, *Woman as 'Nobody' and the Novels of Fanny Burney*. Gainesville: University Press of Florida, 1992.

Darby, Barbara, *Frances Burney, Dramatist: Gender, Performance, and the Late-Eighteenth-Century Stage*. Lexington: University Press of Kentucky, 1997.

Fraiman, Susan, *Unbecoming Women: British Women Writers and the Novel of Development*. New York: Columbia University Press, 1993.

Gallagher, Catherine, *Nobody's Story: The Vanishing Acts of Women Writers in the Marketplace, 1670–1820*. Berkeley: University of California Press, 1994.

Gemmeke, Mascha, *Frances Burney and the Female Bildungsroman: An Interpretation of* The Wanderer; or, Female Difficulties. Frankfurt: Peter Lang, 2004.

Green, Katherine Sobba, *The Courtship Novel 1740–1820: A Feminized Genre*. Lexington: University Press of Kentucky, 1991.

Greenfield, Susan C., *Mothering Daughters: Novels and the Politics of Family Romance: Frances Burney and Jane Austen*. Detroit: Wayne State University Press, 2002.

Johnson, Claudia, *Equivocal Beings: Politics, Gender, and Sentimentality in the 1790s; Wollstonecraft, Radcliffe, Burney, Austen*. Chicago: University of Chicago Press, 1995.

Lynch, Deidre Shauna, *The Economy of Character: Novels, Market Culture, and the Business of Inner Meaning*. Chicago: Chicago University Press, 1998.

Mei, Huang, *Transforming the Cinderella Dream: From Frances Burney to Charlotte Brontë*. New Brunswick and London: Rutgers University Press, 1990.

Rizzo, Betty, *Companions Without Vows: Relationships Among Eighteenth-Century British Women*. Athens and London: University of Georgia Press, 1994.

Rogers, Katharine M., *Frances Burney: The World of 'Female Difficulties'*. New York: Harvester Wheatsheaf, 1990.

Ross, Deborah, *The Excellence of Falsehood: Romance, Realism, and Women's Contribution to the Novel*. Lexington: University Press of Kentucky, 1991.

Sol, Antoinette Marie, *Textual Promiscuities: Eighteenth-Century Critical Rewriting*. Lewisburg: Bucknell University Press; London: Associated University Presses, 2002.

Spencer, Jane, *Literary Relations: Kinship and the Canon 1660–1830*. Oxford: Oxford University Press, 2005.

Turner, Cheryl, *Living by the Pen: Women writers in the Eighteenth century*. London and New York: Routledge, 1992.

Yeazell, Ruth Bernard, *Fictions of Modesty: Women and Courtship in the English Novel*. Chicago: University of Chicago Press, 1991.

Zonitch, Barbara, *Familiar Violence: Gender and Social Upheaval in the Novels of Frances Burney*. Newark: University of Delaware Press, 1997.

Articles and essays

Allen, Emily, 'Staging Identity: Frances Burney's Allegory of Genre', *Eighteenth-Century Studies* 31.4 (1998), 433–51.

Burgess, Miranda J., 'Courting Ruin: The Economic Romances of Frances Burney', *Novel* 28.2 (1995), 131–53.

Campbell, D. Grant, 'Fashionable Suicide: Conspicuous Consumption and the Collapse of Credit in Frances Burney's *Cecilia*', *Studies in Eighteenth-Century Culture* 20 (1990), 131–45.

Campbell, Gina, 'Bringing Belmont to Justice: Burney's Quest for Paternal Recognition in *Evelina*', *Eighteenth-Century Fiction* 3.4 (1991), 321–40.

Clark, Lorna J., 'The Diarist as Novelist: Narrative Strategies in the Journals and Letters of Frances Burney', *English Studies in Canada* 27.3 (2001), 283–302.

Crump, Justine, ' "Turning the World Upside Down": Madness, Moral Management, and Frances Burney's *The Wanderer*', *Eighteenth-Century Fiction* 10.3 (1998), 325–40.

Damoff, Sharon Long, 'The Unaverted Eye: Dangerous Charity in Burney's *Evelina* and *The Wanderer*', *Studies in Eighteenth-Century Culture* 26 (1998), 231–46.

Darby, Barbara, 'Frances Burney's Dramatic Mothers', *English Studies in Canada* 23.1 (1997), 37–58.

Doody, Margaret Anne, 'Beyond *Evelina*: The Individual Novel and the Community of Literature', *Eighteenth-Century Fiction* 3.4 (1991), 358–71.

Dykstal, Timothy, '*Evelina* and the Culture Industry', *Criticism* 37.4 (1995), 559–81.

Epstein, Julia, 'Burney Criticism: Family Romance, Psychobiography, and Social History', *Eighteenth-Century Fiction* 3.4 (1991), 277–82.

'Marginality in Frances Burney's novels', in John Richetti, ed., *The Cambridge Companion to the Eighteenth-Century Novel*. Cambridge: Cambridge University Press, 1996, 198–211.

Greenfield, Susan C., ' "Oh Dear Resemblance of Thy Murdered Mother": Female Authorship in *Evelina*', *Eighteenth-Century Fiction* 3.4 (1991), 301–20.

Gruner, Elisabeth Rose, 'The Bullfinch and the Brother: Marriage and Family in Frances Burney's *Camilla*', *JEGP* 93.1 (1994), 18–34.

Henderson, Andrea, 'Commerce and Masochistic Desire in the 1790s: Frances Burney's *Camilla*', *Eighteenth-Century Studies* 31.1 (1997), 69–86.

Koehler, Martha J. ' "Faultless Monsters" and Monstrous Egos: The Disruption of Model Selves in Frances Burney's *Evelina*', *The Eighteenth Century: Theory and Interpretation* 43.1 (2002), 19–41.

Kowaleski-Wallace, Beth, 'A Night at the Opera: The Body, Class, and Art in *Evelina* and Frances Burney's *Early Diaries*', in *History, Gender & Eighteenth-Century Literature*, ed. Beth Fawkes-Tobin. Athens and London: University of Georgia Press, 1994, 141–58.

Lang-Peralta, Linda, ' "Clandestine Delight": Frances Burney's Life-Writing', in *Women's Life-Writing: Finding Voice/Building Community*, ed. Linda S. Coleman. Bowling Green: Ohio, Bowling Green State University Popular Press, 1997, 23–41.

Lynch, Deidre Shauna, 'Counter Publics: Shopping and Women's Sociability', in *Romantic Sociability: Social Networks and Literary Culture in Britain, 1770–1840*, ed. Gillian Russell and Clara Tuite. Cambridge: Cambridge University Press, 2002, 211–36.

Maunu, Leanne, 'Quelling the French Threat in Frances Burney's *Evelina*', *Studies in Eighteenth-Century Culture* 31 (2002), 99–125.

Oakleaf, David, 'The Name of the Father: Social Identity and the Ambition of *Evelina*', *Eighteenth-Century Fiction* 3.4 (1991), 341–58.

Pawl, Amy J., ' "And What Other Name May I Claim?": Names and Their Owners in Frances Burney's *Evelina*', *Eighteenth-Century Fiction* 3.4 (1991), 283–99.

Sabor, Peter, ' "Alter'd, improved, copied, abridged": Alexandre d'Arblay's Revisions to *Edwy and Elgiva*', *Lumen* 14 (1995), 127–37.

'The Rediscovery of Frances Burney's Plays', *Lumen* 13 (1994), 145–56.

' "A kind of Tax on the Public": The Subscription List to Frances Burney's *Camilla*', in *New Windows on a Woman's World: A Festschrift for Jocelyn Harris*, ed. Colin Gibson and Lisa Marr. Otago: University of Otago Press, I, 299–315.

Salih, Sara, ' "Her Blacks, her whites and her double face!" Altering Alterity in *The Wanderer*', *Eighteenth-Century Fiction* 11.3 (1999), 301–15.

Schellenberg, Betty A. 'From Propensity to Profession: Female Authorship and the Early Career of Frances Burney', *Eighteenth-Century Fiction* 14.3-4 (2002), 345–70.

Severance, Mary, 'An Unerring Rule: The Reformation of the Father in Frances Burney's *Evelina*', *Eighteenth Century: Theory and Interpretation* 36.2 (1995), 119–38.

Shaffer, Julie, 'Not Subordinate: Empowering Women in the Marriage-Plot – The Novels of Frances Burney, Maria Edgeworth, and Jane Austen', *Criticism* 34.1 (1992), 51–73.

Sherman, Sandra, ' "Does Your Ladyship Mean an Extempore?" Wit, Leisure, and the Mode of Production in Frances Burney's *The Witlings*', *Centennial Review* 40.2 (1996), 401–28.

Simons, Judy, 'Fanny Burney: The Tactics of Subversion', in *Living By the Pen: Early British Women Writers*, ed. Dale Spender. New York and London: Teachers College Press, 1992, 126–36.

Straub, Kristina, 'Frances Burney and the Rise of the Woman Novelist', in John Richetti, ed., *The Columbia History of the British Novel*. New York: Columbia University Press, 1994, 199–219.

Thompson, James, 'Burney and Debt', *Models of Value: Eighteenth-Century Political Economy and the Novel*. Durham, N.C.: Duke University Press, 1996, 156–83.

Tieken-Boon van Ostade, Ingrid, 'Stripping the Layers: Language and Content of Fanny Burney's Early Journals', *English Studies* 72.2 (1991), 146–59.

Tucker, Irene, 'Writing Home: *Evelina*, the Epistolary Novel and the Paradox of Property', ELH 60.2 (1993), 419–39.

Wiltshire, John, 'Early Nineteenth-Century Pathography: The Case of Frances Burney', *Literature and History* 2.2 (1993), 9–23.

'Fanny Burney's Face, Madame d'Arblay's Veil', in *Literature and Medicine during the Eighteenth Century*, ed. Marie Mulvey Roberts and Roy Porter. London: Routledge, 1993, 245–65.

'Love unto Death: Fanny Burney's "Narrative of the Last Illness and Death of General d'Arblay" (1820)', *Literature and Medicine* 12.2 (1993), 215–34.

Zomchick, John, 'Satire and the Bourgeois Subject in Frances Burney's Evelina', in James E. Gill, ed. *Cutting Edges: Postmodern Critical Essays on Eighteenth-Century Satire*. Knoxville: University of Tennessee Press, 1995, 347–66.

INDEX

Cambridge Companions to ...

AUTHORS

TOPICS